Cynicism from Diogenes to Dilbert

Cynicism from Diogenes to Dilbert

IAN CUTLER

Foreword by Yiannis Gabriel

McFarland & Company, Inc., Publishers
Jefferson, North Carolina, and London

Library of Congress Online Catalog

Cutler, Ian, 1948–
    Cynicism from Diogenes to Dilbert / Ian Cutler ; foreword by
Yiannis Gabriel.
        p.   cm.
    Includes bibliographical references and index.

    ISBN 0-7864-2093-6 (softcover : 50# alkaline paper) ∞

    1. Cynicism — Social aspects.   2. Cynics (Greek philosophy)
I. Title.
HM1011.C88   2005
                                                    2005016998

British Library cataloguing data are available

On the cover: Jean-Léon Gérôme, *Diogenes*, 1860,
oil on canvas, 29½" × 38⅞" (*clipart.com*)

Manufactured in the United States of America

McFarland & Company, Inc., Publishers
    Box 611, Jefferson, North Carolina 28640
        www.mcfarlandpub.com

For my maternal grandparents Wilhelm and Ella Engelhart who (thanks to the Nazis' obsession with bureaucracy) I know were deported from Vienna on 20th May 1942 and shot in the Blogowshtchina forest Minsk on 26th May 1942 under the orders of Reinhard Heydrich. Heydrich was himself shot by an assassin on the following day, 27th May 1942. But for their murder and my mother Elise's escape neither I nor this book would have existed. Such is the wonder and the absurdity of life.

Acknowledgments

My particular thanks go to Yiannis Gabriel for his tireless support, encouragement and forthright editing suggestions throughout the four years of writing this book; to Luis Navia for his expert knowledge and advice on Classical Cynicism; to Sarah Wild for her encouraging phone calls from Chicago; to Paul and Sarah Briggs for their dedicated friendship and discussions around the kitchen table; and to my wife Angela (the real cynic of the family) for her selfless love and support. Without her own passion for reading, writing and endless debates, this book would have lacked many of its more interesting digressions.

Contents

Restraint is for horses, you can smell it in their shit.
Angela Morgan Cutler

Foreword

BY YIANNIS GABRIEL

You already know the cynic: sarcastic and sardonic, the cynic delights in shooting down every trace of idealism, in wrecking every noble initiative, in questioning every sincere utterance. The cynic is the social toxin, ceaselessly criticizing, undermining and destroying. "Virtue? A fig!"— Iago's signature on behalf of cynics rings across the ages. Yet, of all old philosophies, none appears more attuned to our times than cynicism. Whether listening to politicians, observing the latest prize-winning artistic masterpiece, or merely masticating the daily content of the media, many of us adopt the stance of the cynic, suspecting hidden scenarios and ulterior motives. Cynicism has emerged as a cool choice of attitude in response to spin, sensationalism and manipulation.

It is natural that there is a resurgence of interest in cynicism. Some commentators have castigated it as a social pathology of our times—a chic nihilism that poisons everything. Others have sought to defend it as an efficient defense against the lies and disappointments to which we are daily exposed. Yet others have seen in it a rudimentary form of resistance and even rebellion against a culture of hype and simulation. A different class of commentators have sought to elucidate the nature of "it," the phenomenon of cynicism, looking for historical continuities and fissures, mutations and cross-fertilizations. To the outstanding works of Luis E. Navia and Peter Sloterdijk, we must now add the present volume by Ian Cutler, which offers a far-reaching re-evaluation of cynicism through the ages, a veritable archaeology of a body of ideas and practices that has proven resilient as well as capable of surprising transformations. Both sympathetic and critical, Cutler's work reveals the remarkable ability of cynicism to transubstantiate across discourses and epochs without betraying its unique qualities.

1

Each chapter of this book represents such a transubstantiation of cynicism. The book also reveals the complexities and ambiguities of cynicism that are lost in those commentaries which view it as pathology, defense or resistance.

Cynicism undoubtedly started as a philosophical school. In common with Socrates, one of the undoubted sources of their inspiration, many cynical philosophers did not seek to write down their ideas, least of all to develop some cohesive intellectual system free from contradiction and tension. Instead they sought to live out their philosophy. The absence of a large body of written work made cynicism vulnerable to various slanders by opponents who could attribute to them a variety of moral, philosophical and practical failings. On the other hand, the view that a life can be a statement, a political, aesthetic and moral statement, is one to which our times are well attuned. Cutler is right in viewing cynicism as an art, one that requires considerable practice and sacrifice, one that can be practiced badly or well, one that can be analyzed and studied but cannot be reduced to laws, rules or dogmas. As an art, it is principally a performance art, a fleeting, temporal, yet deeply effective art, that, when well executed, leaves indelible traces. It is not accidental that some of the greatest triumphs of cynicism belong to the realm of the spectacular — Diogenes demanding that Alexander the Great move aside a mite to let the real sun through or masturbating in public and claiming that life would be simple if only he could relieve hunger by stroking his belly. As an art of persuasion based on spectacle, cynicism is particularly compelling at times when faith in rational argument and sensible discussion is tested.

If early cynicism owed much of its notoriety and influence to certain key spectacular interventions, it would be wrong to underestimate the power, originality and pervasiveness of some of its core ideas. Its very unwillingness to engage in a system-building project such as those undertaken by other philosophers grew out of its conviction that theoretical systems are themselves symptoms of an evasion of the fundamental truth that humans are not like animals: they *are* animals (even if they are not *just* animals). In elevating themselves above other creatures of the animal kingdom, the cynics believed that humans indulge in a basic self-deception, whose results are deleterious— exploitation of one person by another, submission to the authority of rulers and loss of freedom. By clothing themselves in rags and celebrating stray dog-like existence, the cynics (from kyon = dog) sought to underline their belief that humans are animals in their very essence and that there is nothing wrong or demeaning about this. Even in our post–Darwinian society, with evolutionary theory making inroads in many areas of the social and human sciences, the cynics' insight retains an ability to stimulate and to provoke.

Stray dogs (unlike well-groomed poodles) recognize no masters and no boundaries. The cynics' disdain for the institutions of the state (including borders, laws, currencies, armies and slavery) finds eloquent expression in their proclamation of cosmopolitanism: citizenship of the world. This oxymoronic proclamation (easily shot down by an Aristotle or a Plato in their different ways) signals the cynics' defiant dismissal of boundaries, passports, citizenship and all the privileges and duties afforded by the state. Being citizens of the world enabled the cynics to claim simultaneously all of the privileges of animals, which can live without respect for human law, and none of the responsibilities of human subjects. It also gave them uniquely global qualities which find much resonance in our times, when capital, information and goods move freely across boundaries, while individuals die in their thousands trying to cross national frontiers in search of a better life.

One final invention of cynicism deserves a special mention here. The claim of the right to speak their mind without fear or restraint, parrhesia, puts the cynics as far away from political correctness as can be imagined today. Not for them, consideration for the feelings and sensitivities of their fellow humans, whether they be the privileged and strong or the marginalized and disenvoiced "others." Nothing could be further away from the cynical attitude than the moral superiority of victimhood, the narcissism of identity politics or the escape in hedonism. The cynics did not wish to be liked and did not wish to be admired for being victims. Their courage and fortitude expressed itself in snarling, outrageous, "in your face" rebelliousness that refuses to be compromised, refuses to be silenced and refuses to be ignored. Not an easy stance to adopt, and one that requires considerable privations (ponos) and exercise (askesis) to attain. This should act as a warning to those who believe in "easy" or "comfortable" cynicism.

The repertoire of practices, aims and ideas initiated by the ancient cynics recur in the pages of this book, as Cutler imaginatively traces them in different cultural and political set-ups, in different discourses and different epochs. It is a measure of their power that they continue to resonate across all these boundaries. And it is a measure of Cutler's success that he has managed to display both the continuity and the richness of cynicism in its different incarnations. As a piece of intellectual archaeology, Cutler combines the obsessive attention to detail characteristic of the detective and the ability to make old themes and old ideas come alive in front of our eyes. The enduring quality of this book is its ability to vindicate cynicism as a defiant and imaginative stance that proudly declines to lapse into narcissism, self-pity or martyrdom, a stance from which we can learn much today.

Yiannis Gabriel is Professor of Organizational Theory at Imperial College, London.

Preface

It is a feature of cynicism, and of the cynical writer, to defy categorization. Nietzsche and Foucault, both of whom are claimed as cynics in this book, confounded their contemporaries who did not know how to categorize their work. Was it history, philosophy, or cultural theory? In writing this book I have encountered just such concern. Is it a scholarly text or cultural critique? Is it written for the academic reader or the inquiring general public? Whether as a personal philosophy or as a feature (negative or positive) of society, cynicism touches us all in one way or another. And yet as a response to the political or moral state of a particular age or society, cynicism has mutated, been forgotten, resuscitated, re-invented, and discarded and has re-emerged in different forms.

The chapters of this book reflect some of this same discontinuity both in style and presentation. From historical research, particularly in Chapter 1 where the foundations of cynicism are established, to a more critiquing style in later chapters, the sources also vary from philosophers (ancient and modern) to television and newspaper journalists, and even cartoon strips. The book focuses as much on significant periods of historical change as it does on the unique personalities that each of these cynical returns has produced. Some of the more consequential cynics are dealt with in their chronological place in history. Nietzsche is allotted an entire chapter because of his pivotal role as classical Cynic revivalist and proto-postmodernist. Yet he and other major cynics, such as Diogenes, also re-occur throughout the entire text. Lesser cynics may appear where their contribution to a particular theme or debate is pertinent. For instance, modern cynics Georges Bataille and Samuel Beckett appear in Chapter 1 because they offer essential insights into the asceticism and abjection of the ancient Greeks. The inclusion of Dilbert cartoons in the penultimate chapter is more than simply an example of the comic strip cynical genre. The significance of Dilbert is that he represents the cynic in all of us.

5

In the first chapter on classical Cynicism, I have relied mainly on secondary texts, first, because I have no pretensions to classical Greek scholarship, but more importantly, because there *are no primary texts* by Diogenes and his near contemporaries, only a few unverifiable fragments. The Cynics generally wrote nothing down. What survives is largely anecdotal, and yet that is one of its major attractions, since the Cynics rejected concepts of truth or historical fact. As Nietzsche maintained, most of history is built on myth and interpretation. The legitimacy of mythology is integral to cynical "scholarship," and in the case of the Cynics, the richness of the Diogenes legends and aphorisms is to be found in their embellishment over time. I make no apologies then, for plundering the secondary texts of both ancient and modern writers for interpretations that best fit my thesis of cynicism as a strategy of survival.

In the chapter on Renaissance cynicism, Chapter 2, I contrast the work of a modern historian with the primary texts of Machiavelli. The Italian Renaissance presents a unique period in the history of cynicism, in which some decidedly cynical features (replacing order with disorder; the flourishing of creative imagination; liberation of the individual; etc.) occur alongside un-cynical behavior such as the acquisition of material wealth and the pursuit of hedonistic pleasure. Machiavelli's cynicism is also considered: If he was a cynic, what kind of cynic was he?

In Chapter 3, Nietzsche's major works are examined alongside secondary texts, not only to present my case that Nietzsche was a cynic, but to demonstrate that he influenced all the major cynical discourses of the twentieth century. In this book, Nietzsche provides the pivotal link between classical Cynicism (of which I claim Nietzsche as the most important modern representative) and postmodern cynicism (of which I equally claim Nietzsche to be one of the primary authors). After discussing ideas familiar to Nietzsche scholars, such as the dichotomy between Dionysus and Apollo, and his Darwinian notion of an *Übermensch*, I concentrate on his more marginal — but for the cynic more significant — ideas such as his writing style, his political incorrectness and his relationship to women.

In my discussion of postmodern cynicism, Chapter 4, I challenge and dismiss notions of modernism and postmodernism as fixed points in cultural history, seeing them rather as opposing mindsets that have existed throughout time. I also describe different and contrasting postmodernisms: the type that will one day be read as a curiosity in the history of ideas, and the live, constantly forward shifting, cynical variety. This chapter does not rehearse the principal ideas of postmodern philosophers; these are far better discussed elsewhere. Instead, I look at some of the marginal ideas that illustrate the cynical side of the postmodernist project.

In Chapter 5, the art movements and isms of the early 20th century are compared to the competing philosophical schools of ancient Greece. A major difference is the speed at which one movement is disrupted and overthrown to create the next. A further parallel is made with the previous discussion as to whether or not postmodernism represents a fixed historical event, i.e., those art historians who wish to define "Avant-Garde" as a fixed point in art history, a showcase of historical art relics of the 1910s and 20s to be studied and revered; as opposed to "avant-garde" in its role of challenging and upsetting that which preceded it. An example is the battle between those who wished to continue presenting Dada, and those who declared it dead, viewing its continuance as a betrayal of everything it stood for. It is the paradox of the avant-garde artist that today's outrageous act of subverting artistic conventions will one day be revered and fixed by art historians as its own convention, to be studied and imitated.

In Chapter 6, I draw on Sloterdijk's assessment that *kynical* anti-philosophy (classical Cynicism) possesses three media by which intelligence can free itself from theory and discourse: *action, laughter, and silence*. From these I expose some figures of our age to cynical treatment.

- *Action*— This section features the polemicist, the columnist, and the film reporter. It distinguishes between two types of cynical journalist: *cynical* in the negative sense of intruding into the lives of the rich and famous simply to titillate a voyeuristic public, and "cynical" in the heroic sense of exposing the great lies of powerful individuals and organizations. Here Auberon Waugh is characterized as the archetypal cynic journalist, a figure in the mold of American columnist H.L. Mencken — someone who always spoke his own mind and was political hostage to no one.

- *Laughter*— Satire and parody, cartoon and comedy. Critique by ridicule is a tradition that can be traced back directly to the Cynics and beyond into carnivalized folklore. The Cynic Menippus of Gadara, through imitations of his work by better known writers such as Lucian, Seneca and William Blake, had a major influence on European satirical literature. This section explores Menippus's modern legacy.

- *Silence*— This section does not concern itself with loud silences, those associated, for instance, with Diogenes or the Dadaists' non-verbal performances. Such gestural rhetoric is well covered elsewhere in this book and is more appropriately regarded as cynical action. The silence discussed here is more an *effect* of cynicism than inherently cynical itself. It is the silence that often *follows* cynical noise, and during which critical reflection takes place. This is the part of the cynical process in which an altered perception of the cynic's target becomes possible: a "cynical enlightenment."

The last chapter looks at cynical responses to the new search for the self. Therapy culture and the new cult of victimhood represent the very antithesis of cynicism, yet they are also a reaction to the present cynical times—"What can we any longer believe?" Here the promises of science, spiritual enlightenment and salvation are put to the test. Cynically speaking, we are living in tame times. The power to ridicule and mock is being slowly smothered beneath a blanket of heightened emotionalism that extinguishes naked cynicism as effectively as any totalitarian regime. In today's self-conscious times, rather than challenge something that angers us, we are more likely to seek some solace for the spiritual void in which we find ourselves.

This book opens with a classical image of Diogenes in his barrel — albeit a rather idealized, athletic looking Diogenes. The space he occupies is the minimum necessary for his needs yet the symbolism is huge. In the penultimate chapter of the book, Scott Adams provides an image of the contemporary cynic: all of us, occupying our tiny workspaces (Dilbert's cubicle in place of Diogenes' barrel) make our own whimper of protest; be it a Dilbert cartoon, an irreverent aphorism, or some other minor act of delinquency. Diogenes and Dilbert share more than dogs for companions and a cubicle from which to challenge the world, both represent an attempt to assert one's individual spirit and integrity. Cynicism is neither a dead philosophy of the ancients nor a destructive toxin that undermines the "wisdom" of the modern world. It is the way in which all of us seek to maintain our sanity, if only by ridiculing our desperate attempts to order and regulate the chaotic world in which we exist.

A note on uses of the terms "cynic/ism": Since at least four different meanings of the terms cynicism and cynic are used in this book, a definition of each is required to ensure that the author's intended meaning is made clear. First, the use of the term with a capital C refers to classical Greek Cynicism and to its adherents. The second use of the term cynicism refers to the positive, modern application highlighted by this book; an orientation to life captured by Peter Sloterdijk's remark that cynicism is the universally widespread way in which enlightened people see to it that they are not taken for suckers. Third, *cynicism* in italics (except where quoted directly) refers to the popular, disparaging use of the term as an attitude that is negative and sneering. The modern nihilistic form (as distinct from the positive or negative forms described above) will be described as such in the text. Wherever possible I will use no emphasis, either to represent a generic term for all the above, because the meaning is obvious in the context, or to have a neutral currency on which the reader may place his or her own interpretation.

1

Classical Foundations of Cynicism

The fountain from which Cynicism sprang among the Greeks is ... an irresistible urge to say "no" to the world that human beings have constructed, because, in the light of *reason* such a world is built on faulty foundations.—*Luis E. Navia*[1]

CYNIC ORIGINS

For those who have heard of the Cynics at all, an image may come to mind of a rather eccentric, unkempt sage, who was supposed to have lived in a barrel and who once walked the streets in daylight with a lighted lamp in search of an honest man. Diogenes of Sinope has become the one enduring symbol of this lesser-known group of classical Greek thinkers. But in often being presented in comic or ridiculous caricature, the serious philosophy underlying the Cynics' more bizarre public performances has been regrettably overlooked.

It is not possible to assign to the birth of Cynicism an exact date or specific individual. Its sources are numerous and varied and so in this sense it was never really founded. Cynicism is best understood as an expression of universal human tendencies, which clearly existed well before Antisthenes (a student of Socrates and supposedly Diogenes' teacher) and also in other sects outside of Greece. Philosophical objections to traditional religions and the sciences, not to mention the ridicule of dogma and hypocrisy in general, had a long pre–Socratic history. Heraclitus, who lived around 200 years before Socrates, was adopted as a Cynic in the *Cynic Epistles*.[2] Hercules was also a model of Cynic ideals; the legendary hero recognized no city or country as his own and accepted no political or social author-

9

ity over himself. His capacity to endure pain and hardship corresponds to Cynic *askesis* and *ponos* (discussed below) and gave him the strength to wander freely as an exile.

Although external influences on the development of Greek thought are denied by many classical Greek scholars, anxious to maintain its purity,[3] there are strong arguments to suggest that Cynicism may have been influenced by Eastern thought and philosophy. Buddhism and Cynicism both hold to the notion that the key to happiness can be achieved by mastering our desires: if one desires nothing, one lacks nothing. It is not inconceivable, then, that Cynic thought was influenced, to some degree at least, by Buddhist teachings. Trade links certainly existed between the Mediterranean and India during the hundred or so years before Cynicism formally emerged. According to Indian records the Buddha died in 483 B.C., 79 years before Diogenes was reportedly born in 404 B.C. Further exchanges must have taken place between Greeks and Indian sages during the campaigns of Alexander.

Like most other philosophical movements of the time, Cynicism was influenced in various ways by sophistry. The early Sophists were the first philosophers to concern themselves with the specific study of human civilization as opposed to the scientific study of nature in general. This interest in the study of human society is said to have grown from the increasing contact that the Greeks had with other advanced civilizations such as the Egyptians and the Babylonians.[4] Evidence that other cultures could develop along different lines posed the question as to whether creation was the work of gods or of humans. These same concerns give Cynicism, and the other Hellenistic philosophies, their cosmopolitan theme. If civilization was socially constructed rather than divinely created, it followed that civilization was capable of change and improvement. Of particular interest concerning the Sophists is the usefulness that others made of the art of pedagogy itself. Both Socrates and Antisthenes owed much of their rhetorical skills to an earlier Sophistical training. They used these skills later to chide the Sophists for what they saw as their imputed wisdom, elusive knowledge, questionable values, compromises, and their quest for wealth.[5]

One of the more interesting — if not dubious — stories about the possible origins of Cynicism involves the Cynosarges (Park of the Agile Dog),[6] a gymnasium and a temple to the worship of Hercules, traceable to the sixth century B.C. The Cynosarges was the only place where Athenian "bastards" were permitted to worship and exercise. Bastards were defined by Athenian law as including anyone with an Athenian father but whose mother was a slave, a prostitute, or a foreigner, as well as those whose parents were not legally married citizens. Although they were generally well-assimilated into Athenian life, a law passed in the fifth century B.C. prohibited bastards from exercising in the gymnasiums. For some reason this law did not extend to the Cynosarges. The Cynosarges thus became a regular gathering place, not only for official bastards, but also self-proclaimed bastards: "men and women who were or felt illegitimate and foreign everywhere, and who lived ill at ease within the established civic community."[7]

And so we are provided with a description of what appears to be a natural breeding ground for Cynicism. Antisthenes, whose mother was a Thracian slave, is reported to have taught regularly at the Cynosarges, and the presence of the Herculean shrine there lends symbolic weight to the theory that this was a possible birthplace of Cynicism. Luis E. Navia even describes Hercules as a "legendary bastard, *par excellence*." [8] Some contemporary historians have argued that these links between a Cynic school (Place of the Agile Dog), Antisthenes (The Absolute Dog), and Diogenes (also known as The Dog), have been conveniently contrived by ancient historians who needed to slot Cynicism in alongside other Greek schools of philosophy with definite founders and places of learning: Plato's Academy, Aristotle's Lyceum, Epicurus' Garden, and Zeno's (Stoicism) Stoa.[9] Yet the fact that Cynicism had neither founder nor place of origin is one of its distinguishing features. Navia maintains that arguments as to whether Antisthenes or Diogenes was the founder of Cynicism are to misunderstand the nature of Cynicism.[10] It was never a school of philosophy; rather it was a loose association of thinkers who opposed the dogmas peddled by all institutions of the time: educational, judicial and religious. Whatever the truth behind the development of Cynicism, the individual historical accounts surrounding the Cynosarges and the individuals associated with it do, when put together, suggest an identifiable group even if they do not provide evidence of a cohesive movement.

The Greek Cynics were given much more to talking (and performing) than they were to writing. Much of their unique philosophy was received through later generations of writers and thinkers, often in the form of anecdotes and witty sayings, or *chreiai*. Nevertheless, there was at one time a considerable body of Cynic texts, which have been lost or possibly destroyed because of ideological objections to their message.[11] Antisthenes is credited with having written more than 70 titles on rhetoric, logic, ethics and politics, as well as literary works. Diogenes himself is variously attributed with a number of dialogues, including a *Republic,* and Crates has been credited as one of the most influential figures of his time, having composed tragedies, elegies, epistles and parodies.[12] Only a few fragments of these original texts survive, so consequently most of what we know of the Cynics is documented and interpreted by others, often in the form of myth or legend which has survived centuries of retelling. There is also much debate about who was and who was not a Cynic. Many of those attributed to the school held conflicting views or branched off into other doctrines such as the Stoics. There are contemporary accounts of Cynicism written by orthodox academics and writers of the time, but because these writers were themselves the butt of Cynic jibes, much of the insight we have into Greek Cynicism is highly critical. Close-hand accounts of Cynicism do exist, most notably in the form of fictional letters written to and between Cynics and their contemporaries, and collected in *The Cynic Epistles.*

Contemporary devotees of classical Greek philosophy tend to steer well clear of the Cynics. In *The Therapy of Desire*, Martha Nussbaum extols the practical importance of the Hellenistic philosophies, stressing their relevance to the "deepest needs" of human beings—the very essence of Cynicism. Yet the Cynics are considered and dismissed in one paragraph of her book because, she says, "regretfully" the paucity of reliable information on Cynicism would have made her text a "scholarly quagmire."[13] This in itself is very revealing, for Cynicism by its very nature defies scholarly interpretation, not because the source material is itself based largely on myth and anecdote, but because Cynicism rejects systems, categories and universal transcendent truths—not least with regard to its own philosophy. If Cynicism has a philosophy at all it is an anti-philosophy, that is, anti philosophy as absolute laws or binding faith. And although Cynics shared certain beliefs and attitudes in common, there was no school or central doctrine to study or learn. Cynicism was a very loose set of values, beliefs, and attitudes, which could be interpreted and practiced according to the individual's own will.

Nussbaum (and Sharples, who also passes over the Cynics[14]) goes on to credit Stoicism with many of the virtues, but none of the vices, attributed to Cynicism by other scholarly sources. This is doubly insulting, since Stoicism was founded by Zeno of Citium, one of the Cynics' legatees. Fortunately, however, other writers have waded through the quagmire, treating the study of Cynicism as a personal challenge. Navia, for instance, provides an annotated bibliography of over 650 texts on the subject.[15]

The term Cynic is derived from the Greek *kynicos*, the adjectival form of the noun for dog,[16] and is a literal reference to dog-like appearance and behavior, such as fornicating and defecating in public, and scavenging for scraps of food. Where others used it with derisory intent, the Cynics embraced the term as a signal for a positive choice of lifestyle.[17] Popular history has it that Diogenes of Sinope (nicknamed "the Dog" because of his growling, snapping demeanor) was the founder of the sect. Other historians argue that Cynicism's precursor was Antisthenes, Diogenes' teacher and Socrates' pupil.[18] Yet, as has been acknowledged, such debates do not add any meaningful understanding to the nature of this loose philosophy. As Navia writes,

> Socrates knew, possibly more than any other human being, how to distinguish reality from appearance, certainty from opinion, and truth from falsehood. He understood with unforgiving clarity the nonsensical character of the games in which politics and social conventions entangle human beings.[19]

What we can say, is that the movement we refer to as Cynicism was born out of the Socratic tradition, and yet, importantly, it stood in opposition to Platonism with its belief in external absolutes. There was a major split in Socrates' philosophical legacy that can be traced back to two of his most famous pupils. Plato took the more accepted academic route and in turn influenced Aristotle. Antisthenes (through Diogenes) influenced Cynicism and to varying degrees the later Hellenistic philosophies. A long feud existed between the two main inheritors of the Socratic school, with Plato frequently on the receiving end of Diogenes' wrath for selling-out to Socrates.[20] Certainly Diogenes faithfully followed Socrates' example of conducting his discourse verbally (and non-verbally) rather than writing down his ideas.

In the same way that many of the Gospel sayings of Jesus of Nazareth were penned by those who had never even met Jesus, so the sayings ascribed to Diogenes (cited in this book by his name in italics) and other leading Cynics, are unlikely to be their own words but interpretations often several sources removed. This of course does not invalidate the authenticity of cynical history, which does not depend for its validity on scholarly interpretation. As is discussed later, with regard to cynical philosophers such as Nietzsche and Foucault, the *truth* of their writings depends as much on allegory and mythology as it does on *fact*—which for the cynic is always fictional in any case.

Diogenes' principal disciple was Crates, who in turn taught Zeno, the founder of Stoicism. Stoicism, although rejecting the Cynics' ascetic, begging life-style, recognized in Cynicism the pure ethical tradition of Socrates of which they were anxious to be the direct inheritors. The following table of dates provides a chronological link between some of these philosophers. The fact that only 136 years separate the approximate birth dates of Socrates and Zeno (many minor schools have been omitted) demonstrates the prolific development of classical Greek philosophy during this period. The reader should perhaps also consider that none of the fundamental debates we have in society today had not been already discussed, arguably with more sophistication, by these same philosophers over two thousand years ago.

Socrates	470–399 B.C.	Aristotle	384–322 B.C.
Antisthenes (Cynic)	c. 445–360 B.C.	Pyrrho (Scepticism)	c. 365–275 B.C.
Aristippus (Hedonism)	c. 435–355 B.C.	Crates (Cynic)	c. 360–280 B.C.
Plato	429–347 B.C.	Epicurus (Epicureanism)	c. 341–270 B.C.
Diogenes (Cynic)	c. 404–323 B.C.	Zeno (Stoicism)	c. 334–262 B.C.[21]

Although reborn many times during the 800-year period between the death of Socrates and the demise of the Roman Empire, and in spite of its popularity spreading from Athens to the Ukraine and from Palestine to Rome, classical Cynicism was never acknowledged as a leading philosophical school. By the middle of the fourth century only the New Academy, the Epicureans, and the Stoics were of any importance. Only the latter recognized the Cynics at all, and then only as poor relations.[22] Cynicism enjoyed renewed outbursts of popularity during its Classical history but reached its peak during the first half of the second century AD with large numbers of Cynics in Rome and Alexandria. There was a great gathering of Cynics from all parts of the Greek-speaking world at the Olympic games in 167 A.D. and a few years later it is reported that the humbler classes were turning Cynic in such numbers that alarm was being expressed at the prospect of work being brought to a standstill.[23] Although Cynicism increased its numbers there is no evidence that it widened its range; most of the known Cynics were of Greek extraction and few could speak Latin.

A study of the periods in which Cynicism enjoyed a growth in popularity indicates possible reasons for its renaissance. Conditions which had proved favorable for the growth of Cynicism after the death of Alexander were also present in the early years of the first century A.D. Political and social vacuums, in which philosophy was involved in an uneasy compromise with rampant luxury, left the ordinary person feeling alienated and abandoned.[24] Parallels can be drawn here with our own increasing interest in consumerism, and the institutionalization and consequent abandonment of social responsibility today. 'There was a demand for a simpler, practical creed, which Cynicism was to meet."[25]

SOME DISTINCTIONS BETWEEN
THE CYNICS AND OTHER SCHOOLS

I do not wish to devote a great deal of space to discussing other individual schools of Greek philosophy. They are not the subject of this book and have all received a great deal more scholarly attention than Cynicism. However, it is only when contrasting Cynicism with these other schools that the novel and uniquely radical stance of the Cynics emerges. For instance, in contrast to other philosophies (which are distinguished by their theoretical assumptions about the world), the essence of Cynicism is to be found in its stylistic nuances and the behavior of its adherents. The distinction between these philosophies will also be important for later discussions in this book. In particular, I do not intend to discuss in any detail the ideas of Plato and Aristotle. This is not to deny the major influence that Plato and Aristotle have had on Western philosophical thought — dominating it for the past two millennia. Nor is it to deny the significance of the battle for Socrates' philosophical inheritance. Indeed, this book would not have been written were it not for this ideological war, a war that is still being waged today. In some respects, contemporary expressions of cynicism can be viewed as a reaction against the Platonic legacy that continues to dominate our social and metaphysical lives.

The predominant feature of Platonism is one that identifies human beings as sophisticated and rational animals, capable through scientific logic and reasoning of progressing to ever greater levels of understanding about themselves and the world they inhabit. Plato's knowledge existed through first principles, pre-existing truths which he held to apply universally, regardless of individual interpretation.[26] It is not difficult to see how the idea of arriving at knowledge through sensory experience — so important to the Cynics, Epicureans, and Hedonists — was devalued by Plato and his devotees, and is still for the most part devalued today. One does not have to look far to locate the contempt with which the Cynics regarded Plato. In Plato and his writings, Antisthenes found everything that he felt adversely afflicted humanity: pride, falsehood, pretentiousness, arrogance, mystification, superstitious and religious humbug, the worship of the state, contempt toward what is concrete, and the misuse of language for the purpose of hiding one's own confusion.[27]

The "march of progress" theories associated with the Platonic and Aristotelian legacy, and the belief in grand narratives explaining our existence, have been continually challenged over the centuries, notably by the Cynics and their legatees but also by modern philosophers such as Nietzsche and some of those labeled as postmodernists. Cynics of all shades can acknowledge the dramatic technical and scientific advancements that feed the myth of progressive enlightenment, but they would question whether such advances have enhanced the quality of human life, or, even sent it into decline. In contrast to the positivist mind set which views the study and manipulation of natural phenomena as the way to advance civilization, cynics point to the numerous examples of humans' continued folly in the management of their lives; in spite of, or even because of, our technological advantages. One obvious example of this is provided by Epicurus (see below) and is as true today as it was in 200 B.C.: people's ability to kill ever greater numbers of their own kind more efficiently.

The cynic, whether Classical, Renaissance, Modern, or Postmodern, regards the course of civilization not as a linear progression toward some ultimate truth or higher state of being, but a cyclical series of beginnings and endings, further beginnings, highs and lows. Each individual and each generation have the same opportunity for success or for failure as the next. A cynical view is put forward to suggest that although science develops in a linear fashion, human beings' sophistication and ability to *manage* their knowledge is as fragile and unpredictable as it ever was.

The four schools outlined below all share with Cynicism some of this antipathy toward Platonism, and in the case of Scepticism, Epicureanism, and Stoicism, the three major schools of the Hellenistic period, were to a greater or lesser extent influenced by the minor school of Cynicism. At times, the distinctions made between different Greek schools of philosophy will appear contradictory, at others so thin that one looks hard for any difference at all. Some individual philosophers had more in common with philosophers from other schools than they did with those from the same school. Disagreements often resulted in splits, defections, or the founding of new schools and therefore the characteristics of each should not necessarily be attributed equally to all its adherents.

Hedonism

The Cyreniac or Hedonistic school is worthy of a brief mention because it shares with Cynicism not only its historical classification as a minor or lesser known school of philosophy, but also the fact that it was founded around the same time as was the Cynic school. Aristippus of Cyrene was a contemporary of Antisthenes and fellow disciple of Socrates. However, at least one historian describes Hedonism as the philosophic doctrine to which Cynicism was most opposed.[28] Aristippus held as his central belief that our actions should be directed to obtaining the greatest amount of pleasure. Cynicism in contrast offered solace in the face of adversity and a strengthening of character aimed at liberating the Cynic from his or her desires and needs.[29] Any happiness a Cynic achieved was obtained by eliminating dependence on material possessions and sensory comforts, not to mention slavish obedience to prevailing cultural, religious or political precepts.

Later Hedonists modified their philosophy in a way that brought it much closer to Cynicism, particularly with regard to its contempt for accepted values.[30] Even Aristippus had acknowledged that extreme self-indulgence could only be acquired at the cost of pain, and recommended that in order to minimize the pain that may accompany pleasure, we should also work at mastering our desires.[31] One of Hedonism's later followers, Hegesias, became so sceptical of attaining contentment through positive enjoyment that he adopted a philosophy of pessimism, declaring happiness to be unattainable. Regardless of this setback, some elements of the Hedonistic school were refined and lived on in Epicureanism, in the same way that the Stoics claimed to have inherited and refined Cynicism. The claim could equally be made, that these later philosophies corrupted the purity and raw idealism of the earlier post–Socratic schools of Cynicism and Hedonism.

Scepticism

A distinction between the terms cynicism and scepticism is particularly important, because in popular usage today they are often, and incorrectly, used inter-changeably. There were some commonalities between the two schools, the "Sceptical way" supposedly having been founded by Pyrrho of Ella in about 300 B.C., during the period that Cynicism itself was emerging.[32] Like Socrates, Pyrrho wrote nothing down. His teachings were recorded by Sextus and others from the writings of Pyrrho's disciple Timon of Phlius, of whom no original writing remains.[33] As with the Cynics, the Sceptics stood in opposition to the Dogmatists, and both involved a tough-minded resistance to gullibility and credulousness. Yet the similarities stop there, because unlike the Sceptics, the Epicureans and the Stoics, the Cynics distanced themselves from these formally established schools, preferring to pour scorn on all of them from the outside.[34]

The literal meaning of sceptic is inquirer. R. W. Sharples informs us that paradoxically, it was the Sceptics' eagerness to find the truth that led them to suspend judgment about it.[35] Suspension of judgment about everything brought freedom from anxiety and disturbance. If one was not of the view that death or illness were great evils one was less inclined to be perturbed by them.[36] This is also a strategy picked up by the Stoics. Bar some refinements, Scepticism is also one of the few classical philosophies to survive almost intact to the present day. In the popular sense, the main distinction between scepticism and cynicism is that, whereas for most sceptics absolute proof is required of something before the sceptic is inclined to accept it, for the cynic, concepts such as proof or truth are irrelevant, the cynic's truth being one of degrees and relative virtues, not one of absolutes.

Epicureanism

Like the Cynics, Epicurus saw a society that was fundamentally flawed. It was a civilization populated by people who, through teaching and social conditioning, had internalized the unhealthy desires of "false social advertising." He challenged the rationalist view of those like Plato and Aristotle who considered that human virtue could be arrived at through philosophical and mathematical reasoning. Unlike Plato's doctrine of first principles, Epicurean knowledge was based on what was received via the senses. Although they believed in gods, the Epicureans maintained that conventional religion was at odds with a tranquil existence. Such religious belief was based on a false fear of gods derived from mental images: "we should rather trust in our eyes."[37] In contrast to Plato's view that society was made up of fundamentally calm, rational people whose beliefs were soundly based, Epicurus saw a society that had been essentially corrupted. As with the Cynics and the Stoics, Epicurus looked to the behavior of animals for inspiration. He held that true human good lay in the healthy desires experienced by animals, and also that of children before being corrupted by teaching and discourse.

Epicureanism offered a practical guide to keeping life free from disturbances. Like the Sophists, the Epicureans taught for money, and like the Hedonists, they adopted the view that pleasure should be the final aim of our actions. Sensual impulses and a rich enjoyment of life were permitted so long as one avoided a dependence on such things. The goal of happiness was to be achieved by balancing the most pleasure with the least pain. This did not necessarily equate to self-indulgence, since pleasure could be achieved as much by altruistic actions as it could by selfish ones—in fact more so. It was the degree to which pain (physical pain and mental anguish) could be removed that was the Epicurean's main criterion of happiness. Furthermore, happiness itself could not be increased exponentially. A lavish banquet, for instance, would not provide a greater degree of pleasure than a crust of bread and a drink of water; if the measure of happiness is the degree to which the pain of thirst or hunger can be vanquished.[38]

According to Lucretius (first century Latin writer and Epicurean), the road to happiness is often an elusive one. For in seeking fame and fortune — a need which, he tells us, is impelled by a desire for security and contentment in life — the opposite fate is in fact often achieved. The resulting, and more lasting pain (including the pain of guilt, envy, regret, etc.) nullify and circumvent any happiness, which may have been achieved. The Cynics were one step ahead of this Epicurean logic, for in attempting to avoid pain and disillusionment, they spent their life training for and subjecting themselves to the worst kind of pain and hardship as an insurance against being cast down. Many instances of this Cynic training (*askesis*) will be discussed later; for example, Diogenes begging alms of a statue in order to get practice in being refused. Living an ascetic lifestyle removed the possibility of destitution because the Cynic had already cast himself down out of a positive choice of lifestyle.

Stoicism

Supposedly founded by Zeno, disciple of the Cynic Crates, Stoicism appears to be a rather strange hybrid between Cynic values and Platonic logic with some unique features of its own thrown in for good measure. Like Plato, the Stoics held that there was a unified, orderly logic to the world giving rise to natural, universal laws.[39] From Plato's school, Zeno borrowed the division of philosophy into logic, physics and ethics, applying his own criteria to these classifications.[40] The Stoics' belief that true morality was impossible without knowledge based on scientific research and fixed methods of proof set them well apart from the Cynics, and yet like the Cynics, the Stoics engaged in attacking what they saw as the false values embodied in orthodox political, philosophical and religious beliefs. But whereas the Cynics simply ridiculed and disregarded such ideas, the Stoics took it as their mission to challenge these ideas through reasoned argument, offering their own brand of truth in its place.

Stoicism further differed from Cynicism in its evangelical stance. It aimed at converting people to the benefits of its philosophy, the brand of which, like Epicureanism, was a medicine for the diseased soul.[41] Stoicism was certainly more popular than Cynicism; it had a major influence over both Greek and Roman society for over 500 years. From Cynicism, the Stoics took their belief that external things should be eliminated from human life, but this included human passion. In marked contrast to the Hedonists and Epicureans, the Stoics claimed that the elimination of passion promised a new basis for political virtue, supporting an ideal, which would lead to a just and humane society.[42]

Like the Sceptics, the Stoics could also be accused of sitting on the fence over a number of important ethical issues. For example, the Stoics refused to adopt a critique concerning the institution of slavery, arguing that the wise and virtuous person was always free regardless of status; no one can own or imprison another's mind.[43] This notion would have provided little comfort to the majority of slaves who were probably not of a Stoic proclivity. The Cynics committed themselves to the view that *all* slaves were equal to *all* other men and women (who were also equal to each other), regardless of their wisdom or virtuosity. In contrast, Aristotle took the view that some people were naturally suited to slavery. It should be finally noted that a major feature, which all the Hellenistic philosophies shared with Cynicism, was a belief in cosmopolitanism as opposed to nationalism. Another was the voluntary withdrawal from life: the right of the individual to commit suicide when life ceased to have any purpose or became intolerable.

CYNIC LIFE: HIGH LIFE OR LOW-LIFE?

> They [the Cynics] attacked and ridiculed religion, philosophy, art, science, literature, love, friendship, good manners, loyalty to parents and the state and even athletics — everything which tended to embellish and enrich life or to give it significance and make it worth living. They did much to prepare the way for Christianity by destroying respect for existing religions, by ignoring distinctions of race and nationality, and by instituting an order of wandering preachers who claimed exceptional freedom in expressing their views.[44]

The passage quoted from Sayre above provides a useful insight into the powerful negative emotions that Cynicism must have generated. It gives equally powerful evidence of the potential — though not intentional — achievements of Cynicism: in this case undertaking the ground clearing that paved the way for Christianity. One possible reason that Cynicism itself did not survive as a movement was that the Cynics were individualistic, having no organization or social cohesion.[45] Another is that the Cynics' rejection of totalizing theories rules it out as a philosophy of social change: It is, rather, a pragmatic philosophy, one that responds to prevailing circumstances rather than initiating them.

Characteristically, the Cynics turned to the habits of lower animals as a source of rhetoric for the most natural way to live. Diogenes' lifestyle, it is said, was inspired by watching a mouse running about: not looking for a place to lie down in, not afraid of the dark, not seeking any of the things which we consider to be dainties.[46] From such observations Diogenes discovered the means of adapting himself to circumstances, as indicated in this passage attributed to Diogenes:

> We should not try to alter circumstances, but to adapt ourselves to them as they really are, as do sailors. They don't try to change the winds or the sea, but take care that they are ready to adapt themselves to conditions. In a dead calm they use the oars, with a following breeze they crowd on sail; with a head wind they shorten sail or heave to. Do you adapt yourself to circumstances in the same way?[47]

As a further example of learning from animals, Diogenes' choice of a large earthenware wine vat as a mobile home is said to have been inspired by his observation of a snail. It was this simple lifestyle, deliberately adopted to contrast with civic society's obsession with luxury and complexity that distinguished Cynics and brought them into ridicule.[48]

The particular modes of discourse employed by the Cynics to deliver their unique form of protest (a language in complete contrast to the verbosity of postmodern cynicism) are exemplified by its minimalism as well as by its power to shock. A clear link will be established between the apparently insignificant though often outrageous actions attributed to certain Cynics, and the powerful ethical stance, which such actions underpinned. Written accounts cover almost every aspect of contra-convention by the Cynics, from incest to defecating in public: "he [Diogenes] saw nothing improper in stealing from the temples, nor from eating the flesh of any animal; nor indeed in cannibalism, for one could find examples of it amongst the customs of foreign nations."[49] But because many of these accounts come from sources hostile to the Cynics, it is difficult to separate malignity from actuality. Whatever the validity of these reports, we do know that the Cynics' actions were supported by strong moral justification. Their practice of living according to nature is partly based on their repudiation of societal laws, which rule certain activities as public and others as private. The Cynic maintained that all human appetites were equal in nature. To explain his habit of masturbating in public, Diogenes is reported to have said, "I only wish I could be rid of hunger by rubbing my belly."[50] It is hardly surprising that Diogenes' antics have attracted a degree of interest and speculation. First century writer and sometime Cynic, Dio Chrysostom, described Diogenes' public masturbation as a demonstration of the folly of those who spend money to satisfy their sexual appetites: "[Diogenes] found Aphrodite everywhere, and for free." And Lucian, second century satirist and Cynic revivalist, claims that Diogenes' public exhibition of relieving himself of his bodily fluids was done in deliberate contrast to those who conceal their bodily functions yet publicly steal, bear false witness, etc., "For what he did was according to our common nature while what they did ... was all carried out because of perversion."[51]

What emerges as a result of examining these (albeit anecdotal) references, is a clear link between even the basest of the Cynics' public behavior and their philosophical and ethical convictions. In rejecting notions of statehood and embracing the larger notion of *citizenship of the world*, the Cynics were prepared to adopt the customs of any alien civilization as ammunition with which to attack and undermine the social norms of their own culture. Some of these customs, though considered taboo at the time, contained ideals to which many still aspire today. Take the issue of euthanasia. As has already been noted, it was the accepted Cynic practice to commit suicide in old age. The most dramatic anecdote recorded involved the Cynic Peregrinus, who said that he wished to put a golden finial to a golden life. After announcing at the Olympic games of 163 B.C. his intention of publicly throwing himself into a burning funeral pyre at the following games, he enjoyed the four years of advertising and speculation and then carried out the performance as promised.[52] Diogenes can perhaps claim the ultimate Cynic statement in subverting social norms. As was his custom of using his own body as a language of protest, he requested that following his death his body should be buried face down, a desire that even in death his body would act as a symbol for the inversion of the social order. He claimed that, in any event, "after a little time down will be converted into up."[53]

The abject lifestyle described above — this living on the edge of society and courting indecency, defilement and death — is as much about embracing a *positive* identity, as it is about simply cocking a snoot at convention. It is helpful to consider Julia Kristeva's thesis in *Powers of Horror: An essay on Abjection* in order to illuminate further this aspect of Cynic life. Kristeva maintains that we are defined by the things that disgust us; the waste of our own bodies is expelled in order that we may live. Our world exists on one side of the border that separates the living "I" from the ultimate waste of our own corpse. Decay and defilement mark out the limits of our own mortality:

> On the edge of non-existence and hallucination, of a reality that, if I acknowledge it, annihilates me. There, abject and abjection are my safeguards. The primers of my culture.... If dung signifies the other side of the border, the place where I am not and which permits me to be, the corpse, the most sickening of wastes, is a border that has encroached upon everything. — *Kristeva*[54]

More than any other modern writer, Samuel Beckett captured the ascetic and abject side of the true Diogenean Cynic. Beckett's heroes (or anti-heroes) are the dispossessed, banished to the absolute margins of society, sometimes contriving elaborate techniques for begging but more often abandoning any responsibility for their own survival whatsoever, obsessed only with their bodily functions. By placing themselves at the very threshold of death (one even encounters monologues from the already dead) Beckett's characters affirm life as only the true cynic can. Unlike *Robinson Crusoe* (of which there are some odd parallels) where Defoe's hero attempts to recreate civilization from the wilderness of his desert island, Beckett's unnamed creature in his novella *The End* seeks less than the minimum necessary to sustain life. Several passages are included below from this one novella to demonstrate Beckett's empathy for the cynic. Beckett's works alone warrant an entire treatise on cynicism, yet this one minor work serves well to highlight Beckett's own cynicism. In the opening scene of *The End*, our hero is ejected from an institution where he has been incarcerated for many years and left to fend for himself with no more than the clothes he stands up in and a small amount of money for food and lodgings. Seeking no more than a place to lie down, perhaps to die quietly and peacefully on his own, he is denied even this luxury. After handing over most of his money to a woman he believes to be the owner of a rat-infested basement, he is then ejected by the real owner: "He said he needed the room immediately for his pig ... I asked if he couldn't let me have another place, any old corner where I could lie down ... I could live here with the pig, I said.... A bus took me to the country. I sat down in a field in the sun.... The night was cold. I wandered round the fields. At last I found a heap of dung.[...]"

Just as the Cynics sought inspiration from the lives of animals, Beckett's character has to give up his abode to a pig only to find warmth and shelter in a dung heap. He is then further shunned by society for his unpleasant appearance and odor:

> One day I met a man I had known in former times. He lived in a cave by the sea ... I reminded him that I wasn't in the habit of staying more than two or three minutes with anyone and that the sea did not agree with me. He seemed deeply grieved to hear it. But to my amazement I got up on the ass and off I went ... little boys jeered and threw stones, but their aim was poor. A policeman stopped us and accused us of disturbing the peace. My friend replied that we were as nature had made us, the boys too were as nature had made them.[...]

In this account we find shades of the Cynic Crate's view that even Diogenes' barrel was a luxury. We are then presented with the stoical manner in which the insults of others are endured and dismissed by the Cynic's philosophical response that man-made laws are at odds with the natural laws of human nature. The character goes to a filthy, decrepit shack in the mountains:

> Nevertheless it was a roof over my head. I rested on a bed of ferns, gathered at great labor with my own hands. One day I couldn't get up. The cow saved me.... She dragged me across the floor, stopping from time to time only to kick me. I did not know our cows could be so inhuman....

The absurdity of life is a hallmark of Beckett's writing, but if Diogenes and Nietzsche mix humor with ridicule and sarcasm, Beckett's work is always presented with a gentle humility and resignation to the bitterness of life. Having already been dispossessed by a pig, our hero is almost thankful for the cow's intervention in removing him from his hovel.

> I unbuttoned my trousers discretely to scratch myself.... Real scratching is superior to masturbation, in my opinion.... Often at the end of the day I discovered the legs of my trousers all wet. That must have been the dogs. I personally pissed very little.[...]

With little else to give meaning to life, the functions and obsessions of the body now become the sole preoccupation of our hero's attention. The pleasure of scratching is further acknowledged on page 26 in an anecdote concerning the Cynic Crates by Marcel Schwob.

> I found a boat, upside down. I righted it.... I made a kind of lid with stray boards.... I pushed it a little towards the stern, climbed into the boat by the bow, crawled to the stern, raised my feet and pushed the lid back towards the bow till it covered me completely.[...]

The various dwelling places of Beckett's character had been secured from necessity rather than deliberate choice as in the case of Diogenes' barrel. He is oblivious to the rest of the world but neither does he ask or expect anything from it. He survives the absurdity of his situation by being totally at one with no more than his own existence and immediate surroundings.

> There were times when I wanted to push away the lid and get out of the boat and couldn't.... So I waited till the desire to shit, even piss, lent me wings.... To contrive a little kingdom, in the midst of the universal muck, then shit on it, ah that was me all over. The excrements were me too, I know, I know, but all the same.— *Samuel Beckett*[55]

Beckett succeeds in transcending completely Kristeva's definition of humanness. He has crossed that border that separates the living "I" from the waste of our own mortality. Diogenes likewise, in his indifference to the waste of his own body, marks himself out from the pretensions of human beings' sham sophistication. He lays bare his own mortality, and in so doing becomes the living embodiment of the mortality and madness of people in general. He reinforces his own position on the margins of society, a society that in turn rejects his Cynic lifestyle as base and inhuman in order to reinforce its own higher level of functioning. When Diogenes pisses, farts, defecates and masturbates in public, he is doing no more than ridiculing the artificial conventions of society around him. Peter Sloterdijk gets straight to the point of this whole issue regarding the Cynics' relationship to human waste and, at the same time, provides us with a description that the reader will find resonates with a later discussion on Menippean satire and the carnivalesque:

> As children of an anal culture, we all have a more or less disturbed relation to our own shit.... The relationship that is drummed into people with regard to their own excretions provides the model for their behavior with all sorts of refuse in their lives.... Diogenes is the only Western philosopher who we know consciously and publicly performed his animal business, and there are reasons to interpret this as a component of a pantomimic theory. It hints at a consciousness of nature that assigns positive values to the animal side of human beings and does not allow any dissociation of what is low or embarrassing. Those who do not want to admit that they produce refuse ... risk suffocating one day in their own shit.[56]

As if in answer to Kristeva's question, "how can I be without border," Diogenes seems to be putting forward a positive alternative to the fragile civilized existence to which conventional society clings.[57] If, as Georges Bataille suggests, abjection is the inability to assume with sufficient strength the imperative act of excluding abject things,[58] it follows that by embracing abject things (Diogenes pissing, passing wind, and defecating in public; Hipparchia, the Cynic wife of Crates, licking clean the purulent sores of the sick, etc.), certain Cynics would have attained a certain spiritual and moral freedom, unavailable to those of us who define our humanness by our need to exclude the abject from our thoughts or actions. The Cynics were not abject, they were simply beyond abjection, and the link between their public behavior and personal philosophy can even be interpreted as a high form of rhetoric. As other philosophies use formal lectures, treatise, and theoretical models to get their philosophy across, so the Cynic — who simply regards such dialogue as hot air — passes wind by way of a critique.

CYNIC VALUES

I was exiled for literally "altering the currency"; my philosophy teaches men to "alter the currency" in another sense. Let us strike out of circulation false standards and values of all kinds.—*Diogenes*[59]

The Cynic sees the domain of ethics as virtually empty, and recognizes and corroborates the brutal fact that, as Schopenhauer suspected, human life must be some kind of mistake.— *Navia*[60]

Disdainful of superficial posturing, the kind demonstrated by today's political correctness, the Cynics took more practical steps to address what they regarded as unfairness and inequality in society. This included the position of women: "The only marriage he [Diogenes] recognized was the union of the man who persuades with the woman who lets herself be persuaded." [61] We might contrast this view with that of Plato, who regarded women as inherently the weaker sex, adding that men in general are better able to carry out most tasks,[62] or Aristotle, who claimed that "by nature the male is more fitted to be in command than the female," and that it was men's nature to be master of the household (the smallest unit of the State) "ruling" over women and children.[63] The Cynic community was an egalitarian one in which all distinctions of rank and birth were to be abolished and even children were held in common.[64] Regarding charges that Diogenes was a misogynist, it should be considered (as discussed later in respect of Nietzsche) that he had nothing good to say about *anyone*, male or female: "He hated evil people for their depravities and good people for their silence in the presence of moral depravity."[65] His comment on seeing a woman hanging from a tree, "I wish every tree bore similar fruit," could equally have applied to men. Diogenes was consistently vicious with his aphoristic quips so it is unremarkable that women should in any way be treated differently from men.

And yet Hipparchia is the only woman Cynic philosopher of whom we have a written account. The sister of Metrocles (a pupil of Crates), Hipparchia came from a wealthy family. One of the most endearing accounts of the life of Crates and Hipparchia is given in a modern fictional account by Marcel Schwob in *The King in the Golden Mask and Other Stories*. Crates was the archetypal Cynic. Originally well born, he considered even Diogenes' barrel a luxury:

He lived stark naked among the sweepings, and he collected crusts of bread, rotten olives and fish bones to fill his wallet ... an unknown skin-disease covered him with swellings. He scratched himself with nails he never trimmed and remarked that from this he drew a double profit, since he wore them down and at the same time experienced relief.[66]

It was with this abject but happy figure that Hipparchia, young, beautiful and well born, fell in love. They married in spite of her parents' objections, and regardless of Crates' warnings to her that they would live like dogs in the street. Both Crates and Hipparchia are remembered for their compassion to the poor and sick. They lived long and happy lives in the streets of Athens and Piraeus, giving to the poor "the mute aid animals give to one another." We do not know of Hipparchia's death, but (according to Schwob's version) when Crates had done with living, as was the Cynic practice, he simply starved himself to death.

The Cynics also spoke out against slavery, and furthermore, the slave turned Cynic would meet with the respect of his equals however much he or she might be despised by civic society at large.[67] The following quotation by the proto–Cynic Heraclitus is consistent with the Cynic stance on this subject:

> What do you think, you men? If God did not make dogs or sheep slaves, nor asses nor horses nor mules, did he then make men slaves? ... They do not reduce one another to slavery, nor does one eagle buy another eagle, nor does one lion pour wine for another lion, nor does one dog castrate another dog, ... Or how can you act piously toward a statue, when you have acted impiously against nature?[68]

As has already been acknowledged, although reviled in conventional circles, the Cynics set some early markers for another creed, one that was to have a more lasting and profound influence on the world — Christianity. F. Gerald Downing in his 1992 study, *Cynics and Christian Origins,* sets out to show how from early days Christianity looked like a variant of Cynicism. Early Christian writers, although very critical of more radical aspects of the Cynic tradition, found the main Cynic strand to be obvious and entirely acceptable. Downing points to the acceptance and widespread use of elements of Cynic tradition as evidence in favor of his case that this must have been how Christianity not only looked but in truth *was,* posing implications for Christian life and beliefs today.[69] It is small wonder that Cynicism itself did not survive as a movement: Cynics were asocial and individualistic. Sayre further suggests, rather malevolently, that their occupation as beggars probably brought them into rivalry with one another.[70] The description of the Cynics as beggars arises frequently in historical writings, particularly by those who would present the Cynics as opting out of society and making themselves dependent on others for their livelihood. Yet this view is at odds with the Cynic ethic of *independence.* Disparaging comparisons have been made to hippies and new age travelers who themselves have often been negatively stereotyped. Undoubtedly, some would have chosen to jump on the Cynic bandwagon in order to opt out, yet many others combined hard work with benevolence, selflessly concerning themselves with the needs of others, as shown by the example of Hipparchia and Crates. If certain Cynic philosophers begged for food or alms, they did so by way of payment for their services either as philosophers or street entertainers, in much the same way that the public give coins to buskers or street corner philosophers today. Greek philosophers from the established schools would almost certainly not have considered providing free public lectures, and in this respect, far from being portrayed as idle, the Cynics should be credited with their generosity.

Diogenes was exiled from Sinope because either he or his father, master of the mint, was caught defacing the local currency. Some historical reports directly link Diogenes to a currency scandal in Sinope in the year 396 B.C.[71] In any event, following a visit Diogenes is reported to have made to the Oracle at Delphi to seek guidance on the matter, the metaphor of re-striking the currency became a major slogan of Cynic philosophy, one in which its adherents were encouraged to test out all usages and laws to see whether or not they had any genuine validity. If they did not, it was the Cynics' role to deface them until they were abandoned.[72] "'Every century needs the presence of a Diogenes,' if nothing else to serve as an awakening call of conscience in the midst of the intellectual slumber and moral moroseness that characterizes the human existence."[73]

Diogenes was unique among philosophers of most generations, not only for his recognition of the spiritual and moral depravity of the world, but also for his courage in being able to denounce such a world "without even a passing thought about the consequences that such a mode of life could bring him."[74] It is this unique combination of profound lucidity, wicked humor, generosity, and indifference to the insults or dangers that his behavior attracted that has made Diogenes the inspirational focus of cynics old and new.

CYNIC TRAINING AND PURPOSE

As the Cynics saw it, their mission was to penetrate more deeply than others into the realm of human experience and like a scout sent into enemy territory, bring back a true report of what lay ahead. Cynicism was a special service for use in an emergency; and the emergency was the chaotic state of human life. Diogenes' own mission became a thorough onslaught on convention, custom, and tradition in all aspects.[75] Contempt for the opinions of others was a manifestation of the Cynic idea of freedom. Since laws and customs were made by men and varied among different cultures, they could have no implicit moral validity.[76] The Cynics also regarded freedom of speech and frankness (*parrhesia*) as their own special privilege,[77] and there is little doubt that during certain periods of their history, Cynics spoke very freely indeed. So freely in fact, that what was tolerated from a Cynic may well have ended in death for another. The following anecdote about Alexander's reported meeting with Diogenes, when the latter was sunning himself in Corinth, has many recorded versions and illustrates that no one was above the Cynics' contempt. When Alexander asked Diogenes to name any boon he wished, he received the unexpected reply from the Cynic: "Stand out of my light."[78] Dio Chrysostom's lengthy version of this story, his *Fourth Discourse on Kingship,* continues the tale with Diogenes baiting Alexander in the following manner:

> "But tell me this: are you the Alexander whom they call a bastard?" At this the king flushed and showed anger, but he controlled himself and regretted that he had deigned to enter into conversation with a man who was both rude and an impostor, as he thought. Diogenes, however, marking his embarrassment, would fain change his throw just like men playing at dice. So when the king said, "What gave you the idea of calling me a bastard?" he replied, "What gave it? Why, I hear that your own mother says this of you. Or is it not Olympias who said that Philip is not your father, as it happens, but a dragon or Ammon or some god … in that case you would certainly be a bastard."
>
> Thereupon Alexander smiled and was pleased as never before, thinking that Diogenes, so far from being rude, was the most tactful of men and the only one who really knew how to pay a compliment.[79]

By more closely examining this particular myth, one is able to expose from beneath the often comical exterior of Cynical discourse some of the Cynics' underlying reason. Michel Foucault devoted his last series of lectures to the study of *parrhesia.* Part of this work includes an in depth analysis of Dio Chrysostom's myth concerning Diogenes and Alexander.[80] According to Foucault, *parrhesia* refers to "a type of relationship between the speaker and what he says. For in *parrhesia,* the speaker makes it manifestly clear and obvious that what he says is his *own* opinion."[81] The parrhesiast relies on the most direct forms of expression deliberately to avoid the kind of rhetorical devices that would veil the parrhesiast's intended meaning. The parrhesiast speaks the truth because it *is* the truth, and, as in the case of Alexander, not always the truth that people wish to hear. It is the courage to say something, which endangers the speaker that distinguishes the parrhesiast from those like the rhetorician who use discourse to seduce.

Foucault adds that to qualify as *parrhesia,* "the *parrhesiastes* is always less powerful than the one with whom he speaks." Furthermore, telling the truth is regarded as a duty. The parrhesiast is not forced to tell the truth, for unlike those who are compelled to tell the truth (say under torture) the parrhesiast is free to remain silent.[82] In common with rhetoric, *parrhesia* is made more effective when supported by practical training (*askesis*), observing rules and principles associated with other arts. We are told that such practice depends, among other things, on the appreciation of the *kairos*, or the "critical moment,"[83] in which *parrhesia* strikes a balance between achieving its maximum affect and losing the interlocutor's cooperation in the parrhesiastic game — in the case of Diogenes and Alexander, of Diogenes losing his life.

But Diogenes' scorn was not reserved for kings and tyrants. His contempt was particularly venomous against the Greek philosophers and scientists whom he could not meet on their own ground. It is not clear if this is because he rejected them, or they he, but in any case he adopted what was the only safe and consistent plan: he ridiculed and denounced all of them.[84] The Cynics' negative attitude toward intellectual, political and other pretensions was simply more than idle dismissal. As the discussion on *parrhesia* shows, the Cynics felt called to challenge others and they worked hard at it. They were renowned for their physical and mental training (*askesis*) and painfully hard work (*ponos*), the consistency and rigor of which carried the main burden of their message.

Implicit in the practice of Cynic *askesis* is the conviction that acting in these particular ways makes a real difference to how things turn out, if only for yourself, the ultimate goal of which is freedom through self-mastery. What appears on the surface to be a life that is simple and minimalist in its needs, is in fact hard-won. *Parrhesia, askesis* and *ponos* are among the better known of Cynic slogans. Some others which have been identified by historians are *anaideia*: shamelessness; *apatheia*: disregard for feelings; and *autarkeia*: self-sufficiency.[85] A critical aspect of these Cynic catchwords was the practical philosophy that underpinned them.

As well as regarding themselves as having control over their own destiny, the Cynics also claimed that one was free, time and again, to change the likely course of events.[86] It followed that if things were not determined in advance, by destiny or fortune, one could make a personal difference to the outcome of one's life. The harder one trained and practiced, whether ridiculing custom and convention or combating the physical elements, the more likely one was to achieve one's personal goals. This would seem to provide the most significant mark of the Cynic, that by training one could arrive at *virtù* (in this sense, excellence).[87] "He [Diogenes] once begged alms of a statue, and when asked why he did so, replied, 'To get practice in being refused.'."[88] Because the Cynics' adherence to acquiring perfection by self-discipline was so visible (intentionally so), crowds of onlookers would often gather to observe the outward spectacle. The public performance was integrally and distinctively Cynic, and always crucially significant.[89]

Cynic virtue, then, was achieved by mastering one's passions, restricting one's needs and interests only to those required by nature, and treating no contingencies as capable of disturbing one's strength of mind. The Cynics' harsh training in respect of their frugal diet and exposure to the elements (not least all manner of microbes) meant that they developed strong immunity to the physical and emotional ill health that afflicted more delicate mortals. Yet few were prepared to embrace this discomfort. The harshness of Cynic *askesis* meant that the list of Diogenes' prospective disciples must have been severely limited. Many students quickly ran away once it became apparent that enjoying the spectacle and charismatic appeal of the master also meant emulating his harsh and meager way of life. Neither is it likely that Diogenes could have warmed to his students: "a man like Diogenes could not have found familiarity and closeness with others but a source of mental torture or at least intolerable boredom."[90] The dumping of the harsher aspects of Cynic life, together with an elevation of Cynic virtue to a goal of happiness, probably accounts for the subsequent success of Epicureanism and the consequent depreciation of Cynicism as a philosophy.

CYNIC PHILOSOPHY

> Law is a good thing, but it is not superior to philosophy. For the former compels a man not to do wrong, but the latter teaches him not to do wrong. To the degree that doing something under compulsion is worse than doing it willingly, to that degree law is worse than philosophy.— *Crates*[91]

Most philosophers are presented in terms of their ideas or systems, possibly with a few characteristic sayings thrown in. In the case of the Cynic philosophers there was very little system to present. Physical and metaphysical theories were despised, leaving little more, we are told, than a "series of brief, incisive and (sometimes) witty sayings and occasionally significant actions with or without further words to explain them."[92] For Diogenes, the only philosophy worth anything was that which could awaken people into action. The rest, as Navia puts it, 'is empty talk and useless games played by philosophers and intellectuals whose major preoccupation is to hide their spiritual emptiness."[93]

It is the insistence on the practical aspect of philosophy, and the consequent depreciation of theory and scientific analysis, that makes Cynic philosophy uniquely fascinating and worthy of more serious analysis. If the theoretical study of a practical philosophy sounds like a contradiction, it may go some way to explain why we know so little about Cynicism, or for that matter, why, following the implosion of theoretical truth and scientific certitude into the anarchy of postmodern theory, we may need a practical cynicism to help us rehabilitate reality. There is in fact a very compelling theoretical stance underpinning the way the Cynics conducted their life, and evidence that they were capable of some reasoning that still eludes us today. Take the issue of sovereignty. In Britain (using currency again as an example) there are still many people who struggle with notions of sacrificing sovereignty, represented by the monarch's head on their money, in exchange for the coinage of a more united world. Diogenes had no such qualms: "The only true commonwealth is that which is as wide as the universe. I am a citizen of the world."[94] The Cynics were the first real cosmopolitans, and for Antisthenes—being the native of a city that proclaimed him a bastard—citizenship of the world had a very poignant significance.

The Cynics' ideal republic then, was not restricted to a geographical place, nor to a racial or ethnic group, nor to historical or cultural traditions. It was a republic without boundaries or social distinctions. The Cynics revolted against the artificiality of a world constructed by human beings. They well understood that the world was not created for the benefit of people alone, and for this reason challenged the way that humans sought to explain, control, and dominate it for their own interests. This rejection of man-made constructs accounts for the Cynics' need for lucidity and an alliance to nature. It also accounts for their resolve to reject the illusions and temptations of a civilized society and why they were willing to embrace the abject side of human nature. For Diogenes, allegiance to a city or nation was a manifestation of sheer stupidity,[95] and Crates, through his understanding that a utopian state could never exist, created his own utopia within himself and his circle of family and friends.[96]

Because of their repudiation of obligations to the state, the Cynics have also been described as anarchists.[97] Not only did they reject ties of patriotism, maintaining that wise people do not fight for their country,[98] but we are also told by Sayre (who maintains the tradition for defaming the Cynics) that they broke ties of family, which in Diogenes' case included suggesting that there should be no gratitude to one's parents for being born, since we were simply creatures generated by nature.[99] It is easy to see how such disingenuous accounts would not have endeared the Cynics to conventional society. Even without the help of their critics, it was a deliberate tactic that the Cynics presented their ideals to the kinds of extremes that were guaranteed to shock and gain them attention. It is also hardly surprising that those like the Stoics and the Christians who wanted a more popular form of philosophy — one which could be mass marketed — would want to jettison the more unsavory aspects of Cynicism.

The Cynics' mission of defacing the currency of false values may have prevented them from announcing their ideas in theoretical systems. Nevertheless, many subsequent writers have attempted to draw together the Cynics' ideas in this way. In Navia's "Twelve Building Blocks of Cynicism," even though these represent the kind of edifice that the Cynics would have found extraneous, we are presented with a summation of Diogenes' thought that captures his philosophy of denunciation (without undermining its integrity) in a systematic way.[100] Yet regardless of its dismissive approach to high-minded ideals in favor of the mundane and the practical, Cynicism is neither a philosophy of nihilism or pessimism:

> ... contrary to what some historians and scholars have argued, Cynicism is *not* a philosophy of despair, an existential plunge into abandonment, that promises no redemption and no escape, but it is a philosophical stance that correctly diagnoses and perhaps cruelly identifies the sorrows and ills that permeate the human condition of this and every other time, and points the way, harsh and brutal as it may be, that can alleviate at least in part those sorrows and ills.—*Navia*[101]

The essence of Cynic virtue was self-mastery; the ability to live happily under even the most adverse of circumstances. The happy person "is the only person who is truly wise, kingly, and free." Those things conventionally deemed necessary for happiness, such as wealth, fame, and political power, have no value in nature. It is this aspect of Cynicism, more than anything else that provided the basis for the Hellenistic philosophies of Epicureanism, Stoicism and Scepticism.[102]

CYNICISM'S APPEAL

Even though it lacked a definite theoretical background, Cynicism had an appeal that lay in the strength and colorful character of many of its adherents. But in this strength lay also its weakness, for when there was no charismatic figure such as Diogenes to lead its followers, Cynicism floundered, having no system or organization to reinforce it.[103] Diogenes must also take some personal responsibility for the negative image of Cynicism. Unlike Crates, who was by all accounts kindness personified, Diogenes has been portrayed as a thoroughly unpleasant character. He regularly insulted people, hit people with his stick, and outraged them by apparently condoning incest and cannibalism, even if he did so simply as a statement of his contempt for Athenian law. These actions may have gone far beyond what other cynics advocated,[104] yet it is Diogenes who stands out as the icon of Greek Cynicism. In spite of his crusty veneer, what also comes across from the numerous anecdotes concerning Diogenes is the image of a rather endearing figure that seems to have had a deep affection for his fellow human beings. Regardless of his outward contempt for people, it was through Diogenes' practice of Cynicism that we also witness his commitment to their moral regeneration. He may have hated the degeneracy of his contemporaries, but Diogenes did not abandon them to "wallow in their moral mire."[105] Cynicism's other appeal lay in its reputation as a "philosophy of the proletariat," contrasting it markedly with the exclusivity of other philosophical schools. In particular, it is easy to understand how Cynicism might have appealed to those who never had any wealth or position but who wanted to elevate themselves a couple of notches in society. Regardless of former wealth or status, in the community of Cynics one was accepted as a social and intellectual equal. For disenfranchised groups such as slaves or women, particularly those who were independent thinkers, Cynicism would have had a particular allure. The Cynic community must have also been a place — without the more sinister motives one associates with the French Foreign Legion or some of the weirder religious sects— where one could bury the past and start a new life with a new identity.

Like early Christianity, Cynicism offered freedom from unhealthy preoccupations with the material world, but unlike Christianity, it offered immediate peace on earth for the individual rather than the promise of a reward in heaven. It was a Cynic slogan that one could lose *material* possessions, yet wisdom and knowledge could never be taken away.[106] Inevitably, there are also negative accounts of why people may have joined the Cynics; the same kind of sentiments applied to beatniks, hippies, and new age travelers who emerged during the latter half of the last century. But it would be a mistake to view the Cynics' life as an easy option. Far from wishing to avoid work and responsibility, most Cynics fully embraced their responsibilities. Many in fact gave away considerable fortunes in order to pursue asceticism as a positive lifestyle. Furthermore, by disseminating their philosophy free to all comers, they arguably contributed far more to society than those who simply chose to sell their wisdom within the exclusivity of schools of learning.

CYNIC GENRES AND LITERARY STYLES

> It is the attitudes and commitments that are expressed in witty say-
> ings, in lively metaphors and parables, and in striking actions, all
> together articulating the life-style that is lived, that show whether
> someone is talking some form of Cynicism or not.— *Downing*[107]

There has been much criticism of Diogenes Laertius' (not to be confused with our own hero) substantial work, *Lives of Eminent Philosophers*,
that it was neither philosophical nor scientific.[108] Such criticism fails to
acknowledge the real importance of Laertius. In a style worthy of the Cynics themselves, truth is not the criteria. What one gets from Laertius— not
always available from more scholarly sources— is a *flavor* and *feeling* for
the minutia of these philosophers' lives. Their non-philosophic likes and
dislikes can be cross referenced by the reader, who can also discover what
each thought about the other, depending on which account one is reading. We are told that Laertius had Epicurean leanings, yet he presents his
(mainly biographical) account of each philosopher impartially. And
although 49 of his own aphorisms are peppered throughout the text, he
adds little interpretive commentary of his own, allowing readers to draw
their own conclusions from the numerous and entertaining stories and
anecdotes provided. Much, but by no means all, of what we do know about
Cynicism can be attributed to Laertius' collection of works, including
different versions of most of the Diogenes *chreia*.

Yet the paucity of original Cynic texts and the reliance on anecdotal
and second-hand tales should in no way diminish the Cynics' contribution
to Western culture. It is precisely their non-literary forms of discourse
that give the Cynics their peculiar authority and resilience,[109] providing
a rich legacy that other writers would adapt and rework over the centuries.
Bracht Branham claims that no other philosophical movement in antiquity left such a literary legacy as did the Cynics, an influence that has
extended far beyond the domain of written discourses associated with other
philosophers. It is the *oral* devices of the Cynics, Branham claims that survive in recognizable genres today. These same oral skills also credit Cynicism as the only literary and philosophical movement that was able to
attract a significant following among the illiterate majority of the time.[110]

The Cynics' oral and non-verbal devices are not normally associated
with the formal treatise of the rhetorician; nevertheless, it is shown here
by Branham how the crude discourse of Cynicism can be reconciled with
the theory and practice of rhetoric. Through his use of the *chreia* and other
verbal adaptations to (usually hostile) circumstances, Diogenes represented a concrete example of applied rhetoric. The way in which Diogenes

chose to deface the currency was to offer *himself* as the medium for argument. He positioned himself in direct violation of the rules and customs he despised; rules that had often become so familiarized that they were rarely articulated, let alone enforced.[111]

Even when unsupported by words, the Cynics' bizarre actions were every bit as much a part of their rhetorical style. In an account by Lucian, there is a display by the Cynic Peregrinus that in spite of its parodic fiction would have been the envy of many contemporary performance artists. In Lucian's story, during his time studying the Cynic way of life in Egypt, Peregrinus is said to have practiced Cynic indifference by appearing in public with half his head shaved, his face covered in mud, and an erect penis. Peregrinus' *askesis* is aimed at achieving indifference through violating commonly accepted forms of behavior.[112] Branham's thesis would allow that such actions by the Cynics are every bit as much examples of the rhetorical art as those normally associated with formal oratory. Diogenes' rhetorical skills, as with the example of Peregrinus, depended on his willingness to make himself an object of ridicule. It was from these "unseemly, shameful, and ridiculous acts," Branham claims, that Diogenes took his moral authority. His performance with his audience is neither mere clowning nor obscene exhibitionism: It represents a dialogue, which is as profoundly philosophical as the more formal lectures of many of his contemporaries. His reward for living as a beggar and acting the fool was his freedom to tell (or act) the truth as he saw it. *Parrhesia* then, in the Cynic context, was more than simply freedom of speech, but the freedom to act out a way of life, which flouted all the normal rules of society. The Cynic claims all acts — right down to his bodily functions — as a language of criticism. Of course, simply lacking in social skills or engaging in vulgar acts did not make one a Cynic. The Cynic goal of achieving indifference, both to the opinions of others and to the physical elements, had to be conceived within a strong philosophical framework of beliefs and required considerable training to carry out with the consummate finesse required of a Cynic.

Because of the enduring utility and influence that written and oral Cynic genres have had on later literary styles, a brief account of each is provided below:

Diatribe

A litigious monologue, the diatribe appeals to an imaginary adversary and as such is an exposition more than an argument, since there is only room for one main speaker.[113] Bion of Borysthenes, a contemporary of Menippus of Gadara (see below), is credited with its invention.[114] The diatribe is also credited with being the prototype for the Christian sermon.[115] In popular usage today the term diatribe is commonly understood to refer to a forceful, verbal attack or piece of bitter criticism.[116] The fragment from Heraclitus on page 27, and the passages by Federman in the Afterword at top of page 196 and bottom of page 197 provide examples.

Chreia

The *chreia* (literal meaning of which is "something useful") accounts for most of the Diogenes stories, being ordinarily a brief statement of an incident or situation followed by a pungent remark.[117] Example would serve best by way of explanation. When asked if he believed in the gods, Diogenes replied, "How can I help believing in them, when I see a god-forsaken wretch like you?"[118] To people who were ridiculing him for walking backward on a porch, he said, "While you are criticizing the way I walk, you are going backward in your way of living." Being reproached for eating in the market place (convention at the time forbade eating in public), "Well, it was in the market-place that I felt hungry."[119] On being asked what wine he enjoyed drinking, Diogenes responded, "That which belongs to some one else."[120] When asked by the Cyreniac Hegesias for a loan of his writings, Diogenes replied, "You are a fool, Hegesias, because you choose painted figs to real figs, and pass over true training and opt for written rules."[121] And in a *chreia* credited to Antisthenes, on it being confirmed to him by a priest that, initiates into the Orphic Mysteries enjoyed certain advantages in Hades, Antisthenes replied, "Why then, don't you die!"[122] Other examples will be recognized elsewhere in this chapter. According to Long, all the Diogenes aphorisms—of which the *chreia* is a very specific type—share three things in common: black humour, paradox or surprise, and ethical seriousness.[123] It is of further interest to note that although Diogenes may have been responsible for popularizing the *chreia* form among the Cynics, there are examples of similarly-styled aphorisms being used as early as the sixth century B.C. The Scythian philosopher Anacharsis, for example, demonstrated his dislike of sea travel, when in response to being asked what vessels were the safest, replied "Those which have been hauled ashore." And when asked which were greater in number, the living or the dead, responded, "In which category, then, do you place those who are on the seas?"[124] Similar explanations are given with regard to Nietzsche's use of aphorisms and are discussed in some detail in that chapter.

Parody

The use of parody as a satirical device is fully discussed later in the book. However, it is worth noting here that Crates has been credited with firmly establishing this mode of discourse as a Cynical tool for defacing traditional values. Menippus, who is said to have been a pupil of Crates, used parody in his own brand of satire (see Menippean Satire below).[125]

Soliloquy

This style of discourse is credited to Antisthenes and is featured by the ability to conduct a dialog with oneself. Aspects of the self are disclosed which are not revealed through passive self-observation.

Symposium

Although not a cynic invention, the symposium has strong links with other cynic genres because of its own origins in the Socratic and the carnivalesque. The symposium has been described as a banquet dialogue in which the discourse assumes special privileges of ease, familiarity, frankness, and eccentricity.[126]

Menippean Satire

Named after the third century B.C. Cynic, Menippus of Gadara, the *menippea* is the most influential and enduring of all Cynic genres. More importantly, all of those styles already discussed above have been absorbed into it. The *menippea* also has roots in carnivalized folklore (see below), and took up elements of Socratic dialogue through Antisthenes, Varro and Bion.[127] Although only fragments of Menippus's work survive, he is credited by Diogenes Laertius as having written 13 books. Menippean satire is better known today through the imitations his work has received by other cynics, and also through classical writers such as Varro, Lucian and Seneca.[128] A modern example of this genre can be found in William Blake's *The Marriage of Heaven and Hell,* in which Blake deliberately reverses notions of good and evil in order to shock the reader into rethinking conventionally-held beliefs. Postmodern examples include the work of John Barth. It is through the work of these later writers that Menippus has been assured a permanent place in literary history and that Cynicism has been credited as a major source of satirical literature in Europe.[129]

Apart from his legacy of a satiric genre, Menippus is most famous for his satirical laughter, referred to by Lucian as "the secret dog who bites as he laughs," even following the dead to Hades to continue his scornful mockery.[130] Menippus combined satire and parody in a way that ridiculed and caricatured pseudo-intellectual and theological fraud. In particular, he parodied the different forms of learned and philosophic discourse of the time by pushing their logic to an absurd extreme. Learned sages were taken literally and incongruous verses, songs, curses, etc., were interjected into the parodied genres to amplify the ridicule.[131]

In his book *Problems of Dostoevesky's Poetics*, Mikhail Bakhtin describes all of the Cynic (and Socratic) genres discussed above under the generic term *serio-comical*.[132] The seriocomic genres of ancient Greece are united by their opposition to what Bakhtin describes as the monological serious genres: those genres that involve a "pedagogical discourse," whereby "someone who knows and possesses the truth instructs someone who is ignorant of it." Bakhtin further sources these serio-comical genres to the oral traditions of carnival folklore. It is the representation in the "living present," the day to day, the mundane, that marks out the serio-comical, contrasting it and distancing it from its serious epic or tragic target.[133]

Carnival

Although not a Cynic genre, because certain aspects of carnival had a probable influence on Cynic' styles of discourse,[134] it is worth briefly discussing what its main dialogic elements were. The main feature of carnival was the reversal of normal positions in society, for example, the fool or clown dominating the proceedings. In carnival mode, one could mock the king or queen and ridicule and pour profanities on other public figures and deities. Whether it was one's essential way of life or a way of letting off steam on festive occasions, the outcome of both Cynicism and carnival was to suspend the laws, prohibitions, and restrictions that determine the structure of civilized, mannered society. This had the leveling effect of freeing people from socio-hierarchical positions of rank, age, property, etc., and liberating them (if only temporarily in the case of carnival) from the normal restraints and restrictions of society. Probably predating the development of sophisticated speech, the difficulty posed by the language of carnival in classical or modern discourse is that it cannot be adequately translated into verbal language. The sensuous orgy of carnival would only have received qualified approval by the Cynics. Their own licentiousness was meant not so much to liberate desire as to shock, to deface the currency of peoples' affectations, not to compensate for it. The upside-down society of carnival was the Cynics' bread and butter, their everyday life, and not some wild interlude away from mundane reality. Yet the Cynics would have welcomed the carnivalesque as an irksome reminder of the hypocrisy, dullness and conventionality of normal life — perpetual carnival rather than perpetual revolution was their ambition.

The essence of Cynicism

> "The characteristic of a human being is that — and this is very much in contrast with other animals — he doesn't know what to do with his shit." ... Occupying an uncertain and troubling space between a nature that is never surpassed and a culture that is never closed off, shit defines civilization. — *Lacan*[135]

> Oh this insane, pathetic beast, ... What ideas he has, what unnaturalness, what paroxysms of nonsense, what *bestiality of thought* erupts as soon as he is prevented just a little from being a *beast in deed.*
> — *Nietzsche*[136]

Much has been made of Cynic references to the behavior of animals as inspirational guidance for the way humans should conduct their lives. A superficial reading of this aspect of Cynicism, coupled with the doggish behavior of many Cynics, may lead one to suppose that Cynics found animal life preferable to human life. Luis Navia challenges this interpretation, offering instead a more perceptive analysis of the Cynics' relationship to animals and providing us with a much deeper insight into this elusive philosophy. In an attempt to consider what might have been the compulsive drive behind the Cynics' unorthodox beliefs and behavior, I contrast Navia's conclusion that Cynic praise of animal life was an ironic device to punctuate humans' betrayal of their true nature, with Georges Bataille's view that humans' denial of their animality (the elevated idealism which Diogenes scorned) *is* their true nature. What both these views emphasize is the self-deception of denying our inescapable animal reality in the pursuit of lofty cerebral ideals.

Navia's interpretation of the Cynics' use of animals in their teaching is not that animal life is preferable, nor that we should adopt animal life as a model for our own. Rather, we should follow, not deny, our own nature in the same way that animals follow theirs. Instead of following our nature, Antisthenes is reported to have claimed that most humans follow conventions. And it is only by divesting ourselves of the artificiality and superficiality with which we deny our true nature, that a happy and virtuous life can be attained: "We must deface the currency that has made us what we were not meant to be."[137] Accounts of the Cynics that imply a life of primitivism and bestiality, are, according to Navia, naive interpretations if not tendentiously misleading. They rely on a selective reading of Cynic rhetoric while ignoring — or failing to grasp — the serious philosophy that underpins it.

Navia proposes that Diogenes' praise of animal nature and his self-characterization as a dog can be interpreted as an ironic strategy, a kind of inverted and rhetorical allegory the purpose of which is to expose "the absurdity of human conduct when it resembles the behavior of nonrational beings." [138] Whether Diogenes did deliberately engage in any such ethical mission we will never know. What is clear, was his ability to exploit a huge credibility gap in human behavior between, on the one hand, people's appetite for instant gratification and hedonism, and on the other their sham sophistication and moralizing idealism.

There are notable periods in history when moral depravity spills out from societies that hold themselves up as models of culture and sophistication. In some cases, such as Renaissance Italy, this represents a positive attempt to reconnect with a glorious (if questionable) pre–Christian past, in others, such as Nazi Germany, we find out just how far human beings are able to depart from what is natural in the name of the civilizing process. The point is, that the Nazis' ability to transgress prohibited forms of behavior indicates the human — not the animal — side of our natures: attempting to legitimize bestiality by creating work of it, and further by enjoying it within the security of group behavior. Abjection is a human construct. Therefore those who transgress their own rules of civilized behavior act in ways that animals never could. And yet paradoxically, animals have become the symbol for that which humans have striven to eject from their own nature.

Navia may be right to propose that Diogenes' rhetoric concerning animals (including his non-verbal rhetoric such as performing his animal business in public) should not be read as a sign that animal life be adopted as a model for our own behavior. Diogenes well understood that people had higher mental functions than lower animals, making their metaphysical pretensions and their depravity all the more irrational. For the Cynics, their abjection, living close to their waste and their own mortality, gave them a spiritual and moral freedom unavailable to those who defined their humanness by the prohibition of abject thoughts and behavior. It also removed any possibility of an Icarian collapse, for the Cynics' asceticism and abjection left them with nowhere to fall.

Regardless of considerable emphasis on the difference between Classical Cynicism and contemporary cynicism, the heritage of Classical Cynicism extends well into the twentieth century. Diogenes' ideas reoccur among such unlikely heirs as the sometime Surrealist, Georges Bataille. Both Diogenes and Bataille draw heavily on animal references to emphasize human pretensions, at the same time acknowledging the important differences between animal nature and human nature. However, what the

Cynics describe as peoples' denial of their nature — their haughty pretensions, their taboos and transgressions, their rise and their consequent fall — becomes in Bataille's view the very thing that marks people out from animals, the essence of human nature. Julia Kristeva highlights a biblical paradox first brought to light by Hegel. Sin leads to death; consequently man without sin is in a state of immortality. Yet man would also become immortal if he ate from the tree of life (knowledge), and in transgressing that prohibition he sinned.[139] That the invitation to achieve perfection is also the invitation to sin confirms Bataille's proposition that taboos are put in place precisely to be broken. That is what makes us human and also what marks us out from other animals; our natural and mortal state. Many mystics and holy men have even regarded the transgression of prohibitions (sinning) as an essential mark of their holiness (Rasputin is an infamous example). As Kristeva puts it, the fall *is* the work of God.[140]

The Cynics managed to shortcut all these feigned devices, at the same time remaining true to their animal *and* human natures. This raises the distinction between *immorality,* which relies on an acceptance of the binary oppositions of good and evil, and the Cynics' *amorality,* which allows them abiding transcendence of the border that the abject keeps in place. And while the search for the meaning of life continues to obsess us, the omnipresent meaning that Cynics acknowledge to be our true nature exists right under our noses. It is disregarded by most of us each day along with our waste and trash as we move forward toward our inevitable deaths, interrupted only by the occasional flashes of joy that separate the mundane from the routine. The Cynic seems to imply that if it were possible to divert our gaze earthward, we might just discover some of that which eludes us in the metaphysical world. Yet paradoxically, it is the false search for rationality itself — expressed through religion, science and philosophy — that creates the mental fog that prevents humans from grasping the fundamentals of their nature. The rational explanations humans seek are obscured and buried beneath false trails and illusory truths created to sooth their anxiety of *not knowing.*

So what *is* human beings' true nature? First, we have Diogenes' view that human nature consists of freedom from mind-obfuscating preoccupations with the metaphysical world, interpreted by Navia as "reason and clarity of mind"[141] (though not in the sense of scientific exactness). Next we have Bataille's view that what makes humans unique is our ability to develop mental constructs that distance us from lower animals; making no value judgment as to whether this is a good or a bad thing. Then, of course, we have the prevailing and opposing view to that of Diogenes, best put by Aristotle, in which he regards the Cynics' self-sufficiency and undermining of the state as a *rejection* of human nature: "The proof that the State is a creation of nature and prior to the individual is that the individual, when isolated is not self-sufficient."[142] Aristotle concludes that only beasts or Gods can live independently of society; no doubt consigning Cynics to the first category! To clarify any confusion arising from the use of the term human nature in the Cynic sense, it might be helpful to refer to humans' essential condition as their animalism, thus distinguishing it either from the nature of lower animals *or* from human nature as defined by Aristotle: the denial of our animal reality. In any event, it would seem that the majority of us probably tend to the latter condition, as T.S. Elliot reminded us when he said that "humankind cannot bear too much reality." Which is why so few among us probably have the stomach to fully engage with cynicism. We prefer instead to shield ourselves from what we "cannot bear" behind a smokescreen of fantastic interpretations about the world and our reason for living in it. But if humans are not to revert to animals, "worse than animals" as Diogenes suggests, and be true to their nature, then the currency of false taboos—presented as laws and prohibitions—must be defaced. So when Diogenes defecates or masturbates in public, he is not breaking any natural taboo, but drawing attention to human beings' greater transgressions: their hypocrisy under the guise of civilized behavior.

Summing Up

> I have told, I have staged the very scene of Diogenes. He is there, in front of his barrel on the public stage, he waits, exhibiting himself. He waits for the Great, hopes for the greatest, waits for the sun.... We spectators hidden in the shadow of the square, we understand, we know that the verminous cynic is destroying the parasites, that he is forsaking intermediaries. Alexander passes. The drama rises to its apex. Alexander and his shadow extend the order of the broken vase, of the discarded coat: all of them screens of the object, of the greatest object, of the sun.—*Michel Serres*[143]

Who, then, was our typical Cynic living around the Mediterranean lands between the third century B.C. and the sixth century A.D.? He or she would have worn similar attire, probably a simple cloak; any meager possessions being carried in a small bag or wallet. We also know, that in spite of their close association with nature and their view that city life was unnatural, they would curiously almost always be seen in urban surroundings. The Cynics had no loyalty to family or state and rejected what they considered to be false values, adopting any customs, which complemented their lifestyle. They considered themselves citizens of the world, or cosmos: the first cosmopolitans. The Cynics' ability to move around freely was further assisted by their resistance to being owned by possessions. They had no interest in trying to convert others to their way of life, but welcomed anyone, regardless of social background or race, to join their ranks. Whatever teaching a Cynic undertook was likely to be performed in public, sometimes in an irreverent or shocking manner, and if a Cynic did something, it was from a desire to do it, not from an external compulsion to do it. Diogenes in particular reminded us that in spite of our pretensions as civilized beings, a denial of our animality was a repudiation of our true nature, an understanding of which required focusing exclusively on the physical world in which we live, and abandoning supernatural and metaphysical beliefs (particularly religious faiths), which could only lead to disillusionment. The Cynic would not, therefore, defer happiness but live each day as though tomorrow might never arrive. Life in any case did not follow a progression toward enlightenment but a cyclical series of mundane repetitions punctuated by occasional highs and lows. The Cynics did not believe in fortune or pre-destiny, but in striving to be masters of their own destiny. *Askesis* and *ponos* were the means by which the Cynic could achieve self-sufficiency and the indifference necessary to cope with all eventualities. If Cynicism was a philosophy at all, it was a practical one, aimed at training for the harsh life, which was the Cynics' expectation. And finally, their mission — certainly Diogenes' — was to deface the currency of human beings' false values and customs and thus discredit the fabrication that was civilized society.

So what possible relevance can Cynicism have for our lives today? If the Cynic's belief in cycles of return has any validity, then we may well currently be experiencing one of those periods in history where civilization has become morally bankrupt. Leaving aside more apocalyptic claims of a return to religious fundamentalism on the scale of the Medieval Crusades, modern cynics would at least agree that current expressions of faith, from belief in deities to company mission statements, have been sanitized, commodified and corrupted to such a degree, that in most cases they have been stripped of any moral or ethical currency. In our present world, more than ever, there is a need for a raw and uncompromising philosophy that will shake us out of our complacency and free us from the soothing illusions that cloud our minds. Or, as Navia puts it: "liberate ourselves from the social and political fetters with which the irrationality of the human world seeks to immobilize us."[144]

2

Renaissance Cynicism: The Limits of Cynicism

> In the Middle Ages both sides of human consciousness—that which was turned within as that which was turned without—lay dreaming or half awake beneath a common veil. The veil was woven of faith, illusion and childish prepossession, through which the world and history were seen clad in strange hues. Man was conscious of himself ... only through some general category. In Italy this veil first melted into air, an *objective* treatment of the state and all the things of this world became possible. The *subjective* side at the same time asserted itself with corresponding emphasis; man became a spiritual individual, and recognized himself as such. In the same way the Greek had once distinguished himself from the barbarian.— *Jacob Burckhardt*[1]

The epochs in history in which cynicism enjoyed a resurgence have already been identified as those periods when moral depravity spilled out from societies that held themselves up as models of culture and sophistication. Political, moral and social vacuums in which the ordinary person felt alienated and abandoned. The Renaissance in Italy was a response to just such a period in history: the bankrupt morality of the Middle Ages. One abuse of power, however, was soon exchanged for another more spirited form: the depraved morality of the despot. Indeed, one of the defining characteristics of the Renaissance is the development of a culture in which examples of gross barbarity are allowed to flourish alongside an explosion of artistic excess. It is within such conditions that we encounter the true cynicism of Renaissance Italy, the audacity of its assault on the prevailing institutions of the time, most notably the Church and the Nobility.

Having acknowledged that the history of Greek Cynicism was built largely on mythology, one might be excused for thinking that by the time we arrive at Renaissance Italy, our history will become more factual. After all, the Renaissance movement was fuelled by the discovery, restoration, translation and dissemination of historical manuscripts. But as Nietzsche and other cynics have maintained, all history is fiction. Each history of the Renaissance simply reflects the historian's view of the world, that version which fits most comfortably with their own truths. For the cynics, the only important truth is their own subjective truth. The real myth is that of objective truth. It is not then surprising that I should choose to draw my images of Renaissance Italy principally from the work of two writers who were themselves cynics. The historian Jacob Burckhardt, and commentator of the time Niccolò Machiavelli. Yet as these are two very different kinds of cynics—one writes at the time while the other writes with five hundred years' hindsight—their perspectives are presented separately in the text.

Burckhardt's account of the Renaissance, a canonical work on the period for many decades, has more recently fallen out of favor with scholars of history precisely because of what is seen as its subjectiveness. But then any rehabilitation of cynicism is incomplete without a rehabilitation of certain historians who, like Burckhardt, are more concerned with the spirit of an age than they are with representing historical accuracies or comprehensive accounts of history. Burckhardt rejected the positivist and scientific view of history as a system.[2] He also rejected (the concept of a *zeitgeist* being an exception) the popular ideas of Hegel, rather being influenced by the young Nietzsche with whom he used to take long walks. Peter Burke considers Burckhardt to be unique among scholars of the Renaissance, describing his work as a socio-cultural history in which marginal aspects such as literature, learning, systems of values (such as chivalry), and even table cloths and table manners, are given emphasis over the grand events and dates of orthodox histories.

> Where positivists saw history as a science and historians as collecting "facts" from the documents and giving what they considered to be an "objective" account of what had actually happened, Burckhardt saw history as art. He regarded history as a form of imaginative literature, akin to poetry.... If Burckhardt has to be labeled, the adjectives "sceptical," "relativist" and, perhaps, "intuitive" are probably less misleading than most.— *Peter Burke*[3]

By the same token that Burckhardt's subjectivity bathes the Renaissance period in a warm glow, so too may he be criticized for dismissing the Middle Ages as some dark, repressed epoch of history. Domestic life during the Middle Ages was seen as a product of popular morals, success and failure presented as divine rewards for virtue and divine punishments for sin. By contrast, scholars at the time of the Renaissance interpreted events as the result of the virtues, aims and resources of human actors.[4] And there can be little doubt that during the Renaissance the common classes were able to rise to positions of power and influence that would have been denied them in other European countries at the time.

At the close of the thirteenth century, Italy was beginning to swarm with individuality and the "ban laid upon human personality was dissolved."[5] So too was there a dissolving of race and a return to the cosmopolitanism of ancient Greece: "The Italians of the fourteenth century knew little of false modesty or of hypocrisy in any shape; not one of them was afraid of singularity, of being and seeming unlike his neighbours." The rejection of the austerity that Christianity had imposed on much of Europe, the yearning for romanticized autonomy and the heroism of ancient times beckoned hedonistic impulses from the past:

> These people [those associated with the tyrannical forces of the Renaissance] were forced to know all the inward resources of their own nature, passing or permanent; and their enjoyment of life was enhanced and concentrated by the desire to obtain the greatest satisfaction from a possibly very brief period of power and influence.— *Burckhardt*[6]

Neither were the lives of many of the subjects of these dynastic families exempt from a life "thriving in the fullest vigour and variety": "The private man, indifferent to politics, and busied partly with serious pursuits, partly with the interests of a dilettante, seems to have been first fully formed in these despotisms of the fourteenth century."[7]

The movement of populations, either as conquerors or those fleeing tyranny, tended to break up parochialism and foster a new cosmopolitan spirit. The philosophy of Diogenes was rekindled by Dante when he said, "my country is the whole world." And by Florentine sculptor Lorenzo Ghiberti when he said "only he who has learned everything is nowhere a stranger; robbed of his fortune and without friends, he is yet the citizen of every country."[8] Consistent with Diogenes' insistence that there was nothing wrong with stealing from temples, Burckhardt relates the story of a man who took away unpunished the lights from the altar on which the crucifix stood and set them by Dante's grave, with the words, "take them; thou art more worthy of them than He, the Crucified One!"[9] However, it was the continued failure of the Church to meet either its own promises or the needs of an emerging intellectual class that ignited the Renaissance phenomena:

> It is not every people which is calm enough, or dull enough, to tolerate a lasting contradiction between a principle and its outward expression. But history does not record a heavier responsibility than that which

rests upon the decaying Church. She set up absolute truth, and by the most violent means, a doctrine which she had distorted to serve her own aggrandizement. Save in the sense of her inviability, she abandoned herself to the most scandalous profligacy, and in order to maintain herself in this state, she leveled mortal blows against the intellect of nations, and drove multitudes of the noblest spirits, whom she had inwardly estranged, into the arms of unbelief and despair.— *Burckhardt*[10]

The roots of this revolution had in fact been planted much earlier. From the time of the Crusades, Italy had been developing close trading relations with the Islamic world not to mention an admiration for its remarkable civilization.[11] Yet when their belief in God began to waiver, softened by their increasing cosmopolitanism, it was not to Islam the Italians turned for alternative models of meeting humanity's needs, but to the pagan beliefs of ancient Greece and Rome. Indeed, it is thanks to the obsessional activities of these Renaissance collectors that we have access to much of the ancient Greek literature we have available today. Both inside and outside Italian universities, oriental and pagan studies were pursued with vigor as was the study of the Greek language itself. But it is from artists and writers that the real spirit of the Renaissance comes alive. It was not simply the language (poetry and philosophical writings) with which these pagan revivalists sought to enhance their own culture but a desire to think and feel as the ancients had done.

The conditions for cynicism could not have been more fertile, yet, once again, cynical responses remained marginalized. By turning to the ancients as a source of inspiration for their lives, the typical Renaissance humanists were not so much engaging in a cynical reaction to the prevailing morality provided by the Church, as they were looking for an alternative utopia, or a return to a romanticized view of a lost utopia. The term humanism, from the Latin *humanitas*, was used in classical times to describe what we still refer to as the humanities today: language, literature, history, moral philosophy, etc.[12] It was closely associated with books: reading them, writing them, producing and marketing them. It is therefore not surprising that humanism achieved new levels of popularity coinciding with the invention of the printing press in the mid-fifteenth century.

The Church was not criticized directly by the humanists, but implicit in the advocacy of pagan cultural values was a view that medieval Christendom lacked the ancient heritage of wisdom, virtue and practical knowledge. "The effort to revivify the classical heritage inevitably brought these (mostly) urban, lay intellectuals into conflict with the established guardians of culture and with the monastic and scholastic traditions of learning they represented."[13] When it became apparent that the Christian project had failed, the humanist sought, not to revel in cynical chaos like the Renaissance despot, but to find an alternative blueprint for human behavior. The ideas of Plato, Aristotle, the Epicureans and the Stoics were used to bolster rather than undermine Christian morality. Many of these works were even rescripted as the true origins of Christianity. Far then from suggesting that the Renaissance represented a rejection of Christian values in favor of pagan values and culture (which Christianity had so successfully extinguished in the first place), Christianity has been credited with making a cold study of ancient culture possible. Even if the spirit of the Renaissance suggests something else, the humanist scholar was not so much responsible for a revival of antiquity, as for a modern study which in its modernity ensured that paganism was kept at a safe historical distance.

There are parallels here with the scepticism of Christian morality today. Even though it would appear that many of those who are obsessed with alternative therapies today are rejecting the orthodox covenants of religion, a belief in God is often implied. As with the current fashion for plundering and packaging other people's beliefs as fast food for the soul, so we cannot be convinced that during the Renaissance, the average citizen was able to see beyond a superficial presentation of Greek philosophy. On Epicureanism, for instance, Burckhardt says that even though the version was sufficient to make people familiar with a godless universe, he questioned the extent to which this teaching was actually understood. Or indeed, if the name of the problematic Greek sage was not simply a catchword.[14] Was the Renaissance no more than a fifteenth century mass marketing of pre-Christian Greek and Latin culture; the kind of cannibalization of styles of the past that we are experiencing in our own postmodern phenomena? Burckhardt's descriptions of Renaissance trivia provide more help in answering this question than traditional histories of the period. There was, for instance, a Renaissance fashion, not only for giving children Greek and Latin names, but Greek and Latin *sounding* names: Jovianus for Giovanni, Petreius for Pietro, Aonius for Antonio, etc.[15]

However, it is not my intention here to present the culture of Renaissance Italy as in any way phony or artificial. The paradox is that there was no need of imitating past or parallel traditions because the Renaissance was a remarkable culture in its own right; not least the tolerance toward other religions and cultures that made this movement possible. But perhaps the most remarkable thing of all about the Renaissance was that the glory of its civilization was achieved through its ability to transgress the normal prohibitions and constraints of civilized society. Therefore, although God remained ever-present in people's lives throughout the period we are discussing, there was also a withdrawal from many of Christianity's controlling dogmas. The need of salvation and the concept of sin gave way to a certain cynical amorality, an appreciation of other life forces that went beyond good and evil. These included an acknowledgement of the caprices of Fortuna and a realization that if one was to attain happiness it could be attained during one's own lifetime — and the sooner the better! Concerns about divine government of the world became secondary to the establishment of more local kingdoms. And, for the first time in hundreds of years, intellectual activity witnessed a victory of philosophy over religious tradition. It assumed, as Burckhardt put it, "a poetic instead of dogmatic form."[16]

With regard to freedom of will, Burckhardt points out that unlike periods of history when religious doctrine was dominant in human affairs — presenting the age-old dilemma of harmonizing free will with the laws of the universe — the Renaissance saw a shift toward a new morality in which people took more responsibility for their own actions. But this morality took different forms; for alongside the hotch-potch of ideas that emerged from the hybrid beliefs of neo-paganism and postmodern Christianity, we must include the amorality of the cynic and the immorality of the despot.

SHADES OF DARK AND LIGHT

> A force which we must constantly take into account in judging the morality of the more highly developed Italian of this period, is that of the imagination. It gives to his virtues and vices a peculiar color, and under its influence his unbridled egotism shows itself in its most terrible shape. — *Burckhardt*[17]

When the ancient Cynics cut loose from man-made laws, religion and morality by decree, they found an alternative code of survival through their harsh training and ascetic lifestyle. By contrast, the typical Renaissance character sought to recreate the perceived glories of the past within a culture constructed from childish fantasy. Selected features of ancient civilizations were fused together with those aspects of their own culture they were unwilling to forego. Consistent with the Renaissance phenomenon as a whole, the zenith of this historical period presented two contradictory but interconnected faces. First is a cynical face, featured by a highly developed sense of individualism which had outgrown the limits of morality and religion; and secondly, made possible by this, is a hedonistic face, the selfishness and corruption born from the uncontrolled (by moral codes that bind a society into its civilized state) appetites of those who were able to indulge their individualism to the limits of their resources. The ultimate downfall of the Renaissance project lay in its inherent failure to achieve its goal of recreating the glories of ancient times. For although the period was certainly fascinating in its own right, it relied on the imitation of a myth, of a culture that had never existed in the first place. There was an unwillingness to jettison completely "the Christian ideal of life" which was simply substituted with "the cult of historical greatness"; or, as Burckhardt further describes it, "a victim of astonishing illusions."[18]

Let us now briefly consider some of these extremes and contradictions of the Renaissance. Hedonism was described earlier as the philosophic doctrine to which Cynicism was most opposed, and yet, in the Renaissance, we find these two impulses, one cynical, the other hedonistic, working harmoniously to breath life into the phenomena we are now discussing. As Burckhardt reminds us, "the Renaissance would not have been the process of worldwide significance which it is, if its elements could be so easily separated one from another."[19] It is also insufficient to suggest that one of these impulses was a force for good and the other of evil. Extremes of good and evil there certainly were, but the alchemy of cynicism and hedonism during the Renaissance produced aspects of a civilization that functioned *beyond* good and evil. And then, true to cynical warnings of Icarian collapse, having reached for the limit of human possibilities, this civilization descended once again into the mundane human existence it had sought to escape.

One may be excused for thinking that cynicism fulfils its own prophecy about the shortcomings of the human world. One criticism frequently leveled against cynicism is that it attempts to undermine the grand cultural, philosophical, religious and political systems of civilization, and yet offers no alternatives to put in their place, the inference being that if cynicism were allowed to flourish, society would become dismantled and chaos and disorder would surely follow. Such a view is to misunderstand the nature of cynicism. Cynicism does not claim to make sense of the human world; its mission is to shake it up — sometimes violently — and to expose it for the unpredictable and often ugly beast that it is. Cynicism merely points to the world in which humans themselves — through their misguided belief that the world can be shaped to their will — create the very chaos and disorder they seek to control. By mirroring life as the cynic sees it we are essentially reminded of who we are. And because true cynicism is amoral, standing as it does outside notions of good and evil, the free will that was released during the Renaissance did not necessarily have civilizing results.

The best we can say of this period was that civilization had a long-earned party. The world of carnival ceased to function as a fiction and spilled out into people's everyday lives, and yet without the protection that masquerade offered. In the darker side of the Renaissance, hedonism had clearly gained the upper hand: "In this country, finally, where individuality of every sort attained its highest development, we find instances of that ideal and absolute wickedness which delight in crimes for their own sake, and not as a means to an end."[20]

Peter Burke describes how the combination of absolute power, "with its temptations to luxury and unbridled selfishness," and the constant perils from enemies and conspirators, turned many of the ruling families into tyrants in the worst sense of the word.[21] Typically, the worst of this tyranny is targeted at members of the tyrant's own family: the aunt of Francesco Sforza who poisoned Sforza's wife and daughter to seize an inheritance; Bernado Varano of Camerino, who killed two of his brothers in order that his property could be divided among his sons;[22] the court of Lodovico Sforza in which daughter was sold by father, wife by husband, and sister by brother.[23] In the family of Este at Ferrara, we are given a report of a virtual epidemic of barbarism:

> a princess was beheaded (1425) for alleged adultery with a step-son, legitimate and illegitimate children fled from the court, and even abroad their lives were threatened by assassins sent in pursuit of them (1471). Plots from without were incessant; the bastard of a bastard tried to wrest the crown from the lawful heir, Ercole 1; this latter is said afterwards (1493) to have poisoned his wife on discovering that she, at the instigation of her brother Ferrante of Naples, was going to poison him. This list of tragedies is closed by the plot of two bastards against their brothers ... Duke Alfonso 1 and Cardinal Ippolito (1506).[24]

Ferrante of Naples himself we are told, excelled in the macabre:

> He liked to have his opponents near him, either alive in well guarded prisons, or dead and embalmed, dressed in the costume which they wore in their lifetime. He would chuckle in talking of the captives with his friends, and made no secret whatever of the museum of mummies.— Burckhardt[25]

But if unbridled hedonism was the primary motivator for such acts of despotism, it was the cynical transcendence of accepted orthodoxies of human behavior that made them possible. Cynicism paved the way for eruptions of unrestrained pleasure-seeking that fell on both sides of a precarious line and made the fusion of artistic excess and despotism possible. For although there was certainly a dark side to life under these Italian princes, who themselves lived under undeniable dangers, so too, was there a consistent quality to life, a situation brought about by the pursuit of an ideal which could only have surfaced under a civilization in which those with certain personal qualities could possibly survive. Not since the ancient Greeks had the idea that one could make a work of art from one's own life been realized.[26]

Out of the Renaissance, Burckhardt describes the emergence of the "all sided man," a superhuman with clear parallels to Nietzsche's *übermensch*. Leon Battista Alberti (1404–1472) was the ultimate model for Burckhardt's "all sided man." In line with his truism that "men can do all things if they will," Alberti followed the Cynic virtues of *askesis* and taking charge of one's own destiny to achieve his own super-human accomplishments. We hear how Alberti excelled in gymnastics and could jump over a man's head with his feet together; how the wildest horses trembled under him; and that he was an accomplished musician and composer yet studied under no master. He studied civil and canonical law, physics and mathematics. He excelled in modeling and painting from memory. He wrote fictional works in prose and verse, a treatise on domestic life in four books, three books on art and 10 volumes on architecture; he was also an innovative and accomplished architect in his own right.[27] Alberti, however, is hardly representative of the typical Renaissance cynic, and certainly too ostentatious for a cynic of the ancient mold. The Renaissance cynic appeared in a variety of different guises, including those more closely resembling their Cynic cousins. We hear of one such teacher, Fabio Calvi of Ravenna, a mentor of the painter Raphael. "He lived to a great age in Rome, eating only pulse ... and dwelt in a hovel little better than the tub of Diogenes. Of the pension which Pope Leo gave him, he spent enough to keep body and soul together and gave the rest away."[28]

In one very fundamental aspect the Renaissance cynic does closely resemble the ancient Cynic. In the face of all objective facts, laws and restraints, by inwardly casting off the authority of a state which they saw as tyrannical and illegitimate, Renaissance cynics retain a feeling of their own sovereignty. In each single instant the decision of the Renaissance character is formed independently, according to honor or interest, passion or calculation, revenge or renunciation.[29] If the cynicism of ancient Greece was identifiable by its individual characters, the cynicism of the Renaissance was represented by the spirit of its age. Sympathetic with Burckhardt's notion of the all-sided man, one of the most remarkable features of the spirit of the Renaissance is the leveling effect it had on its society. In sharp contrast to his contemporaries in the North, the Italian prince was ready to use those from every strata of society. Personal qualifications alone were the criteria for greatness and there was even an indifference to legitimate birth allowing personal fitness to transcend mere bloodline in terms of who obtained power to rule.[30]

AGE OF EQUALITY?

The early humanists had worked hard to plant the conviction into the Italian psyche that personal merit, and not birth, was responsible for nobility. As Franco Sacchetti wrote, "everybody saw how all the work people down to the bakers, how all the wool-carders, usurers, money-changers and blackguards of all descriptions, became knights."[31] And yet, this continued passion for knighthoods during the Renaissance has more the flavor of Quixotian farce than it does humanist principles of egalitarianism. Burckhardt recounts one of Sacchetti's descriptions of just such a 70-year-old holiday cavalier:

> He rides out on horseback to Peretola, where the tournament was cheap, on a jade hired from a dyer. A thistle is stuck by some wag under the tail of the steed, who takes fright, runs away and carries the helmeted rider, bruised and shaken, back into the city. The inevitable conclusion of the story is a severe curtain-lecture from the wife, who is a little enraged at these break neck follies of her husband.[32]

Much has also been made of the equal status enjoyed by Renaissance women with men. Though inequality remained the norm in marriage at the time, there was some evidence of equality of educational opportunity for women of the upper classes.[33] These women often attended the same courses of learning as men, a share of the individuality that was a feature of the time. Yet this one example of equality may have been the only one available to the Renaissance woman. Burckhardt himself puts the lie to claims of women's emancipation in the following lines: "These women had no thought of the public; their function was to influence distinguished men, and to moderate male impulse and caprice." Even women's ability to moderate male caprice has its limits. We are told that once she had left the convent or paternal roof, the educated Renaissance woman was free to develop her individual character, even to the point of taking a lover, so long as the marriage contract was fulfilled (a contract which did not bind the woman's affections). But, adds Burckhardt, "the way is short from such a distinction to complete surrender … [for] where his wife's unfaithfulness exposes him to the derision of outsiders, the affair becomes tragical, and not seldom ends in murder or vengeance of a violent sort."[34] The following passage from Renaissance novelist Matteo Bandello confirms that the idea of the liberated Renaissance woman, which if it existed at all, came at a very high price indeed:

> Would that we were not daily forced to hear that one man has murdered his wife because he suspected her of infidelity; that another man has killed his daughter, on account of a secret marriage; that a third has caused his sister to be murdered, because she would not marry as he wished! It is a great cruelty that we claim the right to do whatever we list, and will not suffer women to do the same. If they do anything which does not please us, there we are at once with our cords and daggers and poison. What folly it is of men to suppose their own and their house's honor depend on the appetite of a woman![35]

So Renaissance woman's individuality was yet subject to her man's individuality. Nevertheless, considering the time (both of the Italian Renaissance and of Burckhardt's writing), a rupturing of the prevailing social position of Western women (up to and including parts of the twentieth century) clearly did take place. For one of those rare cynical periods of history the spirit of Dionysus triumphed as the predominant mode of social intercourse. Yet when we look for the names of the outstanding individual women of the Renaissance we encounter a deafening silence. Burckhardt can only provide us with three, even then acknowledging that they "are the forced result of very unusual circumstances,"[36] and Machiavelli mentions none at all. This is in stark contrast to the civilization of ancient Greece that Renaissance scholars were so keen to imitate. The position of mortal woman during the Renaissance had not recovered from Christianity's total annihilation of the goddess culture on which ancient civilizations thrived.

RIDICULE AND WIT

The savagery of Renaissance despotism was amply matched in this period by the savagery of its satire. At the end of the thirteenth century, Burckhardt describes the aim of literature as "merely to give simple and elegant expression to wise sayings and pretty stories and fables." Most notable, Burckhardt tells us, is the absence of satire. With the arrival of Dante, Petrarch, Sacchetti, Boccaccio and others, a new spirit of defiance, even scorn, entered literature; an attempt to stand the world that existed on its head. Burckhardt describes a vibrant comedy circuit centered on fifteenth century Florence in which the inventors and retailers of jokes, popular figures of the time, had to work hard to stay ahead of changing public taste and appreciation. One form of satire, popular from the end of the fourteenth century, was to send up classics such as the chivalrous poetry of the Middle Ages, parodying both the original genre and affected styles that were in current usage. Indeed, so popular did satire become in Renaissance Italy that it was studied by theorists and taught as an art form.[37]

Burckhardt describes Italy during the Renaissance as a "school for scandal" and repeats the description given to Florentines of the time as sharp-eyed and bad-tongued. Reputations of the rich and famous probably suffered as much under the tongues of Renaissance satirists as they do today under the ever-vigilant gaze of tabloid journalists. Ultimately, however, as with the undercutting cynicism of the early twentieth century art movements, the Renaissance humanists became the targets of the same satire and ridicule that they themselves had made so popular. In the ridicule and wit of the Renaissance we also encounter that cynical reaction to the world described by Sloterdijk as enlightened false consciousness, that instinct of self-preservation that transcends the imposed morality of a culture: "This is that enigmatic mixture of conscience and egotism which often survives in the modern man after he has lost, whether by his own fault or not, faith, hope and love."[38]

FESTIVALS

One of the most visible outward signs of Renaissance cynicism was witnessed in its public festivals. The religious element of these festivals gave way to the secular and "in their best form mark the point of transition from real life into the world of art."[39] The features which contrast these festivals with those of the Middle Ages and the rest of Europe at the time include a greater freedom of intercourse between all classes of society, an appreciation of the meaning of the mythological figures represented in carnival, and "the universal familiarity of the people with the poetical basis of the show."[40]

The Mysteries were a sort of pantomime, one of the most popular forms of festival involving the erection of an extensive three-tier scaffold. The top tier represented paradise and the bottom hell, while the central stage represented the earthly events of the drama. One of the main delights of this form of festival was the elaborate means invented to make figures rise and float in the air. The enjoyment of this spectacle, resided not only in the action itself but in the ridicule made of the inevitable hitches in the performance. Burckhardt describes an elaborate development of this theme invented by Brunellesco for the Feast of the Annunciation. The apparatus consisted of a heavenly globe surrounded by two circles of angels out of which flew the Angel Gabriel in a machine shaped like an almond. Although chiefly secular, these pantomimes presented a bizarre conglomerate of imagery made up of both mythological figures from Greek antiquity and those from Christian symbolism. One of Leonardo da Vinci's machines rivaled even Brunellesco's. It represented all the known heavenly bodies and their movements on a colossal scale.[41] Neither were these extravagances confined to the major cities. The following description by Burckhardt of a carnival event in Reggio is reproduced here in full to allow the reader to visualize the entire scope of the performance, in particular its fantastic, pantomimic mixture of Christian and pagan representation. The role of the seven Virtues, having a symbolic as well as actual role as concubines, is just such a case in point of religious pomposity going hand-in-hand with pagan sexual excess. The comparison between this event and the more elaborate and bizarre creations of the performance art schools of the early twentieth century (discussed in chapter 5) should not be lost:

> When Duke Borso came in 1453 to Reggio, to receive the homage of the city, he was met at the gate by a great machine, on which St Prospero, the patron saint of the town, appeared to float, shaded by a baldachin held by angels, while below him was a revolving disk with eight singing cherubs, two of whom received from the saint the scepter and keys of the city, which they then delivered to the duke, while saints and angels held forth his praise. A chariot drawn by concealed horses now advanced, bearing an empty throne, behind which stood a figure of Justice attended by a genius. At the corners of the chariot stood four grey-headed lawgivers, encircled by angels with banners; by its side rode standard bearers in complete armour. It need hardly be added that the goddess and the genius did not suffer the duke to pass by without an address. A second car, drawn by a unicorn, bore a Caritas with a burning torch. Between the two came the classical spectacle in the form of a ship, moved by men concealed within it. In front of the Church of San Pietro, a halt was again made. The saint, attended by two angels, descended in an aureole from the façade, placed a wreath of laurel on the head of the duke, and then floated back to his former position. The clergy provided another allegory of a purely religious kind. Idolatry and Faith stood on two lofty pillars, and after Faith, represented by a beautiful girl, had uttered her welcome, the other column fell to pieces with the lay figure upon it. Further on, Borso was met by Caesar with seven beautiful women, who were presented to him as the seven Virtues which he was exhorted to pursue. At last the cathedral was reached, but after the service the duke again took his seat on a lofty golden throne, and a second time received the homage of some of the masks already mentioned. To conclude all, three angels flew down from an adjacent building, and, amid songs of joy, delivered to him branches of palm as symbols of peace. — *Burckhardt*[42]

It should further be noted that in Venice, the whole elaborate business of these processions took place on water, descriptions of which are no less fantastic than those already discussed above. The fairytale scene that greeted the princesses of Ferrara in 1941 included countless vessels filled with garlands, hangings, nymphs, and gods floating on machines hung in the air, all of which obliterated the water for a mile around. The air itself was filled with music, sweet odors and the fluttering of embroidered banners.[43]

MACHIAVELLI'S CYNICISM

Niccolò Machiavelli was not a typical Renaissance character of the type we have been discussing. He was not a humanist — rejecting the imitation of pagan culture as superficial. He looked beyond the pieties of ancient *and* modern moralists: "the naive belief that the ancients were somehow made of better human stuff than the moderns."[44] Nor was Machiavelli a despot, nor a satirist, nor a knight, nor an artist. Neither was he an example of Burckhardt's all-sided man. In only one respect does he fit our previous categorizations: He was an *individual,* and of course, he read and he wrote. Machiavelli would have been a cynic regardless of what historical period he had been born into. The fact that he was born into the period we are now discussing has created a uniquely fascinating phenomenon which, although indispensable to a book on cynicism, cannot be extrapolated in any generally useful sense. Machiavelli, the man and his ideas, remains one of those elusive events of fortune (a concept so central to his works) for which forming a thesis becomes a futile exercise.

Georges Bataille maintained that one could use, or abuse, Friedrich Nietzsche's work to support just about any position one wished to take. "It is common," he said, "to retain only one aspect of Nietzsche, suiting the one who assumes the right to choose."[45] The writings of Machiavelli have been used and abused in just such a way to mirror the positions and prejudices of any individual or interest group willing to plunder a passage from his often contradictory counsel. My own abuse is to claim Machiavelli as a cynic, not *cynic* in its negative usage, demonstrated by the use of the disparaging term "machiavellian," but cynical in the positive sense of presenting an honest account of human nature freed from the gloss and sentimentality attached to many orthodox histories. Having said which, many passages of Machiavelli's work simply recount historical names, facts and figures, most notably from Titus Livy's *History of Rome.* The cynicism of Machiavelli lies in the rich interpretations and observations on human nature that he excavates from beneath the exploits (remarkable in themselves) of Renaissance man. Man, because in spite of the yearning for a pre-Christian golden age, very few of the players in Machiavelli's dramas seem to have been women.

Bernard Crick, in the introduction to the 1998 version of *The Discourses*, tells us of Machiavelli that, "One thing alone is clear: he raises strong emotions— mostly of doubtful relevance,"[46] Here we have our first clue to Machiavelli's cynic credentials. The ability to raise strong emotions is an essential qualification for a cynic. But when Crick doubts the *relevance* of the strong emotions produced by Machiavelli, rather than dismissing Machiavelli's critics, Crick is dismissing the very power of Machiavelli's texts. Those who practice the art of *parrhesia* in their discourse are the ones who court the greatest controversy. Rather than apologizing for Machiavelli, the controversy surrounding his writing is the reason he is still relevant today.

So where is the evidence that Machiavelli practiced the art of telling the truth; the naked truth, the truth that has the potential to hurt the teller? After all, the term "Machiavellian" has come to represent someone who is scheming, two-faced and self-interested. The greatest truth of Machiavelli's writing, the truth that is continually reflected throughout his work, is that it accurately reveals the capricious nature of human beings and the world they inhabit. Namely, that there are no universal blueprints by which we can order our lives. This claim will be challenged by those who believe they have discovered laws and guiding principles in the works of Machiavelli. Yet this camp (Machiavelli's advocates, those who claim him as a brilliant political and military strategist) misrepresent Machiavelli as much as do his denigrators, those who brand him with everything that is detested in politics: deviousness, treachery, connivance, manipulation, indeed *Machiavellianism*.

There is plenty in Machiavelli's writing to support all these views, and that *something* is the reason why it is unsafe to rely on Machiavelli's individual maxims as evidence of a definitive doctrine. Most of Machiavelli's advice is directly contradicted elsewhere in his writing. There is a powerful cynical imperative for these contradictions as will be acknowledged later in respect of Nietzsche, and also Foucault, who said "don't ever ask me to remain he same." Machiavelli points out that it is not unreasonable during the course of their lifetime for people to change their judgments and appetites on a whole range of things, even when their circumstances remain the same: "it is impossible that things should look the same to them seeing that they have other appetites, other interests and standpoints, from what they had in their youth."[47] Yet regardless of these apparent contradictions, one should also note a consistent theme that runs through Machiavelli's works: the importance of taking a clear line one way or the other; for as Machiavelli tells us, taking a middle course usually ends in the individual's undoing.[48]

For this reason, any conclusions one may wish to draw from Machiavelli's writings can only be provided by studying his works in their entirety. As with the ancient Cynics, there is no central philosophy or grand narrative to be found in Machiavelli's discourse. What may at first appear to be strategies for social change are more accurately strategies for survival, the pragmatic philosophy of the Cynics which allows one to adapt to prevailing circumstances rather than initiating them. Wisdom there is in abundance, but it is a wisdom that requires Machiavelli's readers to do much of the work in understanding its significance (for them). As Crick says, "He was one of those men who somehow, in a most disorderly and incoherent way, stumble upon certain truths which are important in understanding human society"[49]

Pointing to their startling ability to change sides politically, James Hankins points out that it is typical of Renaissance intellectuals from Petrarch to Machiavelli to lack any ideological commitment, something which seems hypocritical to modern eyes. "Renaissance Italians were not burdened with the cult of sincerity so typical of modern democratic societies." Hankins adds that much ink has been spilled by modern scholars in the vain attempt to find some underlying consistency for this behavior.[50] However, if one views such behavior from the standpoint of a cynic, it is entirely consistent and perfectly understandable. Renaissance cynicism, as with cynicism in general, targeted at least three fronts: humanist idealism, hedonistic materialism, and state legislation and decree. While most people would have no difficulty associating Machiavelli with the first two (philosophical) battles, it may be construed from his writings that far from decrying state interference, he upheld it, and in an extreme manner. But here Machiavelli's advice should rather be viewed as rhetorical and parrhesiastic. He argues from the point of view that humans can alter the circumstances, even taking the extreme position that, where nature fails to refresh humans' tired endeavors with natural disasters, these disasters should be replicated by mortal intervention. Here are also shades of Nietzsche's frustration with God, of wanting to do God's work himself.

On a superficial level, it is of course possible to read Machiavelli like a "Handbook for Despots" or "How to Crush Populations and Maintain Power while Maintaining Your Popularity." Yet the idea that Machiavelli wrote what he wrote simply to ingratiate himself with those in power is probably the greatest myth of all about the writer. Machiavelli had nothing to gain personally from his advice, indeed there is much in his writings that is likely to cause offense and bring cruelty down on his own head. If his primary works, *The Prince* and *The Discourses*, are the equivalent to modern day texts on management theory (they are certainly more honest and realistic in their advice, even if they also rely heavily on smart metaphors) one must consider the climate in which they were written to see just what risks Machiavelli took — assuming of course that his books *were* widely read by despots. Crick denies that Machiavelli's writings were intended to please princes in his one book or republicans in the other: "Many things in both books would please neither; both have a definite slant, but both are incompetent if viewed as pure acts of arse-licking."[51]

I have already asserted my belief that Machiavelli was a parrhesiast. He spoke the truth because he felt obliged to. Machiavelli's truth is a cold and cruel truth, the antithesis of today's stultifying political correctness that smothers truth in sentimentality. The following line is typical of Machiavelli's refreshing advice, which though we would recoil from voicing it at our weekly "team meeting," we cannot avoid its truth: "People should either be caressed or crushed. If you do them minor damage they will get their revenge; but if you cripple them there is nothing they can do."[52] Not all of Machiavelli's advice is so forthright, but any apparent smarminess observed in his other writing comes with the parrhesiast's skill of knowing how to lace truth with flattery in a way that ensures the reception of the message. The role of the parrhesiast, discussed in the previous chapter, is acknowledged by Machiavelli in the following passage:

> My subject is sycophants, who pullulate at court. For men are so easily flattered and are so easily taken in by praise, that it is difficult for them to defend themselves against this plague, and in defending themselves they run the risk of making themselves despicable. For there is no way of protecting oneself against flattery other than by making it clear you do not mind being told the truth; but, when anyone can tell you the truth, then you are not treated with sufficient respect. So a wise ruler ought to find an alternative to flattery and excessive frankness. He ought to choose wise men from among his subjects, and give to them alone freedom to tell the truth.[53]

Machiavelli is a cold pragmatist. Moral distinctions between the different means of acquiring and holding on to power are linked only to the desired outcome. Such an approach is positively cynical, removing sentimentality from truth. For example, in *The Prince* Machiavelli talks of "well-used" as distinct from "abused" forms of cruelty, and of "justified" and "wasted" evil:

> Well-used cruelty (if one can speak well of evil) one may call those

atrocities that are committed at a stroke, in order to secure one's power, and are then not repeated.... If you take control of a state, you should make a list of all the crimes you have to commit and do them all at once. That way you will not have to commit new atrocities every day, and you will be able, by not repeating your evil deeds, to reassure your subjects and to win their support by treating them well. He who acts otherwise, either out of squeamishness or out of bad judgment, has to hold a bloody knife in his hands all the time.... Do all the harm you must do at one and the same time, that way the full extent of it will not be noticed, and will give less offence. One should do good, on the other hand, little by little, so people can fully appreciate it.[54]

And in chapter 17 of *The Prince*, titled "About cruelty and compassion; and about whether it is better to be loved than feared, or the reverse," Machiavelli offers the following advice:

So a ruler ought not to mind the disgrace of being called cruel, if he keeps his subjects peaceful and law-abiding, for it is more compassionate to impose harsh punishments on a few than, out of excessive compassion, to allow disorder to spread, which leads to murders or looting ... this leads us to a question that is in dispute: Is it better to be loved than feared, or vice versa? My reply is one ought to be both loved and feared; but, since it is difficult to accomplish both at the same time, I maintain it is much safer to be feared than loved, if you have to do without one of the two.[55]

By today's standards, the implementation of the advice contained in these two passages would amount at the very least to a gross infringement of human rights. Machiavelli, however, is not concerned with writing politically correct manifestos reflecting how civilized human beings *should* behave. He acknowledges human reality as it is. One can think of many situations in the world today where the intervention of Western powers under banners such as civilized, democratic and Christian, have not only failed to prevent, but in many cases aggravated genocidal human misery. As Crick reminds us: "Far from believing that it is the business of social science to eliminate conflict, we may want, instead, to follow Machiavelli's lead and to define and study it more precisely, so many types of conflict and so many different circumstances."[56]

Machiavelli explains the underlying psychology of the advice he offers above when he describes men to be "ungrateful, fickle, deceptive and deceiving, avoiders of danger, eager to gain. As long as you serve their interests they are devoted to you ... but as soon as you need their help they turn against you,"[57] Yet the psychology Machiavelli uses here is not that branch of the science that clings to testing its truths in double-blind trials: It is more the instinctive and subjective type which relies on stereotyping and generalizations. Machiavelli should not be condemned for that. Anecdote, when it hits the right note, can be a powerful instructor, and as Crick further observes, there is a high degree of consistency among Machiavelli's generalizations.[58]

As has already been acknowledged, Machiavelli has been claimed as many things: theorist, philosopher, political analyst, military strategist, psychologist, social scientist. It is important now to further substantiate my claim on him as a cynic in the classical as well as positive modern sense. There exists in Machiavelli's work, for instance, a version of Diogenes' mission to alter the currency. In the passage that follows Machiavelli suggests employing a deliberate strategy to mirror the energizing effects of a natural disaster, to refresh and renew. This is the kind of vision that the Cynics or the Dadaists could only reference by way of harmless gesture. The act here is one of pure cynicism aimed at subverting the status quo — to turn the world upside down, even if the apparent motive is one of pure selfishness; to give to a new ruler power and authority and to replace the corrupt with a new corruption at the expense of an entire population:

> Should anyone become the ruler either of a city or of a state ... the best thing he could do in order to retain such a principality, given that he be a new prince, is to organize everything in that new state afresh; e.g. in its cities to appoint new governors, with new titles and new authority, the governors themselves being new men. To make the rich poor and the poor rich; as did David when he became king, "*who filled the hungry with good things and the rich sent empty away.*" ; as well as to build new cities, to destroy those already built, and to move the inhabitants from one place to another far distant from it; in short to leave nothing of that province intact.[59]

The Cynics emphasized the lessons of the natural world; so too does Machiavelli continually repeat the obliterating and purging effects in history of floods, pestilences and famines. He draws parallels among these capricious and catastrophic events and the way in which the human body, when it has also accumulated too much superfluous material, also requires purging to restore it to health. When human craftiness and malignity has gone as far as it can go, the world must be purged so that, humbled by adversity, "mankind may adopt a more appropriate form of life and grow better."[60] Machiavelli's counsel is far more significant than that claimed by military, organizational, or political strategists who would have us continue to plod down the same old predictable path of exploiting each other for some short term gain. That is not what these two small immense works are showing us. Machiavelli is prompted by the same cynical emotions as the Dadaist, Richard Huelsenbeck, when Huelsenbeck announced that "things have to collide; things are not proceeding nearly as horribly as they should."[61] Machiavelli is telling us that if the banality of our lives is not rescued by natural disasters, then we must create disasters of our own in order to revitalize the human project.

Machiavelli's theme of purging and renewal is entirely consistent with the whole spirit of the Renaissance, and in particular with the earlier discussion on the stagnation and depravity of the Church. Machiavelli suggests that one need look no further than those people who live in the immediate neighborhood of the Church of Rome itself to witness how little religion was left.[62] Like most other Renaissance thinkers, Machiavelli did not so much condemn Christianity outright, as adopt the cynical view that Christianity had sold out to its original and true ethos and become corrupted. The issue at stake here is between the lost but sustained *virtù* of Greek and Roman paganism and the lost spirit of Christianity. Yet as Hankins points out, Machiavelli's critique of Christianity is far more radical than anything in the humanist tradition. For Machiavelli, "Christian morality is inconsistent with the morality needed to create a successful polity.... He boldly subordinates religion to the interests of civil society."[63] Machiavelli asserts that "the life of all mundane things is of infinite duration," and therefore institutions will only retain their vitality if they 'make frequent renovations possible," or, that they are renovated through some external occurrence. The way to renovate them, he suggests, is to reduce them to their starting-points, to the thing that gave them purpose in the first place. But since this purpose is always corrupted in the process of time, "such a body must of necessity die unless something happens which brings it up to the mark."[64] Machiavelli also recognized, as did Diogenes and Nietzsche, that civil and religious laws have no inherent legitimacy of their own. They were nothing but a collection of decisions, "made by jurists of old, which the jurists of today have tabulated in orderly fashion for our instruction."[65]

There are many other cynical resonances between the thoughts of Machiavelli and those of Nietzsche, and these will become clear when that philosopher is discussed later. Most significant are Machiavelli's often contradictory views of the importance of history, his disregard for binding man-made laws, and personal virtue transcending notions of good and evil:

> Men always, but not always with good reason, praise bygone days and
> criticize the present, and so partial are they to the past that they not
> only admire past ages the knowledge of which has come down to them
> in written records, but also, when they grow old, what they remember
> having seen in their youth.[66]

The causes of this, Machiavelli claims, are first, that the truth of history is filtered to pass over discredited acts and exaggerate that which upholds the reputation of those whom history wishes to exalt, and second, that humans cannot hate the past through fear or envy, the usual reasons for hate. Machiavelli reflects that the world has always been thus, containing good and evil in equal measure, even if, as he says, this good and evil varies from province to province. There is also much evidence that Machiavelli sat on the same lone and lofty perch of world-hating introspection as Sloterdijk's cynic. In his remark that "Nothing is more futile and more inconstant than are the masses,"[67] Machiavelli joins Nietzsche in that philosopher's own undisguised contempt for the domesticated herding human mob. He marks himself out from those who always walk along the beaten path in imitation of what others have done before.[68]

And as if in response to Diogenes' maxim that "we should not try to alter circumstances, but to adapt ourselves to them as they really are," Machiavelli responds with the following:

> One cannot find a man so prudent he knows how to adapt himself to changing circumstances, for he will either be unable to deviate from that style of behavior to which his character inclines him, or, alternatively, having always been successful by adopting one particular style, he will be unable to persuade himself that it is time to change.[69]

Hankins claims that Machiavelli believes survival to be a precondition over all other goods and that there can be no happiness in slavery: "Since survival sometimes requires behavior at variance with traditional morality, one must be prepared to abandon that morality if one is to maintain the minimal condition for happiness, political freedom."[70] Machiavelli's realism is entirely consistent with the beyond good and evil perspective of the Cynics, and the consequent acknowledgement that the meek rarely inherit the earth. Machiavelli's ethics, according to Hankins, embraced a consequentialism in which the goodness of the end must be allowed to trump the goodness of the means: "The prince who allows disorders to arise because he shrinks from cruelty is responsible for the evils resulting from his 'goodness.'"[71] And also like Diogenes, Machiavelli knew that Hedonism was the philosophy *least* likely to free humans from a life of discontentment. He knew that of all the things human beings desire in life they can attain but few, and of those they will also grow weary.[72] It is human nature to be perpetually vexated, to find fault with the present, praise the past, and long for the future — "though for its doing so no rational cause can be assigned."[73]

THE DEATH OF THE RENAISSANCE:
SOME CYNICAL WARNINGS

Picking up on Machiavelli's comment that "we Italians are irreligious and corrupt above others,"[74] Burckhardt considers the triumph and crisis of the Renaissance which had reached its "highest pitch" at the beginning of the sixteenth century. "Political ruin of the nation seemed inevitable," and the early mumblings of "malicious self-conceit" and "abominable profligacy" voiced by the rising powers of the Reformation were also becoming audible.[75]

From the beginnings of its glorious endeavor, the Renaissance had been carelessly sowing the seeds of its own destruction, first through its purging of old systems and structures, creating an ideological vacuum in which new institutions and idealisms could take root, and second by popularizing and giving access to the printed word. Where previously the mass of the educated population were dependent on scholars for their knowledge of antiquity, the spread of printed editions of classical works freed people from their dependence on the humanists. The use of former beliefs and cultural influences from antiquity during the Renaissance—initially employed to annihilate the religious dogma and artistic stagnation at the end of the Middle Ages—ultimately became that which it had sought to destroy, "the model for all thought and action": an idolization of an ancient world which the scholarly processes of the Renaissance had stripped bare of its essential meaning.

In the same way that the Renaissance could never have been anticipated emerging out of the plague-ridden ashes of the Middle Ages, neither could it have been anticipated—at the height of Renaissance frenzy and splendor—that Europe would be plunged once again into the dark ages of religious fear, intolerance and persecution. Such was the fragility of the whole Renaissance project. The cynical abandonment of strict moral and religious codes with no alternative virtues to support the resulting culture, had produced an anarchic situation where jealousy, selfishness, false honor and resentment combined to produce chaotic and tragic results. This is not a condemnation of cynicism, which can only ever offer a strategy of survival to the *individual,* but a warning of the limitations of hedonism as a civilizing or liberating force. Had the freedoms of the Renaissance and the quest for individualism been applied to *all* its citizens, underpinned with a respect for the individual's right to be *truly* an individual, the resulting anarchy and chaos which allowed the Protestant Reformation and Catholic Counter Reformation to firm their grip might yet have been avoided.[76] This is not of course to suggest that cynicism could have provided the model by which the Renaissance might have continued to flourish; it rather provides us, then as now, with the weapon by which we can expose the fragility of the human project in *all* its forms.

Less surprising than the mutated Christian backlash, is the inevitable progression from the Renaissance age of chaos into the scientific Age of Reason. In Foucault's *Madness and Civilization*, we are shown a world that from the close of the Renaissance presented an unassailable dichotomy of reason and unreason, good and evil, order and disorder, completely destroying any unity and equilibrium that may have been given the possibilities to develop out of the Renaissance. In the world that followed, science decided — as it still decides today — what forms of human behavior were deviant or pathological, legislating and prohibiting by penalty of incarceration in jails or asylums those who transgress its newly categorized moral codes. The glory of the Renaissance was also its chaos, but in that chaos also lay its downfall, because typically humans have an obsessional need to create order out of chaos. And thus our cynical cycles of return continue to grind.

3

Nietzschean Cynicism: The Link Between the Ancient and the Modern Forms

Perhaps no other modern philosopher has tried so hard to re-experience the spirit of Socrates and his disciples.— *Walter Kaufmann*[1]

If he was anything in a word, Nietzsche was a Greek born two thousand years too late…. But his Hellenism, I need not add, was anything but the pale neo-Platonism that has run through the thinking of the Western world since the days of the Christian Fathers. From Plato, to be sure, he got what all of us must get, but his real forefather was Heraclitus.— *H.L. Mencken*[2]

The Greeks, the famous people of a past still near to us, had the "unhistorical sense" strongly developed in the period of their greatest power. If a typical child of his age were transported to that world by some enchantment, he would probably find the Greeks very "uneducated." And that discovery would betray the closely guarded secret of modern culture to the laughter of the world. For we moderns have nothing of our own. We only become worth notice by filling ourselves to overflowing with foreign customs, arts, philosophies, religions and sciences: we are wandering encyclopaedias.— *Nietzsche*[3]

We now take a further leap of five hundred years or so to examine the work of Friedrich Nietzsche (1844–1900); not that other cynics were absent during the intervening years between the demise of classical Cynicism and the Renaissance, or between the Renaissance and Nietzsche. Cynics such as Lucian and Blake have not been forgotten; they have their own place in this history, but their work is acknowledged elsewhere where it contributes to a particular theme or discussion. The prominence of the Cynics, the Renaissance and Nietzsche is that of highlighting important historical milestones responsible for the recent and contemporary receptions of cynicism that make up the rest of this book.

It is a credit to Nietzsche that the cynicism he unleashed on the modern world is as contemporary and fresh today as it was one hundred years ago. In comparison, some of the other great thinkers who influenced the twentieth century such as Marx and Freud now appear relative historical curiosities. Their view of the world in terms of categories and classifications, their discourses of truth, their totalitarian theories, and the problem, as Madan Sarup puts it, that "they were weighed down by the cultural baggage of their time,"[4] are some of the features responsible for modernism's failure to stand the test of time. As I intend to demonstrate, it is Nietzsche's role as proto-postmodernist, as well as Greek and Renaissance revivalist, that in contrast to many of his contemporaries gives his philosophy its timeless relevance. As the title of this chapter suggests, it is Nietzsche, not Diogenes, who is the ultimate hero of this book. His role of refreshing the Cynic project for the twentieth century, and the influence of his own philosophical legacy up to the present day, has been huge and uniquely significant — even when he and his Greek forebears remain absent from the credits.

It is not the purpose of this chapter to rehearse many of the existing debates about Nietzsche. There are well over two hundred secondary texts on him from every possible perspective; views which characteristically seem often in opposition. Therefore, if one wishes to read about Nietzsche the misogynist or Nietzsche the "feminist" icon (see below), Nietzsche the self-hating Christian or Nietzsche the self-hating Jew, it is simply a matter of locating the appropriate text. Indeed, as Georges Bataille informs us, the multi-layered irony in Nietzsche's work allows one to use (or abuse) Nietzsche's writings to support just about any position one wishes to take: "It is common to retain only one aspect of Nietzsche, suiting the one who assumes the right to choose."[5] For my own purpose, it suits me to use Nietzsche as a cynic, and I will give my reasons why I feel he meets the criteria required to merit that term. However, I am not the first to claim Nietzsche for this position, even though as Peter Sloterdijk's description of him as a *neo-cyniker* reminds us, Nietzsche's self-characterization as a cynic is often overlooked. References to Nietzsche seem to appear more frequently in texts discussing cynicism than those attributed to any other recent philosopher, Luis Navia even conversely describing Diogenes as a Nietzschean philosopher.[6] This characterization of Nietzsche is also supported by Anthony Long when he emphasizes that "The current willingness of philosophers to take Nietzsche seriously is good news for the ancient Cynics."[7] To which we can add Heinrich Niehues-Probsting's claim that Nietzsche represents the most important stage in the history of the reception of Cynicism into its modern form.[8]

So what then characterizes Nietzsche as a cynic? While evidence of Nietzsche's cynicism will be discussed in more detail later, it is worth summarizing the main features here. In the first place we can draw direct parallels between some of the key features of Nietzsche's work and features of Classical Cynicism discussed in the first chapter, an examination of which reinforces Niehues-Probsting's claim that Nietzsche provides a critical link between ancient and modern forms of cynicism. Both Nietzsche and the Cynics share an objection to scientific and religious dogmatism, and an antipathy toward pre-existing truths. The myth of progressive enlightenment is also dismissed by both the Cynics and Nietzsche, who believed instead in cycles of return. Moreover, although it is by no means conclusive evidence of a cynical stance, we have Nietzsche's and the Cynics' mutual dislike of Plato. Next, we can point to the contempt by both for pretentiousness, the hatred of narrow provincialism, and hostility toward political and other social institutions. Nietzsche and the Cynics saw themselves outside of such narrow preoccupations; they were cosmopolitan: "citizens of the world." And the rejection of systems and totalizing theories was demonstrated by both in the role they adopted of testing out usages and laws. We can also turn to Nietzsche's linguistic style for evidence of a cynical mode of discourse. His use of aphorisms and epigrams to stimulate the reader's senses has strong links with Cynic genres such as the *Chreia*. Compare for example Diogenes' response when asked why he was walking around in broad daylight with a lighted lamp: "I'm looking for an honest man," with Nietzsche's aphorism, "I looked for great human beings, but all I ever found were the *apes* of their ideals."[9]

It is also a claim of this book that Nietzsche provides a powerful connecting philosophical thread linking the Cynics with the postmodernists: a classical scholar who was discussing *post*modernist ideas even before the arrival of "modernism." His contempt for totalizing theories and scientific certitude, and his hostility toward progress and modern ideas at the end of a different century, uncannily echo both the themes of 200 BC and those we are presented with today. According to Sarup, one can see the influence of Nietzsche's philosophy in the work of many postmodernists: the antipathy to any system; the rejection of the Hegelian view of history-as-progress; an awareness of, and criticism of, the increasing pressure for conformity; and an obsession with the subjective and the small story.[10] Nietzsche railed against established views of history, science and knowledge that prevailed during preceding centuries and set the scene for many of the philosophical and cultural genres that appeared and were superseded in relatively quick succession during the following century.

Having summarized some of the philosophical and stylistic links between Nietzsche and the Cynics, we can now turn to Nietzsche's own testimony that he is a cynic. In his final work *Ecce Homo*, in answer to his question "Why I Write Such Good Books," Nietzsche replies, "There is altogether no prouder and at the same time more exquisite kind of book than my books—they attain here and there the highest thing that can be attained on earth, cynicism."[11] And in a letter describing *Ecce Homo* to Georg Brandes, his first biographer and critic, Nietzsche says, "I have now written an account of myself with a cynicism that will become world-historical."[12] The following passage from *Beyond Good and Evil* indicates the value which Nietzsche himself places on Cynicism: "Cynicism is the only form in which base souls approach what is called honesty; and the higher man must open his ears to all the coarser or finer cynicism and congratulate himself when the clown becomes shameless right before him, or the scientific satyr speaks out."[13]

We can also add Nietzsche's opening line of his preface to *The Will to Power*, when he tells us that "Great things require that one be silent about them or talk about them on a grand scale: on a grand scale means cynically and with innocence."[14] For the most part then, when Nietzsche uses the term cynicism — either to describe himself or more generally — he uses it positively: "the highest thing that can be attained on earth." The pejorative use of the term may well appear in Nietzsche's text, but as with much of Nietzsche's writing, readers will need to separate out for themselves Nietzsche's all-too-human comments from his more serious philosophical message.

For yet further evidence of Nietzsche the cynic, let us now turn to his personal life. Nietzsche was preoccupied with self-discipline and testing himself against the elements, in particular his personal struggle against illness. It is from this physical and mental effort described in Chapter 1 as *askesis* and *ponos*, that both Nietzsche and the Cynics aim to become masters of their own destiny. For Nietzsche in particular, self-perfection was the real goal of morality.[15] He sought his happiness in the Cynic sense of living an ascetic life on his meager pension, a life which outwardly exhibited itself as very simple.[16] His total abstinence from alcohol was a denial which even Diogenes did not endure. Nietzsche then, like the Cynics, embraced the minimum necessary for life as a strategy for survival. The tiny room where he lived and worked, devoid of decoration or comfort, has parallels with Diogenes' own choice of dwelling. According to his sister

Elizabeth, "There is no doubt that ... my brother tried a little bit to imitate Diogenes in the tub; he wanted to find out with how little could a philosopher do...."

"Indeed, a minimum of life, an unchaining from all coarser desires, an independence in the middle of all kinds of outer nuisance; a bit of Cynicism, perhaps a bit of 'tub'." — *Nietzsche*[17]

Driven by his need to reach the limits of pain and endurance, one way in which Nietzsche practiced *askesis*— despite his frail health — was to take long walks into the mountains. Nietzsche's typical day would start at five in his small rented room in the Swiss Alpine village of Sils-Maria. He would write until midday and then take long walks up the surrounding peaks, retiring early to bed after a snack of bread and ham or egg alone in his room.[18] An examination of Nietzsche's work reveals many examples of his raging against comfort in all its manifestations: physical, intellectual, and moral. Nietzsche was particularly mindful of the Cynics' avoidance of suffering by affirming life. In his lectures on Greek literature, Nietzsche recalled an anecdote concerning Antisthenes. Plagued by pain and very ill, Antisthenes asks who will free him from his suffering. When Diogenes shows him a dagger, Antisthenes is said to have responded: "I said from suffering, not from life." Nietzsche concludes from this incident the following observation:

> A very profound statement. One cannot get the better of the love of life than by means of a dagger. Yet that is the real suffering. It is obvious that the Cynic clings to life more than the other philosophers: "the shortest way to happiness" is nothing but the love of life in itself and complete needlessness with reference to all other goods.[19]

It is likely, that apart from his one-sided obsession with Wagner's wife, Nietzsche's few relationships with women were purely platonic and based on mutual philosophic interests.[20] Suggestions, for instance, that Nietzsche's dementia had been the result of an earlier syphilitic infection, or that he had deliberately infected himself by twice visiting prostitutes, have no basis in fact. The diagnosis of Nietzsche's illness was never confirmed, and even if it were syphilis, it is quite plausible that this could have been contracted through a skin wound while he administered to sick soldiers during his time as a medical orderly.[21] It is entirely consistent with Nietzsche's philosophical style that his attack on Christianity's denial of sensual pleasure should manifest itself as a plea for hedonistic values, but this approach only reinforces his cynical tendency to set up a critique of one polarized view, by opposing it with another of equal force. Therefore, despite some later references to Nietzsche as an advocate of pleasure, it should not be read into Nietzsche's discourse that proposing sensual enjoyment equates with Nietzsche the hedonist.

Having made a *prima facie* case for Nietzsche the cynic, it is important to understand why this particular aspect of Nietzsche's character has long been sidelined. Starting with his sister's misrepresentation of her brother, ultimately for business considerations, Nietzsche's unpopularity as a result of some of the wilder claims of critics and biographers during the first half of the last century has meant that any serious analysis of Nietzsche's work is relatively recent. Furthermore, ever since Nietzsche's work has been the subject of scholarly investigation, the ambiguity of his philosophical ideas has allowed him to be claimed for just about any cause one cares to make; hence his cynic traits have been lost among many other claims on his character.

For my own part, as well as portraying Nietzsche as a cynic, I have also referred in this chapter to Nietzsche the existentialist, and have alluded to Nietzsche the Epicurean, but no conflict is intended here with his essentially cynical character. Existentialism is not so much a rival philosophy, as a set of themes which share many features in common with cynicism. Like cynicism, it is also a theory of the self, a philosophy of individual autonomy and responsibility concerned with the experience of choice. Such an attitude acknowledges the absurdity of human life rather than a world explained by universal truths.[22] The question of Nietzsche the Epicurean is easily overcome. Although a plea by Nietzsche is presented in this chapter for a return to the sensuality of Epicurean Greece and Rome; and despite providing a definition of truth as "that which produces the most pleasure," there is no evidence to suggest that Nietzsche himself was ever a pleasure seeker. It is the power of cynicism in general, and of Nietzsche's writing in particular, that a dialogue is presented which throws up apparent questions and ambiguities about who the writer was and what his philosophical intentions were; questions which Nietzsche has left us to ponder, perhaps intentionally, long after his death when he says: 'let us assume that people will be allowed to read [my work] in about the year 2000."[23]

Yes, Nietzsche was many other things aside from being a cynic and there have been many other claims to his character. It is not my primary intention to challenge the other claims concerning Nietzsche: I focus on this less-studied aspect of the man simply to increase my own understanding of cynicism. Yet there is one claim about Nietzsche I will challenge. Nietzsche (like the Cynics) has been regarded as a nihilist, precisely because his uncompromising attacks on popular doctrines and values are mistaken for a belief in nothing at all. But the reverse is the case. Nietzsche has a passionate belief in the validity of a search for the real; a search obscured to most of us by the lie of idealism: "The discussion of Nietzsche's 'nihilism' can be looked at in this way. He is a nihilist to those who want to hang on to absolute value systems whether Christian or rationalist. He is seen as an optimist to those who see those tendencies as dangerous or outmoded."[24]

Nietzsche's own definition of nihilism describes the state we experience when the eternal, transcendent truths of grand narratives such as science or Christianity fail to deliver their promises, causing them to self-destruct.[25] When Nietzsche discusses nihilism, he is describing the imminent future of the modern world. And for many postmodern cynics—notably Jean Baudrillard, for whom there is no real left, only simulations—we are now living in the world that Nietzsche predicted.

It is probably appropriate at this juncture to explain to the reader why I have thus far omitted to mention what are considered to be Nietzsche's two central ideas: the Will to Power and the *Übermensch* (overman or superman). For a cynic, it is entirely predictable that these two universal truths of Nietzsche's, adrift in a vast sea of relativism, should be pounced on by many Nietzsche scholars as his central and most important ideas. However, with will to power, Nietzsche falls into the same trap as many postmodernists, that of setting up circular arguments which disappear into a black hole, and of using grand narrative to deny grand narrative:

> His [Nietzsche's] philosophy makes all kinds of pronouncements, some of which are ironic, some of which are purposely designed to shock ... global skepticism always produces paradoxes and empty circularities. How can Nietzsche's own subversive claims to know the limitations of human knowledge survive his own scepticism? If there is no "truth" or "knowledge," how can we accept Nietzsche's epistemological claim that all of reality can be reduced to "energy" or "will to power"?— *Dave Robinson*[26]

> Nietzsche asserts that any attempt to understand the universe is prompted by man's will to power. If so, it would seem that his own conception of the will to power must be admitted by him to be a creation of his own will to power ... Nietzsche was not at his best with problems of this kind.— *Kaufmann*[27]

Yet one could also argue that here is Nietzsche at his paradoxical best, and that the will to power is not what it at first appears. It is at one and the same time a theory of both truth *and* relativism. The will to power asserts that knowledge and truth are subjective human concepts created to serve our own interests and purpose, and that they emerge whenever our survival is at stake, often as a result of the suppression of alternative possibilities. Such human concepts, beliefs and values, then, are the evolutionary result of the competition between warring ideas. They are never, therefore, facts, only interpretations.[28] Only one truth can thus exist: *There is no truth, only the will to power.*

The *Übermensch* is an altogether more fanciful idea, and a natural progression from the will to power. In a Darwinian notion of man being a link between ape and superman, there exists the possibility that some of us ordinary mortals can rise above our own mediocrity and stagnation to attain the qualities that fit Nietzsche's *Übermensch*. These free spirits (powerful, creative beings based on some idealistic notion of Ancient Greek heroes) would, through self-mastery, transcend the restrictions of basic human preoccupations to rule the rest of us willing slaves, not by bullying, but by the sheer force of their personalities. What Nietzsche fails to tell us is how the rest of us mere humans — so impressed by Hollywood film stars, management gurus, and the latest cut-price supermarket deal — would notice an overman if we saw one, or care if we did. We crave external transcendent truths and deceive ourselves with fantasies because we have a need to do so. We are mediocre because we thrive on mediocrity: This is the nature of postmodern man and woman.

Here, we have a complete departure, reversal even, of Cynic philosophy. For while individual Cynics like Diogenes may have fitted the idea of an overman, even viewed themselves as above the preoccupations of mere mortals, they looked not upwards to deities for their inspiration but downwards to animals. Furthermore, like animals, they were for the most part ignored as irrelevant and outside of civilization. And while the Cynics had only disdain for athletes and trials of strength — regarding the whole business as stupid — Nietzsche had undisguised admiration for the heroic Greeks.[29] Allowing then for some fairly minor differences between Nietzsche and the Cynics, we now leave Nietzsche's central ideas to concentrate on his marginal ideas.

DIONYSUS VERSUS APOLLO

For the sake of understanding the older, the still rich and even overflowing Hellenic instinct, I was the first to take seriously that wonderful phenomenon that bears the name of Dionysus: it is explainable only in terms of *too much* energy.... For only in the Dionysian mysteries, in the psychology of the Dionysian condition, does the fundamental fact of the Hellenic instinct express itself — its "will to life." — *Nietzsche*[30]

The dichotomous relationship between the Dionysian and the Apollonian provides a useful metaphor for the philosophical split of Socrates' teachings into those represented by the line of Antisthenes and those represented by the line of Plato. Identifying more with Apollo and the heroic Greeks in his earlier writings, Nietzsche's progressive slide in his writing style to the Dionysian, and strong identification with Dionysus in his later works, provides yet another key to his later philosophical leanings.

The Ancient Greeks achieved a balanced harmony between the rationality and order of Apollo and the frenzied, chaotic love life represented by Dionysus. It is the lack of the Dionysian in post-Socratic, Western civilizations that Nietzsche holds responsible for their failure.[31] Dionysus was the effeminate god of madness, when madness was not yet regarded as outside of normal conventions of behavior. Love, laughter, drama, art, poetry and music arose from the Dionysian ritual. It would be tempting to posit Dionysus as a cynic god (if such a thing could exist), as we are told that Dionysus was "the god of confrontation — the god who startled."[32] We also closely associate Dionysus with carnival. Apollo in contrast never laughed. He was the god of reason: imperious, humorless, intelligent, and aggressive.[33]

But this separation of the Dionysian and the Apollonian did not exist in pre-Socratic Greece. They were simply two sides of the same person: the duality that is the human psyche. And according to Nietzsche, it is the subsequent deprecation of the Dionysian and elevation of the Apollonian that accounts for the inability of modern peoples to live their lives to the full: "From Plato on, there is something essentially amiss."[34] Take for example music. In *Twilight of the Idols*, Nietzsche writes that music as a complete experience remained "a mere residue of Dionysian histrionics" that existed in pre-Socratic Greece. Also a god of music, Apollo was the lyricist to Dionysus' sensual rhythms. Using music as a metaphor for Western philosophy, Nietzsche attempts to rectify the defect that such philosophy is big on lyrics but lacks sensuality. The Dionysian state was the primordial state in which the whole system of our emotions was excited at the same time in an uncontrolled and chaotic state.[35] For Nietzsche, music provided a refuge, a sanctuary,[36] one in which he was able to find his own solace from a hostile world. In the following aphorism, Emile Cioran (born in Rumania 10 years after Nietzsche's death and dying only 10 years ago in Paris in 1995), himself an important cynic philosopher and cosmopolitan, echoes Nietzsche's sentiments on music: "How does music suck our blood? ... The only art capable of bringing comfort, yet it opens up more wounds than all the others! Music is the sound track of *askesis*."[37]

Nietzsche was not to know that one hundred years hence, music was to be the one aspect of our orderly Western lives where the Dionysian eventually triumphed, releasing a passionate and furious energy as though to compensate us for our otherwise routine and mediocre existence. Getting a blood rush after a stressful week in the office from the throb or harmonic cadences of sensual music in clubs and discotheques (with or without the assistance of alcohol), has replaced carnival as an escape from the physical and psychological fetters of constrained society.

The ability to be touched by music in this way, or the willingness to *give* oneself to music in this way, provides a useful insight into the Cynical and Hellenistic belief that the real world is the world we access through our senses rather than through deductive reasoning. Conversely, it demonstrates why Platonist philosophers warn of the dangers of contaminating *their* truths with sensual experiences. That is not to say, of course, that devout rationalists are incapable of sensual pleasure: We all have the Dionysian *and* the Apollonian flowing through our veins. Rather, there are some — as with the celibate priest — who would deny their sensual appetites to achieve a greater spiritual or ideological goal. Although the Cynics operated their own resistance to hedonistic excesses, we should be aware that they were essentially sensual beings, albeit confining their pleasures to those they considered natural. The Cynics' rigorous training was aimed precisely at the removal of cerebral control of social inhibitions.

If the dualities presented in this book — Dionysus and Apollo, Diogenes and Plato — appear familiar, it is because they have been similarly categorized by others under different banners, such as Freud's psychological split between the ego and the id; the head and the heart (or guts); and the biological model of masculine, left brain tendencies (concerned with abstract thinking and linear logic: *doing*) versus feminine, right brain tendencies (concerned with concrete feeling states such as love, humor, and aesthetic appreciation: *being*). Without getting into a tangential discussion about these theories, it is at least important to understand their correspondence to other oppositions discussed elsewhere in this book. Nietzsche does not propose that the Dionysian mode is preferred or that the Apollonian mode is undesirable. Nietzsche believed that by promoting these binary oppositions, putting greater value on one side *or* the other; we perpetuated the dogmatic, patriarchal and moralistic view which has plagued humankind since the time of Plato. To use the left brain/right brain metaphor, the problem is that of reuniting the two hemispheres and not of giving greater value to one or the other, we need both to function completely. Nietzsche's plea for a return to Dionysian rites was an attempt to undermine the relentless dominance of logic over our sensual and intuitive natures. It is also the reason, as I discuss below, why Nietzsche is claimed in the battle against phallocentricity by some feminist writers.

NIETZSCHE'S WRITING STYLE

> They [the Cynics] dared to treat the form [of classical Greek litera-
> ture] as a matter of indifference and mix the styles; they translated
> Socrates as it were into a literary genre complete with the satyr shell
> and the god inside. Thus they became the humorists of antiquity.
> — Nietzsche[38]

> Nietzsche's is the only philosophy that wrenches one away from the
> servitude inherent in philosophical discourse, the only one that
> restores sovereignty to the free spirit.— Georges Bataille[39]

Like Menippus, Nietzsche also mixed his literary style. Polemic, satire,
irony, parody and his preference for the aphorism mark him out as a true
inheritor of the Cynic writing tradition.[40] But in whichever genre Nietzsche
chose to present his writing, it is his biting sarcasm and cynical tone that
most marks him out from other modern writers. This external arrogance
and nastiness— in Nietzsche's case belying a kind and sensitive nature —
provides for the daring honesty and unrestraint that makes a cynic a great
cynic. More importantly, one should not overlook that Nietzsche *knew* he
was being outrageous. It was a deliberate strategy to shock and provoke:
"There is something shrill about much of Nietzsche's writings: he delights
in antithesis to what is current; as if he were swimming against the stream
for its own sake; and he makes a sport of being provocative."[41]

Many have tried simply to write off Nietzsche's unorthodox literary
style as the ravings of a madman. Yet suggestions that Nietzsche's later
works were influenced by madness are refuted by Kaufmann who asserts
that while these later works may indeed have lacked inhibition, large parts
are distinguished by their clarity, lucidity, and startling depth.[42] Nietzsche's
cheekiness is also intensely humorous. It is this appreciation of Nietzsche's
writing art — writing that at times feels more like literary prose than the
dry academic discourse usually associated with philosophy — that draws
many unlikely devotees to his circle of admirers.

Reckoned an arch misogynist, Nietzsche is yet frequently cited by
feminist writers such as Luce Irigaray because they share his rejection of
formal structures in language: "Nietzsche made me take off and go soaring; I had the feeling that I was in the midst of poetry, which made me feel
perfectly happy."[43] The whole debate around Nietzsche and women is a
useful one to test out the many references to Nietzsche's ambiguity and
irony. Nietzsche's writing has been credited with having feminine qualities, yet Nietzsche clearly does not have feminist sympathies. The terms
feminist and feminine in any case have a dichotomous relationship, in
which the feminine equals Dionysian tendencies and feminism equals the
Apollonian side: political dogmatism of the kind which Nietzsche opposed.

In the same way, it would be over simplistic to read Nietzsche's all-too-human comments about women as misogynistic: His relationship with women was too complex for such shallow inferences:

> And truly the feminist women against who Nietzsche multiples his sarcasm are men. Feminism is the operation by means of which woman wishes to resemble man, the dogmatic philosopher, reclaiming truth, science, objectivity, that is, the whole virile illusion, and the effects of castration, attached to it. Feminism wants castration — even that of woman. — *Kaufmann*[44]

Here we have the most novel and apparently contradictory characterization of Nietzsche yet: Nietzsche, the voice of the feminine writer, attacking "men," who are represented by the patriarchal, dogmatic voice of feminism. As Nietzsche himself put it: "There is stupidity in this movement [the feminist movement], an almost masculine stupidity."[45] Some feminists oppose more dogmatic feminist doctrines for the same reasons as Nietzsche does. Hélène Cixous, for example, differs from those who wish either to annihilate or imitate men, believing these to be futile goals. For Cixous, sexual difference is not biological, nor marked by hierarchical opposition: It is located in the libido, which creates the possibility for both women *and* men to engage in feminine writing, writing simply for the pleasure of the text, the kind of writing exampled by Nietzsche, which Luce Irigaray describes as making her take off and go soaring. Cixous refers to this economy of writing and language as either *pre-symbolic*, because of its refusal to be seduced by contemporary modes of thought, or *feminine writing*, because much of the symbolism in modern language and writing is considered to be patriarchal.[46] That Nietzsche should be claimed for writing in a way which opposes patriarchal language is nothing remarkable; the ideas most crucial to Cixous's theorization of feminine writing come almost entirely from studying the texts of male writers, such as James Joyce, E.T.A. Hoffmann, Heinrich von Kleist and Edgar Allen Poe.[47]

Besides the heavy use of metaphor in Nietzsche's work, another feature that demonstrates his feminine, Dionysian style, is his peculiar use of aphorisms and epigrams. In the introduction to *Twilight of the Idols*, Tracy Strong discusses how Nietzsche is able to put over his powerful message without dominating or controlling the reader.[48] If one feels a resonance with one of Nietzsche's pithy comments, a process of critical interpretation automatically takes place in the reader. Not, as Strong points out, to determine what the aphorism *means*, but to make sense of what it is that the aphorism stirred in the reader. By writing in this way — rather than bombarding us with the truths we have come to expect from modern philosophers— Nietzsche helps us to recover, in true Cynic style, *the questions*. He recovers philosophy:

> What? Is humanity just God's mistake? Or God just a mistake of humanity? [49]
>
> It is terrible to die of thirst at sea. Is it necessary that you should so salt your truth that it will no longer — quench thirst? [50]
>
> It is not enough to posses a talent: one must also have your permission to posses it; — eh, my friends? [51]
>
> There is a haughtiness of kindness which has the appearance of wickedness. [52]
>
> Convictions are more dangerous enemies of truth than lies. [53]
>
> In order that a man may respect himself, he must be capable of becoming evil. [54]

The use of ambiguity in Nietzsche's work is the reason why he is often quoted out of context — even though it is not always easy to see whether there *is* a context in his work. Multi-layered irony and seemingly spontaneous ranting account for the apparent paradoxes in the message. To look for an overall system or final truth in Nietzsche will result in the reader becoming hopelessly lost in a maze of contradiction and confusion:

> Nietzsche's books are easier to read but harder to understand than those of almost any other thinker.... As soon as one attempts to penetrate beyond the clever epigrams and well turned insults to grasp their consequences and to coordinate them, one is troubled ... the individual sentences seem clear enough ... it is the total design that puzzles us.— *Kaufmann*[55]

If Nietzsche appears not to have a coherent, unified thesis, it is because he is prepared to think *beyond* those who are simply stuck in the ultimate truth of their presuppositions.[56] For him no one theory can reveal the entire truth; each can only organize a point of view. We must, he says, consider many perspectives and not imprison our thought in any one system.[57] Nietzsche's writing sets up a resonance with his readers' own narrative of life. Often accompanied by mental images and stimulating insights, his words stimulate our senses to wrestle even harder with the questions that continue to trouble us. Another aspect of Nietzsche's writing style is considered by Mencken in his introduction to *The Anti-Christ*. He puts forward the view that unlike Nietzsche, the average philosophical writer believes that the value of his or her writing corresponds in equal weight to the volume and complexity of their words:

> What makes philosophy so garrulous is not the profundity of philosophers, but their lack of art.... There is, too, the endless poll-parroting

that goes on: each new philosopher must prove his learning by laboriously rehearsing the ideas of all previous philosophers.... Nietzsche avoided both faults. He always assumed that his readers knew the books, and that it was thus unnecessary to rewrite them. And, having had an idea that seemed to him to be novel and original, he stated it in as few words as possible, and then shut down ... he never wrote a word too many. He never pumped up an idea to make it appear bigger than it actually was.[58]

In one other important aspect, Nietzsche is distinguished from other philosophers of his time and brought closer to the Cynics. The assumption that in "real" philosophy one must create personal distance between the writer and the object of one's study (to maximize the truth value) is undermined when Nietzsche introduces autobiography into his discourse: 'his eccentric and highly personalized divagations and detours work against the philosophical ideal of lofty disinterestedness."[59]

POLITICAL INCORRECTNESS

Nietzsche is not for the faint hearted, and like Diogenes, he appears, in his commentary at least, to be conceited, intolerant, and annihilating. But this feature of the philosopher, as already acknowledged, is the strength or weakness, depending on your appetite for frankness, of Nietzsche's writing. It is now necessary to juxtapose Nietzsche's total disregard for social approval and his hatred of shallow pretense, with the kind of sentimental, liberal timidity that contemporary discourse is often accused of today—language castrated by the will to power, *political correctness.*

It is a sign of our times that in the 1999 edition of *The Anti-Christ*, the first reprint in 75 years of Nietzsche's penultimate and arguably most vicious work, the publisher feels it necessary to devote two pages at the beginning of the book apologizing, not for Nietzsche's writing, but for translator H.L. Mencken's introduction. Mencken is himself a cynic *par excellence*; who better to translate the one work of Nietzsche that even most Nietzsche devotees have avoided? By apologizing for Mencken, one may assume that the publisher is also apologizing for Nietzsche. The issue at stake is anti-semitism, of which from a politically correct reading of either Nietzsche or Mencken, both would be found equally guilty. The publisher's note on Mencken's introduction includes the following line: "In the wake of the Holocaust, it is acutely uncomfortable for admirers of Mencken — of whom I am one — to read." But, as Kaufmann has suggested, Nietzsche's all-too-human comments—inevitable in his autobiographical style of writing—are philosophically irrelevant.[60] If one really desires to know what Nietzsche felt about race, or for that matter women, disability, or any of the other issues on which the language police might swoop down on us, the answers are there to be found in his work. Dig beneath the all-too-human surface commentary and one can find evidence of profound philosophical thinking. Nietzsche's ambiguity is ultimately a failure in us, his readers, to ask the questions: What did Nietzsche oppose? What did he seek to overcome? What were his problems? Kaufmann says that answers can be found when these questions are recognized.[61]

So what *were* Nietzsche's views on race, and what was behind Nietzsche's own citizen of the world philosophy? For Nietzsche, the power and value of human beings is constructed not biologically according to race, but according to artistic and creative potential. As such, the "valuable specimens" of human kind occur throughout continents and throughout centuries.[62] Nietzsche believed in the hereditary nature of acquired characteristics, in which the mixture of race favored the improvement of culture (both in individuals and in nations) by drawing together what was best among the diverse peoples of the world. Nietzsche's fascination with pre-Socratic Greece included what he regarded as the ancients' readiness to absorb other cultures (e.g., Persian, Egyptian, Indian, Chinese) into their own. "The very reason they got so far is that they knew how to pick up the spear and throw it onward from the point where others had left it. Their art in the skill of fruitful learning was admirable."[63] Nationalism was therefore dangerous to the species, which is why Nietzsche made a plea for intermarriage between nations, even singling out the Jew as a particularly desirable "ingredient."[64] It is clear, therefore, that when carefully selecting the bits of Nietzsche that conveniently support one's own crusade, the Nazi propagandists were as shameless as the rest of us. It is also easy to see how some of Nietzsche's ideas, such as his Darwinian notion of the *Übermensch* and his anti-egalitarian views on society, would have slotted quite conveniently into the Nazis' program of creating a master race. And yet the evidence is there that Nietzsche's views are probably more opposed to those of the Nazis than those of any other German thinker of his time. Consider the evidence borne out in the following extract of a letter from Nietzsche to his sister:

> One of the greatest stupidities you have committed — for yourself and for me! Your association with an anti-Semitic chief express a foreignness to *my* whole life which fills me ever again with ire and melancholy ... it is a matter of honor to me to be absolutely clean and unequivocal regarding anti-Semitism, namely opposed, as I am in my writings.[65]

Of far more interest than any defense of Nietzsche *in absentia*, is that in contrast to our prevailing trend for self-censorship, Nietzsche was completely aware of his all-too-human comments, which were a colorful and necessary element of his discourse. Even more fascinating, is that he was able to predict the kind of mischief that others would make of them in the future. Nietzsche could not have anticipated the full horrors of the events which occurred less than 50 years after his death when he wrote the following words: "I know my fate. One day there will be associated with my name the recollection of something frightful — of a crisis like no other before on earth ... one will guess why I bring out this book before hand; it is intended to prevent people from making mischief with me."[66]

Yet the seizure of ideas for purposes never intended is surely a danger that writers run when they allow their writing to enter the domain of public discourse. As Alan D. Schrift says, "These risks become extreme when a writer chooses to write with the hyperbolic rhetoric that one finds in Nietzsche."[67] Returning to the thesis of Nietzsche the cynic: To in any case take his derogatory remarks about the Jews out of context is to miss completely the point of his message — he despised everybody! Or more accurately, he despised what he felt the mass of people from *any* culture stood for: their closed-mindedness, narrow opinions and absolute beliefs. Nietzsche's own claim is that he never attacked *people*, he simply used them as a "strong magnifying glass" in order to make things visible that would otherwise be hard to get hold of.[68] The following passage is typical of Nietzsche's all-too-human prose:

> What the German spirit *could* be — who hasn't had melancholy thoughts about that! But this people has voluntarily stupefied itself for almost a thousand years: nowhere have the two great European narcotics, alcohol and Christianity, been abused more viciously. Recently they've gotten still another narcotic, which is enough on its own to give the death-blow to all refined and keen suppleness of the spirit: music, our constipated, constipating German music.[69]

Fellow Germans, the English, women, men (particularly businessmen, politicians, lawyers, doctors, academics, and priests); Nietzsche was at war with them all, and none more so than Christians, despite — or maybe because of — the fact that his father and grandfather were Lutheran ministers. It does Nietzsche no credit to judge him in the light of today's politically correct moral values. To confuse the blunt and uncompromising language of the cynic with the xenophobia of the racist is to completely misunderstand the motives behind these two forms of affrontery. The superficiality of much of our contemporary Western values provides a fertile breeding ground for the cynic. If one is looking for a symbol of institutionalized resistance to Diogenes and Nietzsche's citizen of the world philosophy, it is, paradoxically, the prevailing moral virtue represented by the prescribing of acceptable forms of language — language that, while claiming to challenge racist or sexist behavior, denies any real diversification of peoples, who for the most part do not identify with its constant refrains. Political *in*correctness then, far from reflecting a lack of social awareness, represents the cynical conviction that social taboos represent a point of weakness in social discourse that should be attacked.

PROTO-POSTMODERNIST: NIETZSCHE ON KNOWLEDGE, SCIENCE, & TRUTH

> So is Nietzsche a postmodernist? Perhaps. He's been press-ganged as the antecedent for nearly every other philosophical movement this century, so why not? ... Nietzsche is a mirror in which other philosophers can always find their own ideas.... But he still sounds like he is postmodernist. The "grand narratives" of Christianity, Western liberalism, science and progress are bankrupt, says Nietzsche. Entities like "truth" and "knowledge" are illusions, and all the philosopher can do is produce wry aphorisms that draw attention to this melancholy situation.— *Dave Robinson*[70]

I now wish to address the claim made at the beginning of this chapter that Nietzsche was the founder of the perspective we now call the postmodern. Nietzsche sat on the phenomenological side of the fence, where history is myth at best, lies at worst, and science is simply a means of validating the myths and lies and calling them truths:

> History is nothing but the manner in which the spirit of man apprehends facts that are obscure to him, links things together whose connection heaven only knows, replaces the unintelligible by something intelligible, puts his own ideas of causation into the external world, which can perhaps be explained only from within: and assumes the existence of chance, where thousands of small causes may be really at work.— *Nietzsche*[71]

It would seem apparent from the above passage that Nietzsche's cynicism regarding history does in fact invalidate a major part of this book. That is to say, the use of an examination of Greek Cynicism to shed further light on contemporary aspects of cynicism. Nietzsche exposes the dangers of using the past as a model for imitation; the details of past events being a little altered and retouched, and so brought nearer to fiction.[72] But does it matter if one cannot distinguish between a monumental past and a mythical romance if the outcome is the same? In studying Greek Cynicism, or any other aspect of cynicism, it is not the intention here to attempt to discover truth so much as to illuminate meaning. Paradoxically, however, like many postmodern cynics, Nietzsche owes much of his own philosophy concerning history to a classical study of the subject in the first place.

Michel Foucault, in *The Order of Things,* was the first to acknowledge Nietzsche as the founder of postmodernism,[73] and, since Nietzsche often referred to himself posthumously, we may wonder whether those of us reading his work today are in fact Nietzsche's intended audience: "I want to be right not for today or tomorrow but for the millennia."[74] From Nietzsche, Foucault further developed concepts such as the breaking of the present from the past, and relationships between knowledge and power. Jacques Derrida developed some of Nietzsche's ideas concerning language as constraint, and Jean-François Lyotard derived from Nietzsche his ideas about language games. Other ideas associated with both Nietzsche and the postmodernists include the collapse of grand narrative, the cyclical view of human history, anti-enlightenment, hostility to egalitarianism, antipathy to science and politics, and the notion of relativism. Yet it would be a mistake to regard Nietzsche as an aphorist, sowing the seeds of ideas that real philosophers would more fully develop.[75] Many of those later philosophers failed to consider Nietzsche's most important thesis: that trying to turn a philosophy into a system was philosophy's greatest flaw. Alasdair MacIntyre claims that Nietzsche was the only major philosopher not to have flinched from nailing the lie of language as truth, which makes it difficult to nominate any recent philosopher as a worthy inheritor of Nietzsche's mantle.[76]

Nietzsche's position on knowledge mirrors his view of history. It involves the need to let go of the past in order to anticipate what will be needed for the future. To provide further evidence, not only of Nietzsche the proto-postmodernist but his uncanny ability to philosophize posthumously, the following quotation of Nietzsche's could easily be mistaken for Lyotard's critique on the impact of information technology:

> It requires a totally new attitude of mind to be able to look away from the present educational institutions to the strangely different ones that will be necessary for the second or third generation. At present the labors of higher education produce merely the savant or the official or the business man.... But the difficulty lies in unlearning what we know and setting up a new aim.— *Nietzsche*[77]

Nietzsche makes a useful distinction between what he describes as real education and the art of passing examinations: "Imagine a young head, without much experience of life, being stuffed with fifty systems (in the form of words) and fifty criticisms of them, all mixed up together — what an overgrown wilderness he will come to be."[78] Knowledge, he says, taken in excess without hunger, and contrary to desire, has no effect of transforming external life since it remains hidden in a chaotic inner world. For that reason Nietzsche feels that our modern culture is not a living one, but a kind of knowledge *about* culture, a complex web of various thoughts and feelings from which no decision as to its future direction can come.[79] There are many resonances here with today's soundbite politics, corporate images, and *mission statements*, that contain no clue as to what anyone really thinks or feels because they are all written to an agreed script. The cynic's role here is to provide an irreverent stab at this veneer in an attempt to expose any genuine emotions that may lie hidden beneath the surface. Nietzsche's plea for a return to instinct and emotion is most clearly illustrated in his analysis of science: "They cry in triumph that 'science is now beginning to rule life.' Possibly it might; but a life thus ruled is not of much value. It is not such true life, and promises much less for the future than the life that used to be guided not by science, but by instincts and powerful illusions."[80]

Acknowledging that the progress of science had been amazingly rapid in the preceding decade, Nietzsche warned that if we tried to further the progress of science too quickly we would end by destroying real progress. For Nietzsche, the course of civilization is, in any case, not a story of progress toward elevation and advancement. "The European of today, in his essential worth, falls far below the European of the Renaissance."[81] If we can accept the course of history as a series of highs and lows, rather than one of progress toward ultimate truths, then each of us has the same opportunity for acquiring real knowledge (knowledge relevant to our own unique existence) as those who have gone before us and those who will come after:

> Each man has his own individual needs, and so millions of tendencies are running together, straight or crooked, parallel or across, forward or backward, helping or hindering each other. They have all the appearance of chance, and make it impossible, quite apart from all natural influences, to establish any universal lines on which past events must have run.— *Nietzsche*[82]

Nietzsche provides a cynical description of future generations of scientists. Using the metaphor of a hen worn out by being forced to lay too many eggs, he continues, "they can merely cackle more than before, because they lay eggs oftener: but the eggs are always smaller, though their books are bigger." The natural result of this, according to Nietzsche, is the popularizing of science, the habit of cutting the cloth of science to fit the figure of the general public.[83] Nietzsche compares science's relation to wisdom with current morality's relation to holiness: "it is cold and dry, loveless, and ignorant of any deep feeling of dissatisfaction and yearning." Science only sees the problems of knowledge, suffering is something alien and unintelligible to it. And not only suffering: Nietzsche takes the view that scientists and philosophers regard all sensual experience as the enemy of their search for truth. They are obsessed with capturing what *is*, and look for reasons why it is being withheld from them: "There has to be an illusion, a deception at work that prevents us from perceiving what is; 'where's the deceiver?'—'We've got the deceiver!' they cry happily, 'it's sensation! these senses, *which are so immoral anyway*, deceive us about the *true* world.'"[84]

Although, today, we would seem to be witnessing the rediscovery of a human face in politics and other institutions, the cynic would argue that this face actually remains shrouded more than ever by a new morality, one symbolized by positions such as political correctness that hide their insincerity behind the mask of reason and rationalization. Nietzsche, like all cynics, questioned too much and was too inquisitive to be content with crude answers like religion, which he saw as a prohibition against people thinking for themselves.[85] He despised even more the concomitant moral smugness of such belief systems and the way in which moral superiority was equated with goodness and righteousness, and thus *became* morality itself.[86] This theme was to become one of Nietzsche's overriding crusades, as though he saw himself as the new savior with a mission to expose the lie of Christianity. "But my truth is 'dreadful': for hitherto the 'lie' has been called truth.... I am the first 'immoralist': I am therewith the 'destroyer par excellence.'"[87]

Nietzsche would not imprison his thoughts in any one system, rather acknowledging that all we have is a point of view or an individual perspective.[88] Truths are illusions which we have forgotten are illusions; worn out metaphors, "which have been poetically and rhetorically intensified, transferred, and embellished, and which, after long usage, seem to a people to be fixed, canonical, and binding."[89] As Mencken puts it: "The majority of men prefer delusion to truth. It soothes. It is easy to grasp. Above all, it fits more snugly than the truth into a universe of false appearances."[90] Linking the unfamiliar with something familiar alleviates and calms us, as well as providing a feeling of power. The unfamiliar brings with it danger and unrest, "our first instinct is to *do away* with these painful conditions. First principle: some explanation is better than none."[91]

Nietzsche's view of the world seems to be one full of men who "serve truth." Yet because the virtue of justice is seldom present, or even known, it its replaced with a "throng of sham virtues." What Nietzsche claims to possess as the antidote to these sham virtues (historical *fact;* religious *morality;* scientific *certitude;* legal *justice;* philosophical *truths;* and our modern day, political *correctness*— and herein lies the practical element of his cynic mission) is a nose for sniffing out this rhetoric. Nietzsche claims to possess an instinct for cleanliness. The concealed dirt, whitewashed by education, is apparent to him on first contact. "I was the first to sense — 'smell'— the lie as lie ... My genius is in my nostrils."[92]

THE CYNICS' FLIGHT
FROM THE HUMAN HERD

> And a little less well endowed with strength and courage he too would have abandoned and despaired of ever knowing what manner of being he was, and how he was going to live, and lived vanquished, blindly, in a mad world, in the midst of strangers.— *Beckett*[93]

The targets of Nietzsche's attacks, whether history, the law, religion, science, or philosophy, all have one element in common, one that shields the truth more effectively than any other — the suffocating glue of morality. Where ideas are governed by moral reason, sentimentality also rears its head and, as Mencken warns, "sentimentality is as powerful as an army with banners."[94] Nevertheless, it is Nietzsche's *demand* that philosophers place themselves beyond good and evil, put the illusion of moral judgment *beneath* them. This follows from Nietzsche's insight "that there are no moral facts at all."[95] Yet moral facts have been used throughout history as the fuel, the justification, behind the tyranny that human has inflicted upon human, carried along under the banner of improving and enlightening peoples. Nietzsche undermines notions of truth and higher moral virtue, but if it is his mission to expose and tear down false idols (his word for ideals), what does he propose to put in their place? A chief criticism of cynics is that they pull things down but propose nothing new to replace them. The charge against Nietzsche of nihilism stems from his giving the lie to people's elevated view of their own importance in life on earth:

> Once upon a time, in some out of the way corner of that universe which is dispersed into numberless twinkling solar systems, there was a star upon which clever beasts invented knowing. That was the most arrogant and mendacious minute of "world history," but nevertheless, it was only a minute. After nature had drawn a few breaths, the star cooled and congealed, and the clever beasts had to die.— *Nietzsche*[96]

By placing the sum of human existence into such a context, Nietzsche is not dismissing the value of human beings themselves (their individual, existential importance), he is simply amplifying humans' relative insignificance the better to expose their pomposity. Contrast the enormity of the above passage with, for example, table etiquette; that sad pretension that humans employ: first, to distance themselves from lower animals by denying the sensuality involved in devouring food, passing it from plate to mouth without any contact with the hand; and second — depending on the number, complexity, and finery of the implements employed — to distance themselves from lower specimens of humans.

Far from a nihilistic rejection of all theoretical and philosophical systems, cynicism merely seeks to expose the triteness, the mythology, and the hidden agendas that have corrupted such systems, inviting one to rediscover their fundamental meaning and purpose: the simple creed that made them possible in the first place. It does not claim to offer an alternative system. However, having exposed the lie, the question still remains as to whether most of us are prepared to accept the truth.

Nietzsche counters the popular view which asserts that liberal democracies contribute to a project of autonomy: a social space in which individuals not only live the life they please but also attain a degree of moral maturity and independence of judgment.[97] The democratic subject in Nietzsche's view is the typical herd animal. However, among members of the human species are those who are not drawn to what Nietzsche describes as the herd instinct; solitary human beings, who, like Nietzsche and his Cynic ancestors, flee the support and security of the moral community in following more basic needs.[98] It should be noted, for instance in the discussion on the Dilbert cartoon in chapter 6, that individual members of the human herd do remain capable of displaying a certain cynicism, but for the purposes of this discussion Nietzsche is dealing in generalities. For Nietzsche, Christianity is the ultimate example of a herd morality. It attracts and produces people who are "pessimistic and timid." Crucial for Nietzsche is that Christianity's pernicious value system stands in the way of the evolution of a new and superior kind of human being: those who would take up the role of Nietzsche's *Übermenschen*. "As a moral code it [Christianity] produces dull, static and conformist societies that dampen down human potential and achievement."[99]

Hercules, Diogenes, and Nietzsche all fall into this category of solitary individuals with a need to mark themselves out from the herd. It seems to Nietzsche, that a selfish and unreasonable influence ties people down to the same companions and circumstances, and to the daily round of toil. Nietzsche expresses the same citizen of the world sentiments as Diogenes: "Why cling to your bit of earth, or your little business, or listen to what your neighbor says? It is so provincial to bind oneself to views which are no longer binding a couple of hundred miles away."[100] Despite the strong natural forces that compel people to cultivate and protect their community, the cynic has an equally strong and opposing compulsion to reject its values in what Nietzsche describes as an unceasing desire for novelty. It is this very rejection of history and convention, which some regard as disloyalty or rebelliousness, that the cynics see as imperative for their own health and survival. However, true to his contradictory style, while deriding history Nietzsche also bemoans the loss of Classical Greek and Roman culture, whose strong civic traditions were abandoned for Christian mediocrity. We have never recovered, he laments, the instincts of the ancient past.

And yet there is a price to pay for being one of those who is not seduced by the herd and by history, "as everyone knows who has clearly realized the terrible consequences of mere desire for migration and adventure ... the attraction of the new and rare as against the old and tedious."[101] It is a curse characteristic of all forms of cynicism that it is asocial. Cynics feel alienated from the society in which they live *because* they question the world's limits. They feel unable to identify with those they see as being content with the "facility of fiction."[102] Bewes describes the cynic's alienation as 'an ascent into the lone and lofty perch of world-hating introspection."[103] But unlike Bataille, who sees wretchedness in those content with worldly limits, Bewes's cynic feels envy for the metaphysically innocent, those who appear unconcerned at the world's imperfections and even appear to prosper on account of their freedom from such intellectual preoccupations. This is why — unlike the spiritually enlightened, who may exude a privileged smugness at their unique vision of the world — the modern cynic may at times feel handicapped, even tortured by it.

Peter Sloterdijk refers to this feeling as "inner emigration" because cutting oneself off from the fundamental values of society leaves the cynic on the horns of a dilemma: "Get out or collaborate? Flee or stand firm?"[104] There is something childlike about the cynic's compulsion to reject the perceived wisdom of others, but there is also something that the child sees and hears that others do not, and, according to Nietzsche, that something is the most important thing of all.[105]

Nietzsche completed a re-evaluation of his life's work, *Ecce Homo*, in 1888 as he was descending into madness. The work has hints of Nietzsche's impending insanity with grandiose manic pronouncements about his own genius that one is never sure are tongue-in-cheek or in earnest. He shows the frustration that he was a thinker before his time and believes that the cataclysmic impact of his work would only be appreciated by future generations. An instance of Nietzsche's uncanny foresight provides a fitting conclusion to this chapter. In a letter written by Nietzsche to a friend in May of 1888, he describes an image that he had just conjured up: "An old waggoner who with an expression of the most brutal Cynicism, harder even than the winter around him, is peeing against his own horse. The horse, this poor flayed creature, looks around, gratefully, *very* gratefully — ." This apparently unconscious self-parody was realized less than nine months later in the winter of 1888–89, when Nietzsche witnessed an old cart horse being beaten and abused by a coachman in the cab stand outside of his house. Overcome by the spectacle, Nietzsche collapsed weeping around the animal's neck. Some of his acquaintances recall this scene as the first sign of Nietzsche's madness.[106] He died 12 years later in 1900.

4

Postmodern Cynicism

> The cynic is the typical "postmodern" character, a figure alien-
> ated both from society and from his or her own subjectivity.
> 'Cynicism' is a concept mobilized by politicians, critics, and
> commentators as a synonym for postmodernism.— *Timothy
> Bewes*[1]

Bewes, in his 1997 critique, *Cynicism and Postmodernity,* draws a distinction between Greek Cynicism, which he describes as anti-theoretical
and gestural, and postmodern cynicism, which by contrast is weighed down
with theory and paralyzed by contradictions. Yet Classical Cynicism and
postmodern cynicism may well have more in common than the verbosity
of the latter would at first suggest. For in sifting through the blur of postmodernism's tautology, Nietzsche's naked truths are there to be found in
abundance. The aim of this chapter, is to extricate — both from their critics and from those who bestow on them celebrity status— some notable
cynical thinkers from their neglectful categorization as postmodernists.

Many of the ideas and perspectives we call postmodernist are not
unique to the twentieth century. They were flourishing before the modernism of the last century; even, as demonstrated by the Cynics, before
the modernism of Plato. And although the influence of this most recent
variant of the spurning of ideology remains a current, it is also a current
that (stripped of its timeless cynicism) is waning. Neither do the philosophers and theorists cited as postmodernists necessarily share a common
philosophy. They represent a disparate group with little in common other
than the period of history (and place, in the case of the French theorists)
in which they write.

If not all postmodernists are cynics and not all contemporary cynics
are postmodernists, it is necessary to try to understand just what the phenomenon of postmodernism represents. Most answers to the question,
"What is postmodernism?," often add to the mystery by providing incom-

prehensible or contradictory answers. Postmodern theory — unlike postmodern art which claims to speak for itself — is difficult to define, because like cynicism, it appears to stand in opposition to something rather than *for* something: an implosion of master narratives into a black hole of meaningless signs and signifiers. By definition, postmodernism does not use systems or propose a theoretical model of the world because, it would claim, there are no universal theories or systems. It is more of a debunking movement or anti-philosophy than it is an alternative system (Lacan and Kristeva are notable exceptions[2]). In this context, postmodernism expresses a universal and timeless expression of human emotion, a continuity of the Cynical tradition of undercutting the present order, a splitting off from history allowing the future to flourish free from the chains of the stale ideas of the past. A common criticism of postmodernism, and one that will also be addressed in this chapter, is that it consists of nothing *but* theory with no discipline in which to anchor it.

Many postmodernist writers have also become fashionable figures (often with celebrity status) who attract a large following of devotees. And as so often happens through the actions of disciples, the postmodern project has become somewhat corrupted of late. With a new generation of converts eager to expand postmodernism's explanations, neologisms, and impenetrable jargon, it has become that which it sought to destroy, the new truth, the latest grand narrative supporting an ever-booming global industry of literary and scholarly activity. Regardless of its own rhetoric to the contrary, what is loosely categorized as postmodern theory (any discourse of a relativist nature) has become an explosion of alternative truths that often exceed the hyperbole of its quarry.

This chapter discusses both of these postmodernisms: the dead type that will one day be read as a curiosity in the history of ideas, and the live, constantly forward-shifting cynical variety. Chapter 5 contains a critique of avant-gardism that parallels these two faces of postmodernism: those art historians who wish to define Avant-Garde as a fixed point in art history, a showcase of historical art relics of the 1910s and '20s to be studied and revered; as opposed to avant-garde, in its role of challenging and upsetting that which preceded it in a constantly forward-shifting skirmish of generations. As Jürgen Habermas (a defender of modernism) describes it, the formally subversive and embattled styles felt to be scandalous and shocking by one generation, are for the generation which follows "felt to be establishment and the enemy — dead, stifling, canonical, the reified monuments one has *to destroy to do anything new*":

> This means that there will be as many different forms of postmodernism as there were high modernism in place, since the former are at

> least initially specific and local reactions *against* those models. That
> obviously does not make the job of describing postmodernism as a
> coherent thing any easier, since the unity of this new impulse — if it
> had one — is given not in itself but in the very modernism it seeks to
> displace.— *Jürgen Habermas*[3]

In this context, a postmodernism functions as nothing more than a device for refreshing the next modernism, an ever-forward moving hopscotch of ideas, few of which will survive the test of time. Even the *term* postmodernism defies its philosophical intentions. For in appearing to challenge the idea of progressive enlightenment, it actually seems to express the opposite. "Post" suggests a progression on from, and in response to, something else. Why not pre-modernism or anti-modernism? It might excite current philosophers to believe that they have discovered a unique phenomenon in their own time, but in simplistic terms what we call modernism and postmodernism suggests a continuation of the same old dichotomies as are represented by Apollo and Dionysus; Plato and Antisthenes; the left brain versus the right brain; and as one commentator suggests, the ego and the id.[4] Viewed as a dichotomy rather than a progression, modernism and postmodernism simply describe these familiar oppositions, the modernist drive which attempts to explain, categorize and control the world, representing abstract thinking and linear logic — a concern with doing; and postmodern perspectives (those more ready to accept a chaotic and disordered world) representing concrete feeling states such as sexual excitement or aesthetic appreciation — a concern with being. Although the discourses of modernism and postmodernism cannot be simply written off as two opposing human drives (as though there were only two), the point is that modernist and postmodernist perspectives are not a result of progressive fixed points in history so much as one's intrinsic view of the world.

In this sense, what we called modernism and postmodernism continue to march side by side; one is neither the precursor nor the successor of the other. In the history of Western thought, modernism, as we understand it today, could be said to have started with Plato, gathering its momentum with the increasing popularity of scientific, Christian and similar totalizing belief systems (as they replaced more localized traditions and beliefs). Modernism is also constantly shifting as it defines itself in relation to the ancient or the classical. As Habermas put it, "a modern work becomes a classic because it has once been authentically modern."[5] As to the human condition associated with *postmodern* sensibilities, it must have always existed, being free from the formal constraints imposed by the educated, conditioned mind which seeks to order the world it inhabits.

Yet postmodernism, as we understand it today, becomes more acute in opposition to modernist modes of thinking. Neither is it the case that one of these perspectives is right and the other wrong. They are essentially two different ways of seeing the world. It is that the balance has tipped so disproportionately in privileging the Platonic mode of thinking that sparks the cynic's scorn. Those who have acquired a proclivity for the cynical mode are seized by a compulsion to ridicule gross displays of modernist or Platonic thinking. And although the cynic might harbor a secret envy for those who can find peace and fulfillment in a belief in God, science, or moral truths about the world — they just don't happen to buy it themselves.

This feature (one that unites classical and postmodern cynicism) is often dismissed as nihilism, on the basis that those who reject moral, scientific and religious truths must surely believe in nothing at all. Such a belief is a misreading of the cynic's posture as irony, a posture which accounts for the aloof and detached behavior frequently found in cynics of all shades. This facet of cynicism is described by Bewes as "an ascent into the lone and lofty perch of world-hating introspection," and by Peter Sloterdijk as "inner emigration": an alienation and cutting oneself off from the fundamental values of the society in which one lives.[6] Such an attitude is also summed up by Navia, when he writes that "those who find the world something worthy of praise, or who congratulate themselves for having been born into the world, are either intellectually blind or morally perverse."[7] Yet, as already acknowledged, this interpretation of the world may not prevent the cynic from feeling envy for the metaphysically innocent who, on account of their freedom from intellectual preoccupations, enjoy a form of contentment unknown to the cynic.[8] Neither is this something over which the cynic has control, since the cynic is a cynic by nature. It is not something which one elects to become or is even aware of. Navia refers to Diderot's observation that being a cynic is probably the result of a psychological predisposition, even to the extent that if it were absent, one may fail to understand what cynicism actually is.[9] Accepting this endogenous explanation for the phenomenon of cynicism, those not born cynics would remain baffled by the manifestation and teaching of the philosophy. That this claim is hard to substantiate empirically, further reinforces the integrity of Cynicism — defying its own analysis by the means it despises.

What cynics lack in their appreciation of the world, they make up for with the poetry in which they denounce it. So it is with postmodern discourse. Hal Foster provides yet a different perspective on the relationship between modernism and postmodernism, one that is more notable for the style of its delivery than it is for its meaning. Foster's method is typical of the poetic, non-narrative style associated with postmodern writing. One *thinks* one gets it, but it is the mental energy expended in reading the text that both excites and provides deeper insights. Love it or hate it, the combination of poetry and scientific theory employed by certain writers (as will be discussed later) is one aspect of postmodernism that infuriates natural scientists:

> Each epoch dreams the next ... there is no timely transition between the modern and the postmodern. In a sense each comes like sex(uality), too early or too late, and our consciousness of each is premature or after the fact. In this regard modernism and postmodernism must be seen together, in *parallax* (technically, the angle of displacement of an object caused by the movement of its observer), by which I mean that our framings of the two depend on our position in the present *and* that this position is defined in such framings. — *Hal Foster*[10]

Someone once said that the greatest lie of many postmodernist theorists is their assertions that something apocalyptically significant is occurring philosophically or culturally in their time, and that as a project, postmodernism has been more of a whimper than a big bang. Momentous and apocalyptic events *did* occur in the twentieth century: two world wars; Hitler's final solution; the rise and fall of communism; the emergence (or re-emergence) of Islamic fundamentalism; the spread of global capitalism; medical science's development of deadly super-bugs. Such events, often triggered by grand modernist projects to improve or advance civilization (or more often a single interest group of civilization), produced results that were neither planned for nor anticipated, capricious moments in history that we can liken to Foucault's view that history is simply a sequence of turns of life's kaleidoscope. If postmodernism stands for anything, it is the meaningless void left behind in the wake of such failed projects and our inability to predict the next turn of life's kaleidoscope, the realization that human beings are not masters of their own destiny; at least, not in any universal or collective sense; that science, religion and philosophy cannot progress civilization, and that our role in the world is largely a series of (mainly unhappy) accidents.

IRRECONCILABLE TRUTHS

> "Scientific knowledge has brought about a disenchantment with the world." — *Madan Sarup*[11]

> "Many people are simply irritated by the arrogance and empty verbiage of postmodernist discourse and by the spectacle of an intellec-

tual community where everyone repeats sentences and no one under-
stands."— *Sokal and Bricmont*[12]

In the summer of 1996 an academic paper by physicist Alan Sokal,
titled "Transgressing the Boundaries: toward a transformative hermeneutics of quantum gravity," appeared in the critical theory journal *Social
Text*.[13] This particular edition of the journal was to be devoted to rebut-
ting the criticisms leveled against postmodernism. Sokal's paper had been
presented to the publishers as a serious review of the literature in his particular field of research. The prolific and impressive list of references contained in the paper were all genuine. The thesis, Sokal revealed immediately
following publication, was a meaningless and absurd parody of postmodernism's hyperbolic rhetoric. In a gesture worthy of the Cynic Menippus,
Sokal had exposed the vacuity, even fraud, that he claims much of postmodern theory amounts to. In particular, Sokal objected to the appropriation and misuse of hard scientific (and pseudoscientific) theory and
terminology to support nonsensical theories in the humanities.

Following the inevitable backlash against Sokal by critics of his academic lampoon, instead of just standing back and allowing the parody to
speak the volumes it does, he wrote (together with co-author Jean Bricmont) a detailed defense of his actions and an earnest rebuttal of his critics in a book titled *Intellectual Impostures: Postmodern philosophers' abuse
of science*. Any cynical impact of the earlier work was undermined by the
self-conscious justification of it. In its defense of scientific integrity, this
text paradoxically exposes some of the major flaws of the scientific community's own claims, and in so doing has added credibility to the very ideas
the authors sought to condemn. What particularly emerges from the later
work are the very narrow scientific interests of the authors: criticism that,
far from puncturing the real pomposity and nonsense that accounts for
much of so called postmodern theory, is confined to the misappropriation
of theories and terminology from the natural sciences by those in the social
sciences. On the face of it, a rather weak charge: "The authors quoted in
this book clearly do not have more than the vaguest understanding of the
scientific concepts they invoke and, most importantly, they fail to give any
argument justifying the relevance of these scientific concepts to the subjects allegedly under study."[14]

Sokal and Bricmont then go on to analyze often lengthy pieces of
their quarries' texts in the following vein: "... although Lacan uses a few
key words from the mathematical theory of compactness, he mixes them
up arbitrarily and without the slightest regard for their meaning. His
'definition' of compactness is not just false: it is gibberish."[15]

What Sokal and Bricmont's book *does* provide, is an excellent starting point for taking a critical look, both at postmodern theory *and* the positivist, scientific claims used to debunk it. In attempting to expose the
fraud of postmodernist writers, Sokal and Bricmont have also exposed the
very narrow world of science that prompted these postmodern narratives
in the first place. But let us first return to the authors' primary charge:
that some writers in the humanities throw around technical and scientific
terms without being able to explain their relevance or meaning. And further, that this is done in a way designed to intimidate the non-scientific
reader with unintelligible jargon, all the while knowing that "no one is
going to cry out that the king is naked.... If the texts seem incomprehen-
sible, it is for the excellent reason that they mean precisely nothing."[16]

This refreshing assessment of many of the target texts must have come
as some relief to many readers of the more dense and impenetrable postmodernist tomes. For having read and failed to comprehend such works,
many must have convinced themselves that *they* must be lacking in some
way. However, as Sokal and Bricmont's own book unfolds, the major effect
is not so much to damage the reputation of postmodern discourse, as to
seriously throw into question the credibility of science. If one is looking
for ammunition to *support* postmodernism's critique of science it is to be
found here in abundance: "Our goal" say the authors, "is to defend the
canons of rationality and intellectual honesty that are (or should be) common to all scholarly disciplines."[17] If this is a goal, it is a goal that is mis-
calculated, for having set the moral standard on which the authors stake
their truth claims so high, they are not difficult (for the cynic) to dis-
mantle.

Narrative Knowledge vs. Scientific Knowledge

Yet having clearly drawn up the battle lines between modernity and
postmodernity (Platonism and cynicism), this is where the confrontation
may just as well end. Once again we must return to our problem of
definitions. Philosophical questions are clearly very different from scientific questions and cannot be easily compared. They exist in parallel
spheres of understanding, in different universes of discourse. As Jean-
François Lyotard puts it, scientific knowledge does not represent the totality of knowledge but has always existed alongside narrative knowledge
with which it often conflicts.[18] Here, I assume, Lyotard is distinguishing
between knowledge based on philosophic wisdom, as opposed to that presented as scientific fact.

It is imperative for the purposes of this book not to confuse (as Sokal and Bricmont have done) the social or human sciences with true post-modern and philosophic discourse. Sokal and Bricmont choose to draw a dividing line between the natural sciences which they perceive as rational, and the social sciences which they see as relativist hokum. The cynic lumps *all* these sciences, natural and social together, under the one generic heading of *science*, thus distinguishing scientific knowledge from the narrative (or philosophic) knowledge described by Lyotard. As a consequence, we are now presented with the *two* postmodernisms (and two understandings of philosophy) described earlier. The cynical variety and the one which mimics science. That others may have an interest in distinguishing natural science from the pseudo-sciences of the humanities is not of concern to the cynic, who regards *all* scientific knowledge as *pseudo* knowledge. Likewise, what is popularly referred to as philosophy is no more than the grand narratives of science and other modernist discourses. True philosophy (narrative knowledge) is to be found outside as well as inside academia; in the visual arts, literature, theatre, as well as in the everyday language of ordinary thinking people: "A great continuous fault-line divides Western thought.... On one side of the line stands the positive understanding of the human being ... on the other side survive 'the most obscure and most real powers of language,' ... a vestige of the lost world of the Renaissance, 'when words glittered in the universal remembrance of things.'"[19]

It is through positivist human understanding — the breaking up of knowledge into specialist disciplines — that Foucault and other postmodernists claim modern societies control and discipline their populations. They do this by sanctioning the knowledge claims and practices of human sciences such as medicine, psychiatry, psychology, criminology, sociology, and then by legitimizing the practices of teachers, social workers, doctors, judges, policemen and administrators.[20] Baudrillard maintains that it is the non-equivalence of these human spheres of understanding (science, politics, law, aesthetics, etc.) that undermines their reason. They have no meaning outside of themselves because they cannot be exchanged for anything.[21] Laden with signs and meanings that are not connected to any higher reality, each of these systems "generates its own critical mass," "proliferates wildly" and "veers off exponentially." If nihilism is to be found anywhere, it is in the bankruptcy of human knowledge itself, which, according to Baudrillard, is exchangeable for Nothing:

> The transcription and "objective" assessment of an overall system have, ultimately, no more meaning than the assessment of the weight of the earth in millions of billions of tons — a figure which has no meaning outside of a calculation internal to the terrestrial system.

Lyotard

> Metaphysically, it is the same: the values, purposes and causes we delineate are valid only for a form of thought which is human, all too human. They are irrelevant to any other reality whatever.[22]

In trying to compare philosophical questions with scientific questions, Lyotard presents the following paradoxes. In the first place, scientific knowledge cannot know and make known that it is the true knowledge without resorting to narrative knowledge.[23] And secondly, it is impossible to judge the existence or validity of narrative knowledge on the basis of scientific knowledge (or vice versa)—the relevant criteria are different.[24] This does not prevent Sokal and Bricmont, however, from attempting to apply to narrative knowledge the scientific values of truth and falsity, even morality: "Now, both in philosophy and in everyday language, there is a distinction between *knowledge* (understood, roughly, as justified true belief) and mere belief; that is why the word 'knowledge' has a positive connotation, while 'belief' is neutral."[25] And, the authors continue, "if one seeks to have a 'scientific' understanding of anything, one is forced to make a distinction between a good and a bad understanding."[26]

Whatever the incompatibilities between scientific knowledge and narrative knowledge, one must defend Sokal and Bricmont's campaign even if one disagrees with their logic. The relationship between science and philosophy is at the same time antagonistic and symbiotic: the conflict sharpens and invigorates the arguments on both sides. For it is inside the territory created by the incongruity between science and philosophy that cynicism lives and feeds. To cut off this rich source of inspiration and entertainment would be to make the world an altogether dull place. For example, Sokal and Bricmont's criticism of Feyerabend's remark that "love becomes impossible for people who insist on 'objectivity,'" opens up just this kind of vital jousting. Sokal and Bricmont tell us that Feyerabend's opposition to science is not of a cognitive nature but a choice of lifestyle: "he fails to make a clear distinction between factual judgments and value judgments."[27] Such an observation highlights why science might be largely irrelevant, not only for Feyerabend but for all people who prefer to *feel* experience rather than have it *tested*. So what; if we can predict the movements of the planets, show that species evolve, or that matter is made up of atoms? What difference does this knowledge make to the everyday lives of most people? Of course we find using a computer more convenient than writing on papyrus, but are our lives made any happier as a result? Is our writing any more potent?

Relativism

> We are concerned here with a potpourri of ideas, often poorly formu-
> lated, that go under the generic name of "relativism" and are nowadays
> rather influential in some sectors of the academic humanities and
> social sciences.— *Sokal and Bricmont*[28]

The concept of relativism is not, of course, a postmodern invention.
Its importance in the history of Western thought predates that of scientific
knowledge. It became a major feature of the Hellenistic schools discussed
in Chapter 1. Scepticism was the ultimate relativist philosophy — if one is
not of the view that death or illness were great evils, one was less inclined
to be perturbed by them. Or, relative success, as measured in the Stoic's
goal which is not to hit the target but to do everything possible to try. Or,
the Epicurean example of relative pleasure — a drink of water or a crust
of bread to one experiencing the ravages of thirst or hunger giving greater
pleasure than that normally associated with a lavish banquet. Feyerabend
is simply continuing this tradition of relative rather than absolute truth,
a tradition playfully illustrated by the first century Cynic and Stoic writer-
philosopher Dio Chrysostom. In the following extract from his ninth (Isth-
mian) discourse, Dio presents a fictional mix of diatribe and *chreia* attributed
to Diogenes, ridiculing a garlanded and celebrating athlete who had just
broken a record for the 200-yard dash for men.

> "And what does that amount to?" he [Diogenes] inquired; "for you
> certainly have not become a whit more intelligent for having out-
> stripped your competitors.... "No, by heavens," said he, "but I am the
> fastest on foot of all the Greeks." "But not faster than rabbits," said
> Diogenes, "nor deer; and yet these animals, the swiftest of all, are also
> the most cowardly. They are afraid of men and dogs and eagles and
> lead a wretched life. Do you not know," he added, "that speed is the
> mark of cowardice?" ... "Are you not ashamed," he continued, "to take
> pride in an accomplishment in which you are naturally outclassed by
> the meanest of beasts? I do not believe that you can outstrip even a
> fox.... "But," replied he, "I, a man, am the fleetest of men." "What of
> it? Is it not probable that among ants too," Diogenes rejoined, "one is
> swifter than another? Yet they do not admire it, do they? Or would it
> not seem absurd to you if one admired an ant for its speed? Then
> again, if all the runners had been lame, would it have been right for
> you to take on airs because, being lame yourself, you had outstripped
> lame men?"
> As he spoke to the man in this vein, he made the business of foot-
> racing seem cheap in the eyes of many of the bystanders and caused
> the winner himself to go away sorrowing and much meeker. And this
> was no small service he had rendered to mankind whenever he discov-
> ered anyone who was foolishly puffed up and lost to all reason on
> account of some worthless thing; for he would humble the man a little

and relieve him of some small part of his folly, even as one pricks or punctures inflated and swollen parts.[29]

In their attack on relativism and defense of scientific certainty, Sokal and Bricmont cite examples of the moral absolutes of the criminal justice system, confidently bolstered by forensic science. Leaving aside the possibility of human error in collecting, analyzing, interpreting, or presenting forensic evidence, the laws that define whether a particular activity is criminal varies undeniably from one society to another. Even the ultimate crime, the taking of a human life has relative values, as can be clearly demonstrated by the concept of the death penalty. Even if science *could* prove conclusively the author of a particular deed or action, it can shed little light on the relative factors (motive, state of mind, provocation, etc.) on which civilized rather than peremptory justice depends. Science has been used to prop up as many injustices as it has justices.

Sokal and Bricmont further highlight the uncompromising stance of science when they claim certain terminology exclusively for their own discipline, criticizing those who use it outside of the narrow usage to which they apply it themselves. They point out, for example, the two mathematical meanings of the term linear, then criticize postmodernist authors for daring to add a third meaning, "linear thought." Since the term linear was derived from its Latin origin in the seventeenth century, it seems absurd to forbid its use outside of mathematics. Language in general — including scientific language which has absorbed its own share of metaphors, would be much the poorer if words did not evolve new meanings over time. With regard to the term "linear thought," there may be a further underlying objection in as much as it is often applied as a term of denigration by postmodernist writers to describe the one dimensional, positivist mindset of scientists.

Sokal and Bricmont also criticize postmodernists for not sticking to *legitimate* scientific terms: "The concept of 'hyperspace with multiple refractivity' does not exist either in mathematics or physics; it is a Baudrillardian invention."[30] The term might well be hyperbolic, but that should not deny Baudrillard the right to invent and use it. In Baudrillard's case, the use of such language produces critical thought and not a small amount of pleasure; a device antithetical to much of science's dogma which rather demands blind obedience to conventional wisdom. This obsession with conformity is demonstrated by the authors when they say that, 'one finds in Baudrillard's works a profusion of scientific terms, used with total disregard for their meaning.... Moreover, the scientific terminology is mixed up with a non-scientific vocabulary that is employed with equal sloppiness."[31] By the authors' continually comparing the work of postmodernist authors to the very narrow and specialized worlds of physics or mathematics, one cannot help but feel that there must be some profound and hidden irony at work. Can the authors really be serious in their defense of scientific integrity, or are they simply provoking a wider and more interesting philosophical debate?

In attempting to debunk Baudrillard's arguments about the reversal of cause and effect in chaos theory, Sokal and Bricmont pronounce with some sarcasm, that "we seriously doubt that an action in the present could affect an event in the past!"[32] For those trapped within linear thought this may be a perfectly reasonable assumption to make. But it is just such a mindset that Baudrillard is challenging. It is perfectly reasonable to suggest that the significance or meaning of a past event can be changed with the benefit of hindsight or by a future event. New information frequently comes to light that refutes historical truth claims, even challenges that a particular event happened at all. Natural scientists may well be dismissive of relativity, but even so-called facts (particularly those supported by empirical evidence) are disrupted and distorted by communication, selective filtering and even outright fraud. A catastrophe may in hindsight turn out to be beneficial, just as some miracle claims of medical science have turned out to be catastrophic. The momentous social transformation predicted for Marxism that, according to Foucault, historically amounts to no more than a storm in a child's paddling pool,[33] conforms well to Baudrillard's criteria for hurricanes which end in the beating of butterfly wings. In this sense the future does indeed alter the past.

The Delusion of Objectivity

In another reversal of received wisdom, Baudrillard undermines the very foundations on which science attaches its truth claims—that of objective study:

> Ultimately, science has never stopped churning out a reassuring scenario in which the world is being progressively deciphered by the advances of reason. This was the hypothesis with which we "discovered" the world, atoms, molecules, particles, viruses, and so forth. But no one has ever advanced the hypothesis that things may discover us at the same time as we discover them, and that there is a dual relationship in discovery. This is because we do not see the object in its originality. We see it as passive, as waiting to be discovered—a bit like America being discovered by the Spaniards.... But today, before our very eyes, the enigmatic nature of the world is rousing itself, resolved to struggle to retain its mystery. Knowledge is a duel. And this duel

between subject and object brings with it the subject's loss of sovereignty, making the object itself the horizon of its disappearance.

At any rate, it seems that reality, indifferent to any truth, cares not one jot for the knowledge to be derived from observing and analyzing it.[34]

Let us consider Baudrillard's premise measured against the claims of medical science. Sokal and Bricmont provide the example of testing medicine in double-blind protocols as a general methodological principle "that can be justified by rational arguments." One assumes that the rational argument here is that on exposure to certain pharmacological preparations, micro-organisms harmful to humans have been observed to become less harmful. Sokal and Bricmont's first truth claim is then inflated by their further truth claim that "the history of science teaches us that scientific theories come to be accepted above all because of their successes."[35] The following story helps to illustrate both the delusion of scientific success and also Baudrillard's proposition that the *object* of a scientific experiment can learn from the *subject*:

Desiree Williams, a New York woman, is picked up by the police and taken in handcuffs to be forcibly detained in Goldwater Memorial Hospital on an island of the coast of Manhattan. Her crime was that she did not comply with her doctor's request to attend a daily clinic to receive a massive cocktail of toxic drugs and injections that might (in anything up to two years) have cured her multi-drug-resistant strain of tuberculosis. In a TV interview,[36] Dr. Richard Coker, a tuberculosis consultant, explained how New York had recently been compelled to change its public health law to enable the authorities to incarcerate and forcibly treat people in a modern day "leper" colony in order to prevent an epidemic of drug resistant tuberculosis. As Coker explains, 50 years ago people were writing books on the conquest of tuberculosis. The year designated for its final eradication from the planet was 2001. However, medieval plagues and medieval treatments have returned in the twenty-first century and they are visiting the wealthiest cities in the world. Drug resistant forms of tuberculosis are spreading and doctors are having to resort to primitive treatment methods that had been abandoned decades before: "about one out of every five tuberculosis patients in Russia is treated surgically which is to say the drugs don't work anymore, let's go back to the nineteenth century and cut out the infected lung."[37] Neither was tuberculosis the only primitive plague that medical science promised to eradicate with its ever more sophisticated weaponry:

> This evolution of microbes across the planet has produced a super bug for the 21st-century, very different from viruses. Mutant forms of bac-

teria are now threatening to defeat one of our most powerful medical weapons: antibiotics.... When they were first invented they seemed miraculous and saved millions of lives. Antibiotics became the most widely used chemical in medicine and we became completely dependent on them, and then something began to change: nature fought back.[38]

As Robert Daum explains: "Bacteria evolve like humans evolve. The difference is bacteria have a new generation every 20 minutes and humans have a new generation every 25 years, so the pace of bacterial evolution is truly dizzying."[39] In the field of medicine, the significance of Baudrillard's thesis is that bacteria, the *object* of scientific experimentation, clearly have the ability to mutate and adapt to whatever pressure we put on them. Not only are scientific attacks on microbes likely to prove ineffective in the long term, but by continually inventing and creating more and more antibacterial agents, we are also creating ever more dangerous and unpleasant organisms to maim and kill our own species. We also continue to expose ourselves to new, as yet undiscovered, organisms that have lain dormant, such as viruses that are able to mutate and cross the species barrier: Lassa, Rift Valley Fever, the Ebola virus, and of course AIDS, of which an estimated fifteen million people had died by the end of the last millennium.[40] As if living out the script of a science fiction fantasy we are now reaping the sinister rewards of our scientific egotism.

Sokal and Bricmont provide us with yet more evidence of the obstinacy (in its obsession with realizing the world) of scientific endeavor when they tell us that "it is perhaps unpleasant to learn that a specific object of interest (such as the weather in 3 weeks' time) escapes our ability to predict it, but this does not stop the development of science."[41] In a similar vein, the authors counter Bruno Latour's ridicule of the scientific controversy regarding the number of sub-atomic neutrinos emitted by the sun. They express their hope that the question will indeed one day be settled, not to end the controversy, "but because sufficiently powerful empirical data will become available."[42] Again, Sokal and Bricmont fail to explain how such knowledge might possibly benefit humankind. What emerges from these writings is simply science for science's sake, an obsession with providing answers to a whole host of questions, the outcome of which merely allows one camp or another to claim success and publish its findings. But as with the example of the development of super-bugs, success is illusory and posterity often reaps some very unpleasant rewards from these scientific enterprises. Baudrillard poses questions that go far beyond this narrow domain of science: He is not attempting to *be* scientific but to show us the limits of science.

POSTMODERNISM'S MODERNIST LEGACY

One criticism leveled against Lyotard is that he lumps all grand narratives together. Sarup questions why even if some grand narratives are dubious should we reject them all?[43] Breaking up of grand narratives, he says, leads to disillusionment and a severing of the social bond and cohesive fabric which clothes society. Lyotard contends that this notion of a lost paradise, the paradise of an *organic* society, never existed in the first place. But how do we deal with Sarup's further criticism that "While Lyotard resists grand narratives, it is impossible to discern how one can have a theory of postmodernism without one."[44] My own reading of postmodernist texts (the truly cynical ones) is that its authors are not so much engaged in proposing theories as they are in debunking the totalizing theories of others. Where philosophical or narrative theories *are* put forward they tend to be speculative rather than dogmatic. To make a crude distinction between pure philosophy and pure science (as opposed to the psuedo-types, e.g., social science, in which the one borrows its legitimacy from the truth claims of the other), philosophy simply *advances* theories, whereas science is concerned with *proving* its theories and turning them into *facts*.

That a new generation of so called postmodern writers (Sokal and Bricmont's literary critics and cultural theorists) are engaged in replacing the old master narratives with new ones, is indicative of a *post*-postmodernism — to be blunt, a return to plain old modernism. So when Sarup criticizes Lyotard for ruling out the sort of critical social theory which employs categories like gender, race and class to support theories of dominance and subordination [45] he is simply stating the obvious. Why would Lyotard have any truck with such banality? He's a cynic (even if, like Foucault, he is also falsely labeled a social scientist)! Convenient political slogans such as gender, race and class have no place in the cynic's vocabulary. Through their use in the formation of positions such as victimhood, these tired slogans represent the very antithesis of cynicism; a target of, and a threat to, cynical reason. No contradiction is intended here with, on the one hand, the cynic's trust of existential truth (experiences of the self such as Feyerabend's understanding of lovemaking), and on the other hand, what many might claim to be the voice of experience articulated through the politics of gender, class, race, etc. The former represents concrete emotion with no further claim to moral value or higher purpose, whereas the latter represents those abstract emotions that nourish and promote dogmas of truth and falsehood, right and wrong. And it is precisely those theorists who claim the moral high ground with the rhetoric of gender, class and race, who then apply the term neo-conservatives to those postmodernist writers who refuse to engage with such naive prescriptions in the first place. Postmodern cynics do not acknowledge the narrow politics of left and right. Is being a conservative, a liberal or a nihilist the only choice there is? Is there really no other category to which one can belong?

> Politically, it is clear that thinkers such as Lyotard and Foucault are neo-conservatives. They take away the dynamic upon which liberal social thought has traditionally relied. They offer us no theoretical reason to move in one social direction or another.— *Sarup*[46]

And in a passage that could equally have come from Sokal and Bricmont, Sarup tells us: "I believe that it is important for people to support the Enlightenment project because education is closely connected with the notion of a change of consciousness; gaining a wider, deeper understanding of the world represents a change for the better."[47]

It is hard to believe that Sarup is not also being ironic when, having provided us with such illuminating insights into postmodernism, he then, in his summings up and conclusion, exchanges the cynic's reason for easy liberal clichés and a plea for a return to Enlightenment. Sarup accuses Derrida, Foucault and "other modern Nietzscheans" of viewing the end of history in the sense of dying. "Having lost faith in the progressive character of history, they are reacting against thinkers of the Enlightenment. They assert that the Enlightenment project of modernity has failed."[48] Adds Sarup, "I would argue that the more people believe that history should be moving towards the establishment of a rational society, the more likely history will be moving towards it. By making this link between theory and practice we make history conform to our notion of it."[49]

Plato may well have come to the same conclusion as Sarup, who is simply providing us here with a plea for continuing the relentless march of progress toward our ultimate enlightenment and salvation. And Sokal and Bricmont are only too ready to warn us of the dangers posed by postmodern cynics when they tell us that "it is irresponsible, to say the least, to treat with such casualness what has historically been the principal defence against these follies, namely a rational vision of the world."[50]

> The main reason for believing in scientific theories (at least the best-verified ones) is that they explain the coherence of our experience.... The experimental conformations of the best-established scientific theories, taken together, are evidence that we really have acquired an objective (albeit approximate and incomplete) knowledge of the natural world.[51]

Sarup's claims for the moral high ground in the social or human sciences are as flawed as Sokal and Bricmont's claims for the indisputable facts of natural science. Both remain stubbornly attached to a linear view of history that ends in enlightenment and utopia. Why are both social and natural scientists so terrified of postmodern notions of an end to history? The idea, after all, is simply a metaphor for an end to the credibility of the Enlightenment and modernist projects. Postmodernists are not suggesting some apocalyptic end to the physical world, even if this is entirely compatible with science's big bang theory for explaining the *start* of the world, and of history — as if *that* is not the most monumental cop-out!

Baudrillard's World of Hyper-reality

It is not difficult to see why Sokal and Bricmont are so hostile to writers like Jean Baudrillard, who applies the charge of intellectual dishonesty so mercilessly against scientists. Baudrillard is the ultimate postmodern philosopher: His descriptions of a world stripped of any real meaning by science's attempt to understand, categorize and control it are simply dismissed by his critics as a belief in nothing at all. Even those, like Sarup, who are prepared to engage with and represent Baudrillard's ideas have difficulty with his uncompromising stand: "In Baudrillard's world, truth and falsity are wholly indistinguishable, a position which I believe leads to moral and political nihilism."[52] But far from representing a belief in nothing, Baudrillard and other cynics feel liberated by a world outside of simple dichotomies like truth and falsehood. Baudrillard's is a critique beyond Good and Evil, one which eloquently dismisses Sarup's criticisms: "It is a diabolical temptation to wish for the Reign of Good, since to do so is to prepare the way for absolute Evil. If Good has a monopoly of this world, then the other will be the monopoly of Evil. We shall not escape the reversal of values, and the world become the field of the metastasis of the death of God."[53]

Baudrillard is describing the world we have created for ourselves, and if that world has become meaningless, it is the price scientists and others have paid for trying to realize its secrets. Even if there *were* objective laws to the universe, Baudrillard claims that humans (because they are human) would anyway interpret and use them in a way that would result in chaos. As Louise-Ferdinand Céline put it: "Men don't have to be drunk to make havoc of heaven and earth. *With them carnage is ingrained!*"[54]

Sadly (or thankfully), only cynics and the mad feel alienated in the orderly world presented by scientists, politicians and priests. The rest maintain a blessed illusion that life continues along rational lines on an earth created for them: its wise custodians. Baudrillard eloquently explodes these sham beliefs. In Baudrillard's world everything is hyper-reality (the blurring of distinctions between reality and illusion). This borderline world, "more real than real," has become the only existence. Baudrillard says that we have tried to realize the world by stripping it of any metaphysical dimension, and that by trying to express everything, we are left with nothing. In our search to find the real, we have forced out the real.

One of the main criticisms leveled against Baudrillard, and one that signals his characterization as a nihilist (and a neo-conservative), is that he sees no positive features in the postmodern world, rather he seems to be expressing a nostalgia for some imperfect but contented world still full of secrets. Positive, Baudrillard may not be, but the real charge of nihilism must ultimately be reserved for the scientists themselves, who in their own obsession with uncovering truth, have found and lost the greatest truth of all: "If the world emerged at a single stroke it cannot have any determinate meaning or end."[55] Or, as Emile Cioran puts it, "we are not failures until we believe life has a meaning — and from that point on we are all failures because it hasn't."[56] Baudrillard's view of the world *is* apocalyptic, the modern has come and gone, and now all we are left with is the fragmentation of the social, the political, and the moral. But then Nietzsche was making the same predictions at the end of the nineteenth century and here we still are struggling with the same old debates. Baudrillard's vision is important because it reminds us that the world described by Nietzsche one hundred years ago is the one we currently inhabit. It continually fails to achieve the objectives set out by modernists, and has done so for the past two thousand years.

An interesting postscript to a discussion on Baudrillard is the extent to which postmodern philosophers may not be able to resist talking up their own fictions. The destruction of the twin towers of the World Trade Center on September 11th, 2001, represented a truly spectacular example of the fusing together of fantasy and reality. And if the Baudrillardian significance of this event was to realize the dreams of movie makers and catastrophists, it also provided trendy philosophers like Baudrillard, Slavoj Zizek and Paul Virilio with the ideal opportunity to thrust their ideas into the spotlight. They published a trilogy of texts in time for the first anniversary of the event![57] "... we might even be said to have before us the absolute event, the 'mother' of all events, the pure event uniting with itself all the events that have never taken place."[58]

With these comments on September 11th, Baudrillard cashed in his store of philosophical predictions for one orgiastic pronouncement. But what if the planes that crashed into the twin towers had been armed with nuclear warheads and had wiped out the entire population of New York? The thought must have crossed people's minds. Is the collapse of the twin towers any more spectacular, ichnographically speaking, than the nuclear mushroom clouds that enveloped the cities of Hiroshima and Nagasaki, events produced in response to the largest suicide bombing campaign in history? Is not that other holocaust, the one perpetrated by the nation that bequeathed to the world the ideas of Kant, Hegel, Schopenhauer, Marx, Nietzsche, Einstein, et al., even more fantastic and unbelievable than September 11th, both in its cool and meticulous planning and the extent of its murderous design? And yet, in the presence of a contemporary event as mesmerizing as September 11th, even Baudrillard has been carried away by the possibility of history as progress toward the ultimate event, "the mother of all events"; momentarily forgetting his cynical view of the world as capricious and cyclical. And the script of this particular drama is indeed still being written. But, as just acknowledged, have we not already been there before, two generations ago? No, we are told, this is something new, the globalization of terror is what makes this different. Yet one can look back to the Medieval Crusades at least, to realize that global terrorism is not a new phenomenon. A cynical response to the philosophical signifi-cance of September 11th might be, that whether the interests behind ter-ror are national, religious or economic, whether its victims die by the sword or the bomb, the effects are surely the same: catastrophe for some, a talk-ing point for others, while the rest of human kind continue the business of living out their lives. The truly unique nature of September 11th was that it was *our* catastrophe; not just ours concerning its proximity in time (after all, thousands of people are dying of starvation, AIDS, earthquakes, wars and internal terrorism on a routine basis), but that it affected busi-ness-suited Westerners in a place hitherto considered immune from dis-aster, if not symbolic of security and success, a symbolism replaced so suddenly and dramatically by Icarian collapse. We will have to wait for history to rewrite this event with the hindsight of future events (not least the current Christian and Muslim war), before we are able to say just how "absolute" it was.

MICHEL FOUCAULT: RESCUING PHILOSOPHY FROM THE STRAITJACKET OF SCIENCE

Hostile to the encyclopaedic ideal in the human sciences.... Foucault left behind no synoptic critique of society, no system of ethics, no comprehensive theory of power, not even ... a generally useful histori-cal method.— *James Miller*[59]

It can be no accident that in researching *parrhesia* during the final months of his life, in particular the compulsion to tell the truth about himself, Michel Foucault should have focused on no less a figure than Diogenes of Sinope as the main precursor for the strange mode of his own philosophical life.[60] In his book *The Passion of Michel Foucault*, James Miller describes how having first researched Socrates as an exemplar for his ideas, Foucault was then to reject Socrates in favor of Diogenes; a much closer ideal for the way Foucault formulated the meaning of his own life.[61] That Foucault was to return to Diogenes as a model for his own personal philosophy during the final months of his life is consistent with an earlier observation by Miller, that it was Nietzsche who marked the end of Foucault's philosophical apprenticeship.[62] For in spite of the twists and turns in Foucault's philosophical beliefs and the different truth claims of others on behalf of Foucault's philosophy, a consistent cynical thread is clearly visible running throughout his life. Miller declares his book to be "a narrative account of one man's lifelong struggle to honor Nietzsche's injunction, 'to become what one is.'"[63] Like Nietzsche, Foucault would have recognized that living one's philosophy was the aim of all cynics from Diogenes onwards: "The key to the personal poetic attitude of a philosopher is not to be sought in his ideas, as if it could be deduced from them, but rather in his philosophy-as-life, in his philosophical life, his ethos."[61]

Typical of mainstream scholarship, most of the texts on Foucault have ignored his cynicism, trawling instead for master narratives and then presenting his work in the inaccessible diffuseness of critical and cultural theory. This compulsion for using the unpronounceable and the unintelligible, for creating neologisms (imagine the effect of every scholar adding only one new term to the lexicon of scholastic verbiage), and for taking three pages to say something that could more effectively be communicated in three lines, has become a defining feature of contemporary theory:

> The volcanic 'eruption' of his own singular prose produced a kind of soft black ash, easy to use for drawing new faces.... Quoted, imitated, travestied.... Flashed at academic conferences as a kind of off-the-rack fashion statement, Foucault's work became at last truly, and deeply, "anonymous," lost in the great murmur of discourses held today.
> — *Miller*[65]

Miller claims that liberals and socialists have over the years reduced Foucault's works to a set of popular slogans, a phenomenon that Foucault himself acknowledged in his own lifetime.[66] Fredric Jameson is one of those who cannot distinguish the real Foucault from the caricature that his ideas have come to represent:

> Today, increasingly, we have a new kind of writing simply called "theory".... This new kind of discourse generally associated with France

and so called French theory, is becoming widespread and marks the
end of philosophy as such. Is the work of Michel Foucault to be called
philosophy, history, social theory, or political science?[67]

That Jameson is unable to pigeonhole Foucault's work is evidence
that the postmodernist project has been a success. Foucault is one (like
Nietzsche) who has succeeded in breaking free from the meaningless categories of a failed modernism. Jameson's concern that this phenomenon
(he calls it theory) is a manifestation of postmodernism, should rather be
celebrated as a return to *true* philosophy, liberated from its prevailing
orthodoxies and illegitimate disciplines. Foucault's unconventional writing style was noted from the beginning of his academic career by the professors who reviewed his doctoral thesis, *Madness and Civilization*:
"...dazzled by the author's erudition and command of hitherto untapped
archival sources ... they all appreciated its exceptional intelligence.... But
the book's central argument — and, even more its intricate literary form —
they found puzzling, even vaguely disturbing."— Miller[68]

As one of the scholarly jury noted, the uses of allegories, mythical concepts, and fictional characters from history "allow a sort of metaphysical
incursion into history, which in a fashion transform the narrative into
epic, and history into an allegorical drama, bringing to life a philosophy."[69] Miller poses the professors' dilemma (the same dilemma as that
posed by Jameson): if the book was not a conventional work of history,
what was it? Foucault's literary style, like Bataille's and Nietzsche's, is cynical. It ignores conventional academic methodologies preferring instead to
draw from any sources the writer feels may assist in illuminating his thesis. In addition to scholarly texts, the cynical scholar will use personal
experience, fictional works, mythology, art, as well as borrowing and con-
structing aphorisms. Cynical scholarship represents an incursion of the
Dionysian into the formal and limiting structures (and laws) of academia:
"no matter how strenuously a culture tried to outlaw the Dionysian
impulse, it could only be fettered, never transcended: after all, Dionysus,
in the Nietzschean view, symbolized the power of transcendence itself."[70]

Discussing both Nietzsche and Foucault, Miller describes the out-
wardly-aimed violence of the Dionysian philosopher: "taking joy in destroying whatever mutilates life, and malicious delight in translating 'man back
into nature.'"[71] Unlike, then, the previous generation of philosophers, those
who sought one universal truth to replace another (Marxism for imperial-
ism, socialism for fascism, etc.), Miller contends that Foucault's generation: "felt no such need for morality, for compasses, for fixed road maps of
reality.... Hegel's vision of a harmonious synthesis of reason and freedom,
seemed to them little short of a failure of philosophical nerve."[72]

But Foucault's generation as not the first to abandon such comforting truths and certainties. These postmodernist philosophers follow a long line of others who were not short on the philosophical nerve of the cynic. From Diogenes through Nietzsche and Heidegger to Foucault himself, there has existed a shared belief in the power of the individual "to start over, to begin anew — to take up, reshape and transform the world"[73] (if only *their* world). Whatever the slogan: "will to power," "being," "transcendence," a core belief exists forming a continuous thread that links the central figures discussed in this book. Even though Foucault backed up his ideas with scientific and historical references (Nietzsche's included) dressed up in his own metaphors and neologisms, he could not, according to Miller, go past Nietzsche's hypothesis. But then, of course, neither could Nietzsche! If postmodernism could be surpassed, then what would postmodernism stand for?

Like Nietzsche, Foucault employs a genealogical approach. This method of understanding the past (seemingly at odds with the common usage of the term genealogy) replaces conventional history's grand spectacles and famous dates for the forgotten and marginal events (for example Cynicism itself) which have been discredited. Discredited, precisely because they do not support the prevailing and privileged view of history in which historical events are seen as rational building block towards greater enlightenment. Instead, we are presented with a series of disconnected and arbitrary events in which humans are the objects rather than the authors of change.

> Foucault ... approached the past as if it were a kaleidoscope.... The sequence of patterns obeyed no inner logic, conformed to no universal norm of reason, and evidenced no higher purpose; it could therefore not be regarded as a form of "progress," for the latest pattern is neither more true nor false than those that preceded it.[74]

With one such twist of the kaleidoscope Foucault dismisses Marxism (declared by Sartre only six years earlier as unsurpassable). Marxism may have created "a few waves," but these "are no more than storms in a child's paddling pool."[75] The truths of Foucault, like the truths of Nietzsche, have been misappropriated by those who wish to maintain a positive view of the world. And don't look to postmodernism's inheritors to uphold its mission. What was initially a rebellion against modernism's codes and categories, has itself become coded and categorized. Indeed, one gets a better understanding of postmodernism from reading its critics than one does from its zealots. It is, for example, Sarup's *criticisms* of Foucault's writings that bring to light the philosopher's genuine, cynical integrity:

> Foucault refuses to be committed to a general ontology of history, society or the human subject, or to advance any general theory of

power.... Foucault's refusal to deal with epistemological questions means that it is difficult to evaluate them. As he does not present his own methodological protocols we do not know what standards should be used to assess his work.... If we are to engage seriously with Foucault's writings, considerable theoretical work on his epistemological and ontological protocols will have to be done.[76]

Having provided such a cogent summary of Foucault's main ideas (insights to which I am much indebted), by then applying scientific criteria to Foucault's work, Sarup would seem to have completely missed its philosophical importance. The generosity of cynics such as Nietzsche and Foucault, is that having provided so much creative raw material, they stand back and allow others (so called Nietzscheans and Foucauldians) to formulate and peddle the smart theories and grand narratives that were never intended in the first place, paradoxically acquiring tribute for that which they spent their lives ridiculing.

Sarup also criticizes Foucault for not inspiring revolution in his comment that 'he offers no grounds for encouraging resistance or struggle."[77] If Foucault did not see it as his responsibility to ferment revolution, he was certainly not averse to participating in violent insurrection. Foucault was disenchanted with party politics, Marxism in particular; it is therefore incongruous that Sarup should revert to the rhetoric of Marxism when he declares that "Foucault disregards the fact that domination has its basis in the relations of production and exploitation and in the organization of the state."[78] Why should Foucault agree with such an assumption? Foucault's treatise on power is clear and unambiguous: the origin of power is not in a structure, it is not something that can be acquired or seized, since it comes from below as much as it does from above. Power relations do not exist outside other types of relations but are immanent to them. To conceive of power simply as repression, constraint or prohibition is inadequate.[79] In the following critique, Sarup at the same time both illuminates and attacks Foucault's view of power. Here the plea for some rational solution to oppressive societal structures is audible, even though both Nietzsche and Foucault are clearly describing what *is* rather than what *should be*:

> But if all relations are power relations, how do we choose between one society and another? When Foucault had to answer a question such as this he became evasive. Theoretically he had put himself in a situation where he could not use terms like equality, freedom, justice. These concepts are merely tokens in a game, an interplay of forces. This is a viewpoint very much like that of Nietzsche (who wrote "when the oppressed want justice it is just a pretext for the fact that they want power for themselves"). History according to this view, is an endless play of domination.[80]

Far from trying to be evasive, both Nietzsche and Foucault rejected notions such as equality, freedom and justice precisely because they did not believe them to have any meaning, or if they did, that their significance was as perverse as Nietzsche's example above makes clear. That is not to say that the cynic has no social conscience, nor that he or she is indifferent to injustice (in its non-statutory, non-totalizing sense). The cynic's contribution to social change takes place at the margins of universal notions of equality, justice or freedom. Theirs is a local struggle which affects the cynic's immediate environment. Indeed, in spite of Sarup's criticisms, Foucault was to effect localized social change in a very significant way through his long-term personal commitment (not without considerable risk) to prison reform.

Foucault as Parrhesiast

It is in Foucault's discourse on death that we finally encounter his true cynicism. As with the Cynic and Stoic belief in determining one's own end, Foucault viewed (and welcomed) death as the fulfillment of one's existence.

> It is in death, that the individual becomes at one with himself, escaping from monotonous lives and their leveling effect; in the slow, half-subterranean, but already visible approach of death, the dull, common life at last becomes an individuality; a black border isolates it, and gives it the style of its truth.— Foucault[81]

This becoming at one with oneself in death — escaping the expectations of the other: parents, children, spouses, communities, societies — is something the Cynics sought to achieve in life. Like Peregrinus (who carefully arranged his pyre and announced the event of his suicide before dramatically flinging himself into the flames), Foucault viewed death as the ultimate human experience, to be prepared for carefully, to savor. To organize it "bit by bit, decorate it, arrange the details, find the ingredients, imagine it, choose it, get advice on it, shape it into a work without spectators [unlike Peregrinus], one which exists only for oneself, just for that shortest little moment of life."[82] Foucault even fantasized about setting up an institute where people could plan and arrange their deaths, a place to enjoy and savor one's final moments. Not in a violent, sordid way by, say, hanging, gassing or shooting oneself in a garage. But in a celebratory way with the help of drugs, even in the company of others planning a similar event. For Foucault, to die is to experience the "formless form of an absolutely simple pleasure," a "limitless pleasure whose patient preparation, with neither rest nor predetermination, will illuminate the entirety of your life."[83]

We will never know if Foucault found truth in the final pleasure of his dying. But like his Cynic ancestors, he did leave behind a rich legacy of knowledge to be explored. As Thomas Flynn reminds, there is something Greek about Foucault's "tragic passing and about the philosophical torso he left behind."[84]

Foucault was uncompromising about truth telling, presenting it in his final lectures as a moral virtue; "you admitted the truth even if it cost you your self-image."[85] He viewed the parrhesiast as the open contrary of the rhetorician, who did not have to meet the prior conditions of truth to enter into discourse. That is, "he did not have to believe what he said.... Moreover, unlike the parrhesiast, he was a professional in classical society with a metier of his own."[86] In Flynn's view, "the 'ethical' parrhesiast thus emerges in a tradition from Diogenes to Nietzsche as an alternative, not a complement, to his moral counterpart."[87]

> The Cynic was characterized by friend and foe alike as a parrhesiast, indeed, as a kind of prophet of truth telling. His deliberately unconventional lifestyle freed him for the task. In fact, the Cynics made their lives a liturgy of truth-telling.... Foucault sees the Cynics' extreme, indeed scandalous, pursuit of the true life as an inversion of, a kind of carnivalesque grimace directed toward the Platonic tradition.[88]

In the same way that the Cynics lived according to their nature, so Foucault claimed that his own personal philosophy, indeed everything he had written, grew in part out of direct personal experience. Neither, did he claim, was there any systematic method to his work. His nature and his knowledge he put to the test in his very existence.[89] Nor do Foucault's constantly shifting beliefs detract from his cynic credentials. "Don't ever ask me," he said, "to remain the same." He was a structuralist who demonstrated his post-structuralism in as much as he could never settle on a system that captured what he wanted to illustrate or what he felt. Indeed, almost everything about Foucault seems contradictory. Although he always remained a scholar, he claims that his real desire was to write fiction. Then again, Foucault's obsessive historical scholarship was based on the old premise that truth *is* stranger than fiction, and also that, in any case, historical studies *were* to some extent fictional. The true cynic philosopher, then, must accept one's self and one's own experiences as the primary locus for one's investigations. In this regard, I propose that the contention of Bewes, Sloterdijk and others that Greek Cynicism differs markedly from contemporary cynicism, is challenged by the examples of those like Foucault, Artaud, Nietzsche and Bataille, whose writings simply reflect the truth about themselves, rather than representing externalized and abstract theories.

GREEK CYNICISM'S
POSTMODERN LEGACY

Bewes describes contemporary cynicism as "a strategic mode of thinking" which, in Sloterdijk's words, "is the universally widespread way in which enlightened people see to it that they are not taken for suckers."[90] But was this not also a strategy of the Greek Cynics? What provoked Diogenes is unlikely to be fundamentally different from that which provoked Nietzsche or Baudrillard. Diogenes' reaction to Plato is Nietzsche's reaction to Hegel or Sloterdijk's reaction to Kant. All that changes is the historical context and the effect on the individual cynic. The fact that Sloterdijk and others contrast classical Cynicism and contemporary cynicism does not mean that the underlying critique of Greek Cynicism no longer applies, nor that it has developed into a different set of attitudes or behaviors. That postmodernists are not to be found lined up in the streets half naked in tubs does not deny the fact that Diogenes' practical Cynicism still survives today alongside its more nihilistic and theoretical cousins. Likewise nihilistic cynicism or the negative, disparaging attitude mis-designated *cynicism*, would have also existed alongside the Cynicism of the Greeks.

That the mode of discourse currently referred to as postmodernism seems paradoxically to represent the grand narratives it critiques, merely alerts us to the fact that such a critique is no longer cynically postmodern. In the same way, what we are often presented with as philosophy is in reality scientific or pseudo-scientific doctrine. Thus it has always been with expressions of rebellion against dogma and logical explanations about our illogical world. There are always those waiting to hijack spontaneous protest and turn it into a movement. Witness the split between those who wished to declare Dada dead because it had outlived its usefulness and those who wished to preserve its artistic form(ula), or, the specious truths attributed to Jesus Christ (of whom no original sayings exist) which became one of the major narratives of the last two millennia. Much of modern dogma results in this way, from the appropriation of basic human instincts and emotions, re-scripted as blueprints by which others are urged to order their lives, following exclusive bodies of knowledge that discard (by their nature) the simple truths that gave birth to them.

That Nietzsche, Foucault, Baudrillard, and Lyotard have all published polemical arguments against institutionalized knowledge through the very medium which they rail against, may seem paradoxical. Cynicism appears ill at ease in an academic forum; it is, after all, not so much a philosophy as an everyday reaction to the gap which some people perceive to exist between what they are told and what they instinctively feel. Neither does cynicism rely on verbal dialogue. A non-verbal message can prove just as powerful, if not more so, than the spoken word. Even the way one chooses to dress or act can say more about what one thinks (both of one's self and of others) than the spoken word ever could. The message is simple and lasting. Even the absence of speech at the appropriate moment can be a more powerful tool than making an utterance. As will be shown in the following chapter, modern-day examples of Diogenean cynicism do exist; in the chaotic anarchy of the performance artist every bit as much as in the poetry of Baudrillard's written polemics.

5

Return of the Dog Cynics: 20th Century Performance Art

The world was for them [the Cynics] a senseless circus, and because of this, they wasted no opportunity to mount the stage ... and present themselves as accomplished exhibitionists. In a literal sense, then, they expressed their convictions by putting themselves on exhibition. Their lives were collections of performance pieces carefully arranged and methodically worked out...— *Navia*[1]

With Dada, the first neokynicism of the twentieth century strides on stage. Its thrust is directed against everything that takes itself "seriously"— whether it be in the area of culture and the arts, in politics or in public life. Nothing else in our century [twentieth] has so furiously smashed the *esprit de serieux* as the dadaist rabble. Dada is basically neither an art movement nor an anti-art movement, but a radical "philosophical action." It practices the art of a militant irony.— *Sloterdijk*[2]

In his defense after being jailed for biting members of the audience at a Stockholm performance, Russian artist Oleg Kulik laid the blame for his behavior on the organizers of the show who had called the police to arrest him. First, it was they who had invited him to give the performance, in the full knowledge that he had been previously arrested at a show in Zurich for the same offense. Kulik's second defense was that the audience had begun to treat him like the dog he played, teasing him and kicking him in the head. Furthermore, the show's organizers had put Kulik on too long a chain, which allowed him to venture beyond the bounds of the warning sign "Dangerous Dog." It was essential for Kulik-the-person, who spent day and night naked and chained in and around his dog house, not to take responsibility for Kulik-the-dog, hence he always traveled with his owner (his wife). This chapter reveals that Kulik was by no means unique among twentieth century performance artists in replicating Diogenes' use of animal behavior as rhetoric,[3] a theme that recurs in many disparate forms throughout this book such as Beuys with his hare and Dilbert's companion Dogbert in the cartoon strip of the same name.

The story of art from the late nineteenth century onwards reveals a breeding ground and rich platform for cynics of all shades. Even so, identifying cynical movements and genres becomes problematic due to the rapidly changing fashions and contradictory meanings even within the same art movements. Profoundly cynical actions take place alongside exhibitions of gross decadence, and the daring or the avant-garde could become clichéd or sell out sometimes within a matter of weeks. Cynical artists and dogmatists often inhabit for a time the same school. Later, for instance, the rift is discussed between those Dadaists who felt the movement had served its purpose and wished to kill it off, and those who wanted to preserve the genre as a permanent showcase. Furthermore, the early twentieth century was an intensely political era. Eastern and Western Europe were going through a period of rampant grassroots ideological fervor and modernist manifestos. The relationship of cynicism (even returns of Classical Cynicism) to the political was no longer one of pure aversion. For example, the Futurists and the Dadaists were undoubtedly cynical, but they were also considerably more political in their purpose than, say, the Bauhaus school, which in spite of jettisoning much of the political subtext of the Dadaists, was considerably less cynical in the work it produced.

Other theatre genres—though clearly aimed at debunking representative, oppressive structures through the use of cynical tools such as irony, parody and satire — were entirely political in their aim. Heavily influenced by modernist theatre in the rest of Europe, Spain's *Teatro de Urgencia* (Theatre of Urgency) was developed with the primary aim of promoting Republican ideology within the context of the civil war. Jim McCarthy defines *Teatro de Urgencia* as inculcating values that would "nurture the spectator as an ideal Republican combatant or citizen."[4] The role of theatre in this context was an agent of social change. With the fall of the Republic *Teatro de Urgencia* as a theatre genre simply disappeared.

Previous definitions of cynicism in this book as apolitical now require further review in the context of art and performance during the first half of the twentieth century. Classical Cynicism, Nietzschean cynicism, and to a lesser extent postmodern cynicism, relied on standing outside the political as a major feature of their cynical tone. The cynicism of early twentieth century art (for different reasons than the cynicism of Machiavelli) clearly does not. The question then becomes, whether in times of intense political upheaval the cynic can, or would want to, stand outside of politics. Cynicism has already been characterized as an opportunistic philosophy, one that responds to the prevailing social climate. Although *Teatro de Urgencia,* with its heavily ideological agenda, does not fit our neat definition of cynicism, it did develop in an opportunistic fashion: a response to Spanish Nationalism which it sought to undermine using cynical weapons to deliver its attack. In the following pages we encounter some challenging contradictions to my so far more precise definitions of cynicism: Futurism and Dadaism being cynical *and* political; Bauhaus and Surrealism being apolitical yet decidedly modernist; Joseph Beuys for combining cynicism with spiritual idealism; and Stuart Brisley, "the curator of shit," for taking himself seriously.

For much of this chapter I am indebted to RoseLee Goldberg's book *Performance Art: From Futurism to the Present.* This text provides a consistent historical thread on which it is possible to hang the more inconsistent and contradictory features of performance art as a cynical critique. And yet Goldberg invites challenge when she tells us that performance art as a legitimate form of artistic expression in its own right, was born during the 1970s. Before this, she says, performance often formed a demonstration or execution of ideas that supported other media of conceptual art. From a cynical perspective, the problem here is Goldberg's use of the word "legitimate." Is she de-legitimizing any performance that was not accepted by art schools or the art establishment? The cynic does not question the legitimacy of Diogenes masturbating in public simply because the action was performed outside of the normal discourse of academia. Diogenes' reception both then as now — that we are able to read about him at all — is what legitimizes his actions. The same criteria should be applied to performance art, of which Diogenes is claimed as an early exponent:

> He [Diogenes] presents himself to the world as a performer and an exhibitionist, and every idea and belief of his takes on the garb of a *physical* gesture or is expressed by him in apothegms in which the language denotes unmistakably *physical* functions.... We witness him in a series of "performance pieces" that abound with grossness and display a tremendous sense of humor. In every instance, he must initiate his Cynicism by means of concrete physical gestures or acts.... The man is undoubtedly a walking riot, a clownish character, a *performer* of the highest caliber, who knows well how to mingle with his sarcasm and diatribal tone an extraordinary amount of humor and joking, mixing a liberal dosage of vulgarity and grossness in his innumerable antics with a great deal of unrelenting moralizing. His outrageous and caustic remarks and acts still make us laugh, as much as they probably did his amused and disbelieving contemporaries, but we would be mis-

taken, were we to conclude that such behavior was meant only to amuse or call attention to himself.— *Navia*[5]

There can be no doubt that the Cynics' public performances, particularly their *reasons* for performing (already well established in this book), contain all the ingredients and motives we find employed by their contemporary associates. "Live gestures," Goldberg tells us, "have constantly been used as a weapon against the conventions of established art."[6] If we consider the more theatrical aspects of the Cynics (Diogenes and his lamp, begging alms of a statue, walking into a theatre as others were leaving; or Peregrinus, practicing the art of indifference to convention by appearing in public with half his head shaved, his face covered in mud, and an exposed erection), then we can establish a tradition where the entire lifestyle of a community represented a weapon, not only against art but against every aspect of human civilization:

> Performance manifestos, from the Futurist to the present, have been the expressions of dissidents who have attempted to find another means to evaluate art experience in every day life. Performance has been a way of appealing directly to a large public, as well as shocking audiences into reassessing their own notions of art and its relation to culture.... Unlike theatre, the performer *is* the artist, seldom a character like an actor, and the content rarely follows a traditional plot or narrative.... For this reason its base has always been anarchic.— *Goldberg*[7]

One distinguishing feature of cynical artists of the twentieth century was that their self-professed aim as dissident avant-gardists left them in constant danger of becoming the target of other, newer dissident artists. In the rapidly changing and developing movements of twentieth century art, performance appeared at the leading edge of artistic expression, yet it is the art *objects* and *visual images* of movements such as Futurism, Dadaism, Surrealism and Bauhaus by which these styles are usually identified today.

Discussions concerning the different styles and schools that made up the various art movements of the twentieth century are of more interest to scholars of art history than they are to scholars of cynicism. Therefore, in describing these different movements, the discussion here will focus on those individual performances that made twentieth century art vibrant, fresh, challenging and cynical. Of all the arts, with the possible exception of music, it is fine art: painting, sculpture, photography, performance, etc., that has in recent times been the most innovative and challenging of the artistic genres due to its inherently avant-garde nature. Cinema and television can be left to one side here because as art they often include a fusion (both positive and negative) of other art media.

DADA AND OTHER ISMS OF
THE EARLY 20TH CENTURY

With an act of violence, they [the Dadaists] equated art with what at
the time was contemptuously called "arts and crafts" — with innocuous
decorative art that accommodated the need for the upright citizen for
being cheered up and a diversion from reality.... Here, the handwrit-
ing of kynical modernity appears for the first time: the affirmation of
reality as reality in order to be able to smash in the face everything
that is merely "aesthetic thinking." — *Sloterdijk*[8]

A radio discussion on Surrealism, broadcast in 2001, opened with an
opinion that the "creative idealism" of the Surrealists was one of the positive things to have come out of the "nihilistic aggression" of Dada.[9] Dada
was simply dismissed as though its only contribution to art and ideas was
that it had spawned André Breton and the Surrealist movement. Cynics
may well be excused for turning this assessment on its head. The Dadaists,
having put so much passion and energy into smashing down aesthetics and
idealism in art, were sold out by Breton (with his obsession in Freudian
psychoanalysis and claims of having discovered how to interpret the mysteries of dreams), who presented a new aesthetic in art. Having collabo-
rated with Dadaists, whom he and other emerging Surrealists saw as a
vehicle for their own beliefs, Breton became a central figure in its demise
(Anti-Dada also became a distinct artistic form of expression at this time).
This included a mock trial and several ugly brawls in which one performer
suffered a broken arm. But Surrealism was to suffer its own factionalism
and discord, and although it abandoned the cynical discourse of Dada for
a belief, as its name suggests, in a higher reality, it also generated one of
the most important cynics of the twentieth century — Georges Bataille.
Bataille defined his cynicism, not through his one-time association with
the Surrealists, but by his subsequent rejection of it, and in particular his
enmity, even hatred, of André Breton. Bataille's rift with Breton illuminates through his writings one of the essentials of cynicism: the rejection
of human beings' Icarian impulse to elevate themselves morally and spiritually above their animal nature.[10] If Dadaism represented the militant
cynicism that Sloterdijk suggests it does, then Surrealism becomes cynicism's very reverse, sarcastically dismissed by Bataille as:

the transformations of Icarian reflexes into a pathetic-comic and gratuitous literature ... the Icarian movement consists precisely of acting
and even thinking as if they [the Surrealists] had attained without
laughter the spiritual elevation that is only empty rumbling of their
words.[11]

The schools and isms that emerged from early twentieth century art movements present a unique historical phenomena. Born under the influential shadow, not only of idealists such as Marx and Freud, but also notable cynics like Nietzsche, performance art was an early test bed for the emergence and subsequent clash between the high modernist and nihilistic postmodernist forms that dominated twentieth century Western art. Unlike the ancient Greek schools of philosophy, which lasted for several hundred years, disciples of movements like Futurism, Dadaism and Surrealism were to be as actively involved in subverting and demolishing their philosophical creations as they were involved in giving them life. Given the individualistic and egotistical nature of many of these artists, it is incredible that they ever created any unified movements at all. It is also unhelpful, given the manner in which one movement was born out of another in such rapid succession, to try to draw too firm a distinction between any inherent characteristics that each may present. After all, sometime Surrealist Bataille was an arch cynic and sometime Dadaist Breton was an arch idealist. Rather than attempt to explore the genre, it makes more sense to focus on the cynical features and characters that emerge from this unique, but brief, period in the history of ideas. But first, let us again question the provenance of performance art itself.

Goldberg gives the start date of performance art as 20th February 1909, when Filippo Tommaso Marinetti published the first Futurist manifesto in *Le Figaro*, a large circulation daily newspaper in Paris. The article attacked establishment values of the painting and literary academies in their cultural capital.[12] Yet from accounts contained elsewhere in this book, it becomes clear that the history of performance art precedes this date by several thousand years, surfacing in a spectacular form during the Renaissance. It is not unusual, however, for each new generation to claim something it regards as having special significance for its time as invented by its near contemporaries. The claim that performance art had a prior tradition can be demonstrated in showing that the intention of these early twentieth century performance artists was identical to that of their ancient Greek predecessors—to provoke and enrage their public. Violent scenes at early Futurist performances led to arrests, convictions, and a couple of days in jail which provided free publicity for future events. And like the Cynics, Futurist performances were seeking not applause from their audiences but jeering and hostility. Missiles were frequently thrown at performers which brought the response on one occasion, "throw an idea instead of potatoes, idiots!"[13] In his article *"The Pleasure of Being Booed,"* Marinetti insisted that the performer should be despised by the audience.

Applause, he insisted, merely indicated "something mediocre, dull, regurgitated or too well digested."

> Booing assured the actor that the audience was alive, not simply
> blinded by "intellectual intoxication." He [Marinetti] suggested vari-
> ous tricks designed to infuriate the audience: double booking the
> auditorium, coating the seats with glue. And he encouraged his friends
> to do whatever came to mind on stage.[14]

Variety theatre became the model for Futurist performance, having "no tradition, no masters, no dogma." Furthermore, variety was just what the name implied. As with the *menippea*,[15] the Futurists subverted traditional genres, mixing film, acrobatics, song and dance, clowning and 'the whole gamut of stupidity, imbecility, doltishness, and absurdity, insensibility pushing the intelligence to the very border of madness."[16] The *raison-detre* of Futurist performance became that which continually invented new areas of astonishment to coerce the audience into collaboration and liberate it from its passive role as "stupid voyeurs." By co-operating with the actors' fantasy, the action of variety and cabaret developed simultaneously on stage, in the boxes and in the orchestra. The choice of performance as the vehicle to shock, as well as their clearly stated mission to undermine the conventions and values of their own time, marked the Futurists out as modern day cynics in the Diogenes mold: "'anti-academic, primitive and naive, hence the more significant for the unexpectedness of its discoveries and the simplicity of its means.' Consequently, in the flow of Marinetti's logic, variety theatre 'destroys the Solemn, the Sacred. the Serious and the Sublime in Art with a capital A.'"[17]

Like Menippean Satire, Futurist performance made use of ironic and parodic insertions, and the mixing of different styles into a single brief performance. Synthetic Theatre, for example, suggested mixing together all of the Greek, Italian, and French tragedies into a condensed comic mix.[18] Futurist performances became more and more elaborate involving not just the stage but the whole auditorium with constantly changing scenes combining sound, human performance, elaborate lighting, and shifting decor. Descriptions of elaborate music hall and circus themes by later Russian performers have strong associations with the extravagances of Renaissance street theatre: "He [Sergei Yutkevich] devised a fully mobile environment with moving steps and treadmill, trampolines, flashing electric signs and cinema posters, rotating decor and flying lights." Circus, music hall, variety, Japanese theatre and puppet show were all considered for their possibilities of arriving at a popular entertainment form that would appeal to "large and not necessarily educated audiences."[19]

In the same way that Cynicism has been described as the philosophy of the proletariat, so we are now provided with a description of *art* being claimed back on behalf of the proletariat. However, because of the period of history with which we now concern ourselves, associations with the term proletariat itself become problematical, for in trying to identify pure forms of cynicism in Futurism, Dadaism or other art movements, we also encounter their Marxist associations. Much of twentieth century performance art, like other art forms of the time, also took on the form of political propaganda. In some cases, both the mode and the purpose of performance art during this period demonstrates the very antithesis of cynical discourse. Far from attacking grand narrative and established modes of discourse, Russian Agit-train and Agit-street performance (prototypes for the later Agit-prop, or "living newspaper"), as with *Teatro de Urgencia*, fully embraced and glorified the prevailing revolutionary fervor. Yet as a pragmatic philosophy able to adapt itself to prevailing circumstances, we can identify the decidedly cynical character of our philosophy emerging from beneath the political veil that now enshrouds it.

Early performance artists practiced their own form of *askesis*. The bio-mechanical movements of Futurist performers, actors, dancers, and acrobats required rigorous training to perfect the precise and strenuous moves required.[20] Yet in such discipline and perfecting of style, also lay the downfall of each new art movement as avant-garde. The perfecting of artistic styles and genres demonstrates Bataille's Icarian complex. The paradox here, is the cynical undermining of high art only to then develop a facsimile of that whose arrogance one sought to puncture in the first place. To highlight how rapidly Futurist performance evolved, from its early cynical beginnings toward a triumph of modernist high art, one need only look to later performances which employed Taylor's efficiency theories to underpin the perfection of its delivery.

Dada drew on the cynical origins of Futurism, rejecting their later extravagant performances. Dada's roots were in the sleazy, dimly lit cafes and clubs of Munich, a city with an already strong tradition of cabaret. One of the eccentric figures of this "intimate theatre" scene was Frank Wedekind, a notoriously provocative performer and playwright. Wedekind would urinate, masturbate, and sometimes induce convulsions on stage.[21] Each of Wedekind's plays were censored by the authorities so that he was forced to exist on the fringes of the theatre world. He eked out a living on the cabaret circuit surviving censorship, trials, prison sentences and the nervousness of producers. It was a life which suited Wedekind and made him a popular figure among Munich's bohemian artistic community. One prominent member of this community, and co-founder of the Cabaret Voltaire, Hugo Ball, said of Wedekind: "To me the theatre meant inconceivable freedom. My strongest impression was of the poet as a fearful cynical spectacle.... In the theatre he was struggling to eliminate both himself and the last remains of a once firmly established civilization."[22]

And in Goldberg's own view, "Wedekind's performances reveled in the license given to the artist to be the mad outsider, exempt from society's normal behavior. But he knew that such license was given only because the role of the artist was considered utterly insignificant, more tolerated than accepted."[23]

After fleeing Germany for draft dodging, Hugo Ball and his future wife, Emmy Hennings, opened the Cabaret Voltaire in Zurich on 5th February 1916 and Dada was born. The name Dada was coined by Ball and Richard Huelsenbeck (a friend who joined Ball from Munich) from a German-French dictionary. The meaning being rocking-horse or hobby horse in French; and for the Germans "a sign of foolish naivety, joy in procreation, and preoccupation with the baby carriage."[24] The pace and energy of the Dadaists' nightly performances at the Cabaret Voltaire (paintings, dance, music, poetry, performance, storytelling; all interspersed with drunkenness and violence) could not be sustained for more than five months. When Huelsenbeck returned to Berlin in 1917, Dada returned to its more anarchic roots of provoking the audience with ironic gestures and skits, not to mention performances that lacked any irony at all, such as Grosz urinating on an expressionist painting on stage. Indeed, childlike and infantile behavior was an intentional and necessary part of Dada philosophy. Ball's stated desire was to achieve "a magical return to a state of infantilism," a return to the primitivism which the Dadaists sought to achieve through reduction, abstraction, and deliberate childishness.[25] Yet it was precisely through the seemingly childish, senseless games in which the Dadaists engaged, coupled with their arrogance and "dandyish absurdism" that we find the serious side of their philosophy — an all-out assault on meaning and language. As Sloterdijk tells us, the Dadaists' aim was to disrupt the orderly, comfortable, civilizing process that the rest of us buy into in order to maintain the illusion that life is controllable, predictable and explainable, and instead, expose us to the chaotic reality that life is. As Ball and Huelsenbeck put it in their 1915 *Memorial Reading for Fallen Poets,* "We want to provoke, perturb, bewilder, tease, tickle to death, confuse, without any context. Be reckless, negators."[26] The Dadaists made sense of the capricious nature of the world, Sloterdijk says, by trumping unhappiness with a "self intended 'high' misery." As positivists continued their search for a better life in the conviction that the world should, and could, be a better place, the Dadaists, like their Cynic ancestors, held no such illusions and celebrated their hatred of the world's pretensions by raging against it. As we are further reminded by Sloterdijk, Dada had always existed throughout history and throughout the world in various forms: "In the beginning was the chaos into which people, in their debility and hunger for meaning, dream a cosmos.... At the zero point of meaning, only a pathetic contempt for meaning still stirs itself — an all penetrating nausea about 'positivity.'" [27]

One of the achievements of Dada, then, was to give meaning back to the world in the form of the meaninglessness they felt it truly represented. Their strategy was to give themselves over to the senseless vagaries that human life presented: "If what drives us is brutal, then so are we. Dada does not look onto an ordered cosmos. What is important for it is presence of mind in the chaos." [28] The Dadaists were literally at war with the prevailing culture and one of their weapons is described by Sloterdijk as the ironical-polemic: "The art of declaring oneself, in an ironic, dirty way, to be in agreement with the worst possible things." An example of such a strategy can be seen in Richard Huelsenbeck's first Dada speech in Berlin, in February, 1918, when he declared to his audience that Dadaism was in favor of war. "Things have to collide; things are not proceeding nearly as horribly as they should." [29] Not since Nietzsche, Sloterdijk says, had anyone tried to take up the return of the repressed from a positive angle: "With cynical speeches he [Huelsenbeck] produced an ego beyond good and evil that wanted to be like its mad epoch." [30] And also like Nietzsche, the Dadaists' rage was fuelled by an intense irritation at the appropriation of language as a weapon in the war of self-righteousness:

> Ball believed that under the influence of Kant and German idealism, as well as Lutheran sobriety, language had been made abstract and thus debased into a utilitarianism that allowed it to be plundered by jingoism, literary professionalism, journalism and intellectual vacuity. It had become a tool for upholding the ruling value systems and the rational and intellectualizing orientation that had produced Western philosophy, art, music and religion.— *Malcolm Green* [31]

Even though much of the rhetoric of Dada (like that of the Cynics) relied on gestural and verbal polemics, there were also some notable attempts by the Dadaists to challenge meaning in literature through their own writing. Sloterdijk describes Walter Serner's writing as affirming the unbearable "chaos of unbearable sentences" that constitute our knowledge about the world in order to outdo the "confusion of 'facts' that whirl about together." [32] Dadaists sought to expose the deceitful language games that pose as an understanding of the world — the "formal-logical corsets" that positivists put on their facts— by demolishing the very structural foundations on which the logical world fixes its truths. In a review of Serner's

Last Loosening Manifesto, Zurich Dadaist Hans Richter, gives notice of the Dadaists' philosophical aims: "Everything must be loosened; not a screw must remain in its place; the holes in which they once fitted must be torn out; screws and humanity on their way to new functions which can only be recognized once all that was has been negated."[33]

But Dada reserved its main contempt for other artists, those who sought to portray comfortable ideals about the world around us, misrepresenting its tarnished reality with aesthetically pleasing images to adorn private and public spaces, offering soothing reassurance in the face of chaos. This is an incongruity which anyone will understand who has been irritated by having to look at some insipid chocolate box print of pastel washed flowers while listening to the dentist's drill in the next room. The established art world had turned its back on jolting people into a state of critical reflection, in favor of producing saleable craft products that reinforced the received truths and values by which most people ordered their lives:

> Dada turns against art as a technique of bestowing meaning. Dada is
> anti-semantics. It rejects "style" as a pretence of meaning just as much
> as the deceitful "beautifying" of things.... Wherever firm "values,"
> higher meanings, and deeper significances emerge, Dada attempts a
> disordering of meaning.... [it] pulls the ground out from under all
> faith in universal concepts, formulas for the world, and totalizations.
> — *Sloterdijk*[34]

In the same year that Huelsenbeck returned to Berlin, Marcel Duchamp attempted to exhibit his urinal at the *Independents Exhibition* of 1917 in New York. This single event represented a symbolic turning point in the history of visual art. For though performance artists had already staked the claim that the concepts and ideas of the artist overrode the end product, this was the first time that the idea had been applied to an art object itself. The urinal did not represent the end product in terms of the artist's physical craft, but that of a mass produced item that had been claimed as art and bore the artist's signature. This was a significantly cynical act; for more than simply outraging the art orthodoxy of the time, Duchamp permanently introduced the idea of conceptual art into art's own showcase: the gallery space.

Not all performance art movements of the early twentieth century were associated with cynical rebellion. Unlike the cafe culture in which Futurism and Dada thrived, Bauhaus, in spite of its radical aim of transcending traditional art disciplines and categories, developed its philosophy within the community of an academic institution. Opened in 1919 as a teaching institution for the arts, the aim of Bauhaus was to break down the barriers between the different art media and create a unification of the arts. Not for the first time did the provincial and conservative town of Weimar play host to some very unconventional residents. The former homes of Goethe and Nietzsche were among the residences occupied by the numerous artists and their families who flocked to Weimar to teach at the Bauhaus. The first course on performance art was among a wide variety of subjects taught at this new institution, yet we associate Bauhaus not with anarchy or ridicule but with high modernism. Even so, the program's second director, Oskar Schlemmer, well understood the essential role of Dada: "It was probably a legacy of the Dadaists to ridicule automatically everything that smacked of solemnity or ethical precepts ... it [the grotesque] found its nourishment in travesty and in mocking the anti-quated forms of the contemporary theatre."[35]

Schlemmer's theory of performance centered on the problem inher-ent in any educational program, that between theory and practice. His model was the opposition between Apollo and Dionysus, with painting representing the intellectual Apollonian side, and experimental theatre representing the unadulterated pleasure of Dionysus. For Schlemmer these two aspects of art were complementary; his painting providing the theo-retical research from which his practice of performance emerged: "The dance is Dionysian and wholly emotional in origin ... I struggle between two souls in my breast — one painting-orientated, or rather philosophical artistic; the other theatrical; or, to put it bluntly, an ethical soul and an aesthetic one."[36]

Regardless of his intentions, Schlemmer's painting (his theoretical Apollonian side) also featured heavily in his performance. His sets, props, masks, costumes, and the strict mechanical, geometric discipline, not only of the sets but the dance moves themselves, were anything but Dionysian. Indeed, one could argue that these aesthetic representations of the indus-trialized machine age (theatre which resembled a factory production line complete with human robots), in parodying modernity, simply reinforced it. Every aspect of modern technology: lifting gear, optical and reflecting instruments, neon lighting, remote control backdrops, moving stage sets, even an airplane, were employed. The carefully choreographed and designed productions, though having a playful and satirical side, contained neither the overt provocation of the early Futurists or Dadaists, nor their Dionysian orgies of excess. The complex stage designs had more in com-mon with today's Broadway and West End musical extravaganzas than with the cabaret arena.

In 1920, a year after the Bauhaus had opened, Dada arrived in Paris. Having become stale in Zurich, its anarchy required a fresh audience eager to be insulted and provoked, and Paris audiences were not disappointed.

Yet although they participated in the plot of Dada (the demolition of conventional art) it seems that the avant-garde, art-wise Parisians were still shocked and outraged by the totality of that annihilation. One poetry reading turned out to be no more than the text of a cheap newspaper column accompanied by a cacophony of bells and rattles; another audience, lured by a booked appearance of Charlie Chaplin, was harangued by a barrage of insults including a warning that their decaying teeth, ears, and tongues full of sores would be pulled out and their "putrid bones" broken.[37] Events surrounding the demise of Dada set the scene for much of art's development throughout the rest of the twentieth century: the continual undercutting of styles and genres, as new artists subverted old in an attempt to stay fresh and one step ahead of the stale and of ridicule. A furious battle broke out between those who wished to continue presenting Dada and those who declared it dead, viewing its continuance as a betrayal of everything it stood for. Art could never again rest on its laurels. An artistic statement or concept once in the public arena rapidly became passé. In twentieth century art the Cynicism of the ancient Greeks now reaches hyper velocity as cynical artists strive to avoid becoming the cynic's next target.

AVANT-GARDE VS. AVANT-GARDE

No gentlemen art is not in danger —for art no longer exists. It is dead ... it was a beautiful illusion proceeding from a sunny serene feeling towards life (!)—and now nothing elevates us any longer, nothing at all! ... Oh Expressionism, you turning point in the world of romantic falsehood.— *Raoul Hausmann* [38]

In discussing art as cynical, avant-garde will not be presented here in the way it is normally presented by art critics and historians. Hal Foster, for example, describes how the neo-avant-gardists of the 1950s and '60s engaged in a representation of 1910 to '20s Avant-Gardism, this time employing such techniques as collage, assemblage, the readymade, and monochrome painting.[39] Here we are provided with a description of two fixed points in art history that are identifiable by their genre. By employing the label neo-avant-garde we have undermined what avant-garde stood for: challenging, subverting, overturning, and undermining the clichés that former artistic styles and images had come to represent. Approached from an art history perspective, one's view of any avant-garde movement will be shaped by the mindset of the teacher or the student (whether cynic or dogmatist) as to whether avant-garde represents a kick in the pants or a paradigm of high art. It is the paradox of the avant-garde that today's outrageous act of artistic expression will one day be revered and fixed forever as a historical truth, to be learned, studied and respected. Whatever intrinsic value historical artworks might have, cynical artists know instinctively that they must discover and create their own images and ideas and reflect on what is important for *them*. The Dadaist Hugo Ball well understood this need to break continually with the past when he wrote in his diary that "the sceptical artist should enter the flow of the times," destroy in order to build anew, break down handed-down meanings in order to be free to use one's unfettered imagination: unleash the imaginative process in order to "bring those things back to light which have crossed the threshold of consciousness intact."[40]

For the purposes of a discussion on cynicism, it is avant-garde as an ongoing movement rather than as an artistic style that concerns us. In this context, we can regard avant-garde as the cutting edge that defaces the currency of false or defunct ideas, styles, and customs in the world of Western art — the compulsive cynical act of keeping art awake and on its toes. Whether performer, musician, comic, writer, or painter, one can identify the traditionalist from the cynic by observing those who hang onto the past, attempting to enshrine style, form and structure within a recognizable school or genre, as distinct from those who view the annihilation or abandonment of the tried and familiar as the very essence of creativity in art. What artists of all shades must find painful, is any acceptance that the world may have moved on; for to do so is to acknowledge that they have been left behind in the perpetual dance of generations.

After Duchamp had placed his urinal in a gallery and declared it art, the unique concept that an everyday manufactured object could *be* art was used up. Duchamp's original use of the readymade subverted the exchange, exhibition value of art by substituting objects of utility for the purely aesthetic, and likewise, the aesthetic for the practical, for example using a Rembrandt as an ironing board.[41] And while today the exhibition, exchange value of the readymade has equaled that of more traditional art objects, the thousands of art installations employing such everyday objects in the wake of Duchamp's original statement will always have a blunt edge to their message. The cynical genius of Duchamp was the appearance of this abject utensil in a gallery space: the ultimate heresy of defiling the altar of high art.

Cynical art, then, is represented in two complementary ways. It is iconoclastic: rupturing and smashing images and ideas, and it is avant-gardist: creating new images and ideas. If it is to work in this way it must push aside the tired images of its own creations as much as those it identifies as the work of others. Neither should it try to repeat or revisit previous cynical actions. The danger with neos and returns are that the expectations of the original will create the opposite effect from the one intended. For example, the neo-avant-garde institutionalizing the Avant-Garde. Foster criticizes Peter Bürger for romanticizing the historical avant-garde and failing to acknowledge the success of the neo-avant-garde,[42] and yet both Foster *and* Bürger are engaged in fixing these movements as historical genres, overlooking the more important and cynical feature of avant-garde which must always be constantly shifting ahead of itself.

Neither should the continual shifting forward of ideas in art be seen as a forward move toward enlightenment. Such a concept would indicate a final point, the death of art, which although it has been hailed many times continues to be defied. Art simply refuses to die, rising like a phoenix from the ashes left by its latest executioner. At its most acute, this impulsive, headlong drive for the new and the fresh is illustrated in the way that for some artists, an individual artwork becomes dead the moment it has been completed, when the creative process that executed the work itself becomes redundant. Bataille captures this elusive quality of an individual work of art when he tells us that the will to fix the instant in painting or writing can only "evoke" but never "make substantial" that which once appeared:

> This gives rise to a mixture of unhappiness and exultation, of disgust and insolence; nothing seems more miserable and more dead than the stabilized thing, nothing is more desirable than what will soon disappear. But, as he feels what he loves escaping, the painter or writer trembles from the cold of extreme want; vain efforts are expended to create pathways permitting the endless reattainment of that which flees.[43]

We should not, then, look to avant-garde to revolutionize an artistic end-product; that is to miss the point of avant-garde. At its most basic, avant-garde is simply a means of moving art forward and leaving the past behind, in the same way that today's mouthwatering meal becomes tomorrow's excrement. Unlike the production of an art object, such as a painting or sculpture, performance art does not need to concern itself with this problem since it is always immediate, and — unless it is to become theatre — not repeatable. Only the ideas that gave birth to a particular performance can become hackneyed, because there is nothing to gather dust in a museum or to become a saleable commodity. The acknowledgement here, of course, is that the truly cynical performance can never be translated into success as defined by mass sales. Disregarding some early notable collaborative performances, it was Surrealist film and literature, not performance, that went on to achieve the lasting popularity that (perhaps deliberately) eluded Futurism and Dada.

Of course, being shocking or avant-garde is not of itself cynical, at least, not in our positive use of the term. The power to shock and be different are now indispensable strategies for staying ahead in the ever-competitive art market. Damien Hirst became familiar with the general public for his pickled carcasses, yet Hirst knows that he cannot sustain his international artistic reputation unless he continually re-invents himself. Emerging after four years in "hiding," preparing for a major new exhibition in New York, Hirst was quick to ridicule himself, thereby denying others the opportunity: "You know me, I'm the bloke who cuts cows in half." The critics had already been writing Hirst's obituaries ("Whatever happened to Damien Hirst?"), but just as they were writing him off, up he popped again. Yet apart from one or two interesting new works, the exhibition was padded out with much of Hirst's recurring imagery, safe in the knowledge that anything bearing his signature would fetch a good price. Not that one should blame any artist for exploiting a good thing when possible. Hirst was caught between his need to be recognized as a serious artist producing new work, and the huge market that exists for familiar images: the dilemma between producing art or craft. It is not only avant-garde artists, then, who threaten those at the peak of success; it is often their own consumers demanding more of the same. Hirst's most memorable work has become its own metaphor — to become suspended by his public in his own formaldehyde.

KITSCH CHRIST OR CYNICAL IDEALIST?

Regardless of its political and spiritual undertones, not until the work of Joseph Beuys in the 1960s were we to witness a return to the kind of Diogenean posturing associated with the early Dadaists. Beuys may not have been an archetypal cynic, but there was much in his work and his life that warrants his inclusion in this book; not least his inherent distrust of humankind and the use he made of animals in his rhetoric. In one of his early exhibitions, his hair covered in honey and gold leaf, Beuys held a dead hare in his arms. After "letting" the hare touch his paintings and drawings with its paws, he sat on a stool in the corner of the gallery and proceeded to explain to the dead animal the meanings of his works— since "even in death a hare has more sensitivity and instinctive understanding than some men with their stubborn rationality."[44]

Another feature supporting Beuys' characterization as a cynic is that his art was his way of life in the same way that the Cynics lived according to their philosophy. In both his art and his life he sought to excel, presenting us with his own brand of *askesis*. Indeed whole chapters of Beuys' life were performances in their own right. As a radio operator in the *Luftwaffe*, Beuys' Stuka plane was shot down over the Crimea. During his 20-day coma he had imagined that he had been rescued by a tribe of Tartars who had wrapped him in fat and felt to keep him warm. For years Beuys perpetuated the myth that this incident had really occurred (we can never be certain that it had not, such is the mythology surrounding Beuys) and that his survival and recovery at the hands of the Tartars was responsible for a recurring theme in his work: the therapeutic powers of fat and felt.[45] Donald Kuspit considers that the authenticity of Beuys' World War II story is, in any case, irrelevant.[46] It was part of the mythology surrounding Beuys and also part of Beuys' mythology about himself. This view is consistent with the mythology surrounding Diogenes and also with the type of cynical scholarship engaged in by Nietzsche where fact and fiction are intertwined to produce clarity of thought.

Much of the truth about Beuys is more bizarre than the myth. The reason he always wore a hat was to stop the steel plate inserted into his skull (as a result of his plane crash) from overheating in the sun. Kuspit goes on to suggest that Beuys' experience among the Tartars, whether fictional or not, represented Beuys' artistic birth. He took Duchamp's statement about the urinal into another dimension by endowing with mystical properties the otherwise uninspiring materials of fat and felt. The use of animal fat in Beuys' sculptures has been given many interpretations. Andrea Duncan presents the symbolism in Beuys' sculpture as the antithesis of early Christian practices of defying death. Virginity was the closest to the Christian ideal of maleness representing the inviolate whole object. In death, Christians plugged and sealed the body to prevent the escape of its liquid content. In contrast, the Greeks embraced the exchange between life and death, unhindering the "living vital sap" from leaving the body after death; the body ceasing to become a "containing body."[47] In Beuys' fat sculpture we have an art object that is not contained but is free to change form and to decompose in response to the heat of the gallery space.

However interesting such discursive theories might be, from a cynical point of view Beuys' fascination lay in the paradox and the enigma of the man himself. Like Nietzsche, Beuys confounds his critics and admirers alike, the same critic for instance, describing him as, "a bullshit artist of unrivalled ambition and stamina, and dazzling aesthetic refinement," and, "an important figure precisely because we suspect that his myth was pure hokum and yet we readily succumb to its lyricism."[48] The self-creation of the myth in his own lifetime can only reinforce that Beuys was a performance artist of unrivalled brilliance. Cynic he certainly was, yet, like Nietzsche, one could equally claim him for many other camps. His mission to heal mankind also leaves Beuys a strong candidate to be claimed as a Stoic artist. And if Nietzsche has been characterized as an anti-Christ and scapegoated for the Germans' loss of humanity, then Beuys has been cast as a *kistch Christ* and spiritual savior of the Germans' conscience, allowing them to reclaim it.

Beuys became professor of sculpture at the Düsseldorf academy in 1961, then followed a 10-year career distinguished by polemical anti-art attitudes and confrontations with the authorities. He was eventually dismissed from his post in 1971 because, as his associate Johannes Cladders tells us, the director of the academy correctly perceived that Beuys intended to convert the academy into an institute for his own ideology. Beuys was now free to concentrate on his own career as an artist, which included many unique and memorable performances. However, unlike the irony of the Cynics or the Dadaists, Beuys' performances were immersed in conspicuous symbolism and meaning. Regardless of this, the cynicism of Beuys' discourse in its power to shock and disturb the status quo was no less forceful. In 1974 Beuys spent seven days in a cage with a wild coyote performing daily rituals and introducing the animal to man-made objects. This included a fresh copy each day of the *Wall Street Journal* on which the animal urinated. The obvious symbolism of the performance, *I Like America and America Likes Me*, was that for Beuys, America stood for its natural inhabitants and not the legacy of its European colonizers. One can only guess what the coyote might have gained from the experience.

"Social sculpture" was Beuys' contribution to the history of ideas. In keeping with Cynic teaching that humans can influence their destiny and are not innocently carried along by some pre-determined plan, Beuys believed that everyone was potentially an artist or a creative being, and further, that "social sculpture" could mobilize this latent individual creativity to mold the society of the future. In spite of Beuys' idealism, criticism that his work was subjective[49] endears him to the cynical view that what we experience through our senses is the only truth. Beuys' loose organization, the Free University for Creativity and Interdisciplinary Research, was also based on his premise of the power of individual creativity harnessed to a common purpose. In it Beuys sought to create an international network of artists, economists, psychologists and others as an alternative to the traditional closed institutions he viewed as responsible for the corrupt state of society.

BODY ART AND BODY WASTE

It is with some relief that we are now able to leave behind political posturing in art for a more direct, personal statement. If Beuys' work had attempted to stimulate his audiences' awareness of the wider social environment, the work of New York artist Vito Acconi was aimed at making his own body, his physical presence, the center of his art. In *Following Piece* (1969) he simply followed individuals at random, abandoning them when they entered a private space such as a building to follow another. Though Acconi was very much aware of his own part in the performance, he was invisible to his audience, which was totally unaware of its involvement. In another performance entitled *Seed Bed* (1971), Acconi sought to involve his audience more fully. As visitors to the gallery walked over a specially constructed ramp, Acconi could be seen reclined and masturbating below them, setting up an "intimate power play" between artist and public.[50] In his role as beggar, Diogenes may well have been impressed at just how easily Acconi could get his audience to part with money to watch him masturbate. In Diogenes' case (even if like Acconi there was some underlying moral message to his actions) he would at best have been indifferent to his public, and at worst simply out to provoke them.

From the 1960s onwards, body art has provided the kind of abject realism that the Cynics introduced 2,300 years earlier. Though the Cynics may not have presented themselves as artists, their own public performances must have created power-fields between performer and public very similar to those of contemporary body artists. As if providing a critique of Cynic *askesis*, Californian artist Chris Burden surpassed the kind of physical endurance that most people are prepared to tolerate by continually placing himself at the border of his own mortality. In *Shooting Piece* he was shot in the arm by a friend, and in *Dead Man* he was left in the center of a busy Los Angeles boulevard inside a canvas bag.[51]

Whatever might be the stated or implied aim of an artistic performance, one is bound to speculate about the underlying drive of artists who repeatedly seek to mutilate themselves in public. These include artists like Gina Pane, for example, performing self-inflicted cuts to her face and body, or lying on an iron bed over lighted candles;[52] Ulay sewing his mouth shut;[53] or Orlan having her face repeatedly sculpted by plastic surgery while giving a video-taped commentary.[54] Or the work of Marina Abramovic, in which she allowed a room full of spectators to abuse her for six hours using instruments of pain and pleasure left in the gallery space for their convenience, performance that was only brought to an end by a fight between her tormentors after her clothes had been cut from her body with razor blades, her skin slashed, and a loaded gun had been held to her head.[55] Whatever meaning such performances are trying to research: convincing the public that the body is artistic material? investigating the ritualized pain of self-abuse? exploring a relationship with the artist's public? one cannot help but speculate whether the psychological state that the artist realizes by engaging in self-mutilation (or prompting an abusive act by others) is any different from that experienced by the non-artist involved in a similar act. A theme that has not yet been discussed with regard to the Cynics is the energizing effect that Burden claims to have experienced as a result of his near-death exploits. Similar experiences claimed by non-artists who deliberately self-harm may go some way to explaining the use of self-mutilation as a relief from unbearable psychological tension. Discussing Burden's performance *Shoot*, Kathy O'Dell poses the question: "Is such an action 'masochistic' in the popular sense of the term? Does it suggest pleasure in being subjected to pain?"[56] There are many theories as to why people subject their own bodies to pain or mutilation. Renata Salecl puts forward the view that one's body is the only thing left over which the individual still retains power, and that body mutilation is a means of radical individualization in a world where traditional forms of identity are breaking down.[57] Consider Salecl's proposition in the context of Kristeva's thesis on abjection. Discussing Levitical laws that uphold purity and protect humans from defilement, Kristeva writes that:

> The body must bear no trace of its debt to nature: it must be clean and proper in order to be fully symbolic. In order to confirm that it should endure no gash other than that of circumcision, equivalent to sexual separation and/or separation from the mother. Any other mark would be the sign of belonging to the impure, the non-separate, the non-symbolic, the non-holy: ... [and from Leviticus] "Ye shall not make any cuttings in your flesh for the dead nor print any marks upon you."[58]

Giles Deleuze's study of masochism both confirms and goes beyond O'Dell's question when he identifies a "super personal" aspect of masochism. Deleuze likens his "birth of a new Man" to Nietzsche's dream of the *Übermensch*.[59] And just such a metamorphosis, so we are told, Foucault submitted himself to with his sadomasochistic excesses in the San Fransisco clubs and bath houses in the final years before his death. The "creation of new possibilities of pleasure, which people had no idea about previously." A pleasure "so deep, so intense, so overwhelming that I couldn't survive it ... complete total pleasure ... for me, it's related to death."[60]

To what extent, then, may the Cynics' own extremes of corporeal endurance have produced sensations of *physical* as well as psychological well-being? Odd as it seems, to suggest that the ancient Cynics engaged with masochism in its modern sense, the "super personal" outcomes of some modern-day masochists may not be that removed from the Cynics' own transcendence of pain and discomfort. Through their *askesis* the Cynics were able to rise above and outside of the constraints of conventional society; not to mention the insults and abuse they must have received on a frequent basis. In the same way that Foucault discusses finding truth through his involvement with sadomasochistic practices, or certain performance artists find truth through near-death experiences, so the Cynics found truth in their harsh training and way of life. Another uniting feature of self-inflicted pain (whether Cynic *ponos*; the body artist; or those who self-harm in desperation or despair) is the failure of language to articulate the thing being felt — even to help one feel at all. It is an irresistible compulsion to express the unspeakable.

The mind-altering effects of being exposed to danger, either through self-mutilation or death-defying feats such as sky diving or bungee jumping, are well known: that sudden injection of Dionysian abandonment that disorients and jerks the body out its claustrophobic numbness. We may then consider whether the ancient Cynics' willingness to court extreme physical hardship in their way of life, was in some way driven by this physical and psychological high that would have enabled them to feign smug indifference in the face of adversity. Did they enjoy exposing themselves in public? Does the hidden drive of Acconi's exhibitionist performance involve the same perverse pleasure as that experienced by the flasher in the park? On the face of it, the only difference between the two performances would appear to be that the one gets his audience to pay to see his erection, even receiving critical acclaim, and the other gets thrown in jail and labeled a pervert. But there is an essential difference between these two actions, and for many artists the experience can be anything but pleasurable. André Stitt describes his own emotional response to his work: "Every time I perform I'm frightened to death. Afterwards I maintain an initial high, then get terribly depressed. Its exhausting mentally, and my own assimilation of the work only connects months later."[61]

But more importantly, in contrast to the unwilling, trapped spectator in the case of the flasher, the artist's audience is in most cases compliant and free to walk out. In Marina Abramovic's work (described above) O'Dell actually places the balance of responsibility for the limits of the performance on the audience. There is a contract between the performer and the audience in which the audience *allows* the performer to play with danger and self-abuse. By not intervening to prevent harm to the performer the audience is giving tacit agreement for the act to take place.

And, discussing Stitt, Simon Herbert describes a voyeuristic audience of the kind that probably also enjoyed Diogenes' performances: "Whilst watching him eating dog food, wearing a Mickey Mouse hat, or shooting himself in the head with blanks, we are forced to recognize our own emotional bankruptcy, our greed for visceral consumption."[62]

In meeting this need to consume the visceral, Austrian artist Herman Nitsch draws from the Futurist sentiment, "you must paint, as drunkards sing and vomit sounds, noises and smells." In order to engage with the Dionysian, Nitsch's "actions" include ritual animal slaughter, disemboweling animals and pouring buckets of blood and entrails over nude actors. Such ritual performances serve as a reminder of the more brutal and abject side of human nature, a side denied and sanitized not only in aesthetic art, but also in modern religions such as Christianity. O'Dell's interpretation is that Nitsch's destruction of animal carcasses was meant to represent the "pleasurable renewal of the human body through its interaction with the animal world,"[63] work, incidentally, in which we also witness a symbolic return to the kind of ancient religious observances that so fascinated Bataille:

> The Mithraic cult of the sun led to a very widespread religious practice: people stripped in a kind of pit that was covered in a wooden scaffold, on which a priest slashed the throat of a bull; thus they were suddenly doused with hot blood, to the accompaniment of the bull's boisterous struggle and bellowing — a simple way of reaping the moral benefits of the blinding sun. Of course the bull himself is also an image of the sun, but only with his throat slit.[64]

In Nitsch's work, animal carcasses become substitutes for human bodies, because, as Nitsch says, he is denied access to the real thing: "If medical students can perform with human bodies, why not artists?" Nitsch's duty is to the truth in all its visceral gore. His aim, like Bataille's, is to cut through all the uplifting spirituality associated with Christianity and reclaim our gore. The work uses Christian symbolism, such as representations of the crucifixion, to further subvert Christianity's preoccupation with insulating the civilized world from the unclean and the disgusting. We witness this same obsessive denial of the abject in today's cathedral to cleanliness and order — the supermarket. The clinical environment and careful packaging of the supermarket (a denial that it is full of animal carcasses) reinforces the Christian infatuation with the sanitization and sanctification of death which many cynical artists aim to negate: "Many modern artists take us into the territory that disgusts us. They look behind the scenes of our sanitised, packaged lives and face us with the bloody, dirty, smelly reality. For them, rubbish, sex, ageing flesh, slaughter, birth and death are art — reality is art."[65]

This theme, the fragile relationship between our sophisticated egos and the death and decay that our own bodies must ultimately become, unites both the Cynics and these contemporary artists. Through the creation of religious or societal taboos and prohibitions humans have marked themselves out from the abject world of other animals. The Christian practice of plugging the body's orifices following death — the symbolic control of our bodily fluids in death — was discussed earlier. This attempt to reinforce the barrier between our inner and outer worlds is a defiance of our living fragility and a refusal to accept our ever present mortality. In corporeal terms, it is our skin that marks out the border between purity and defilement, and throughout major parts of history what lay beneath our skin was a mystery.

At the turn of this millennium a major row has broken out about the morality of one of the last taboos in art, the use of human corpses in the gallery space. Preserved by his technique of plastination, artist-anatomist Gunther von Hagens puts on public display flayed corpses and body parts that are as fascinating for their aesthetic splendor as they are for their anatomical revelations. "We should not fear what lies beneath the skin" von Hagens says, "we should revel in its magnificence."[66] In a process that takes around one year and costs up to £35,000 per corpse, von Hagens extracts the fluids from the human tissues and replaces them with plastics. "The result is a specimen which is anatomically perfect and identical, except the new necro-body can be bent and stretched like a Barbie doll."[67] Von Hagens' work has provoked considerable controversy, yet he is continuing the established tradition of the artist-anatomist which has continually pushed against strict taboos about the use of dead people and body parts as a form of discourse. Von Hagens differs from his predecessors in that the volume of his operation is on a factory scale, complete with production lines. And whatever artistic pretensions von Hagens may have, he is involved in big business supported by a slick publicity machine. Entrance prices to his exhibitions are far in excess of equivalent museum or gallery fees, reinforcing charges of the commercialization of death.

In spite of their hunger for knowledge, the Greeks had resisted the temptation to dissect the human body (even for the purposes of anatomical research) up until their conquest of Egypt in 280 B.C. The Egyptians had no such qualms. Quick to exploit their dominance in the field of learning, the Greeks established the first school of anatomy (The Temple of the Muses) in Alexandria. Not only did they dissect dead bodies, but they also scoured Alexandria for convicted criminals on which to perform living autopsies. The end of Greek occupation after only 40 years and the subsequent destruction of the anatomy school ensured that previously accepted beliefs about the functioning of the human body persisted. It was not until the Roman amphitheatre that the next opportunity for anatomical research arose. It was also the first manifestation of the showman anatomist; although in the case of Galen of Pergamum (ca. 130 — 200), surgeon to the gladiators, he still had to confine his public anatomy demonstrations to animals.

In Renaissance Italy anatomy and art became finally and gloriously integrated. Like Michelangelo, who is reported to have flayed dead bodies to discover the secrets of anatomy, Leonardo da Vinci, by his own account, dissected more than 30 corpses. As with von Hagens, da Vinci was interested in the emotional as well as the purely scientific effects of anatomy. But it was the Flemish physician Andreas Vesalius (1514 —1564) who came closest to von Hagens in productivity. Performing detailed dissections to record the structure of the human body, Vesalius teamed up with students from the studio of Renaissance artist Titian to illustrate *Fabrica*, the first comprehensive textbook of anatomy. In one painting a weary skeleton leans on a spade, and another sits on a ledge looking melancholy.[68] Von Hagens' *Bodyworks* have taken these Renaissance prototypes much further, both in their anatomical reality and their aesthetic fortitude:

> Von Hagens based his Runner, where the muscles have been splayed out aerodynamically like a fan, on Italian futurist Boccioni's Prototypes of Movement in Space. The Open Drawer model, where the body is prized open in chunks, is based on Anthropomorphic Cupboard by Dali; the Muscle Man, with his skin draped over his arm is based on Bartholomew in the Sistine Chapel; the chess player, bent over the board, brain exposed deep in concentration, on a Cézanne ... the newest addition, Horse and Rider, which looks like it has leapt straight out of the Four Horsemen of the Apocalypse, work brilliantly. Man and beast, stripped of skin and fur merge as a single being. Man is portrayed as animal but nonetheless the greatest of them, holding the horse's brain, tiny in proportion to its body, in one hand and whipping him on with the other. Another piece, a pregnant woman presented reclining in an Ingres-like posture, with stomach open to reveal a five-month-old foetus, seriously pushes the bounds of taste.[69]

In a TV interview, gleefully gamboling around his factory and showing off his latest publicity merchandise such as T-shirts and cuddly toys which unzip to reveal their anatomical contents, von Hagens embraces charges like the disneyfication of death. Beneath von Hagens' delight in upsetting both the art and scientific establishments (not to mention the squeamish general public), and regardless of his commercial exploitation of the dead, an important cynical discourse is taking place. Why are we so anxious about what lies underneath our skin? The faces of the thousands of visitors who flock to von Hagens' exhibitions speak for themselves. Initial disgust quickly gives way to awed fascination. Once the taboo of turning the body inside-out has been breached, what is there after all to be disgusted by? The fragility of our corporeality is a much-needed antidote to human vanity and pretense. Moralistic whining about the dignity of death evaporates in the face of the thousands of requests von Hagens receives from those eager to have their bodies immortalized in plastic. It is typical of human hypocrisy, and the arrogance of science, that we are happy for human corpses to be dissected and pickled in the name of medical research, yet the aesthetic use of corpses is viewed with revulsion. As for countering the charge that some of von Hagens' initial artworks were not aware they would be exhibited in public, one need look no further than the scientific community's own showcase: Egyptian and other mummified remains ripped from their final resting places and displayed in our municipal museums. Scientific interest and the distance of time and culture, it seems, have a soothing effect on our moral conscience.

British artist Stuart Brisley, like von Hagens and Nitsch, is also concerned that the denial of our visceral reality, and of our vomit, blood, feces and other bodily fluids, demeans the wholeness of human experience. Dubbed the "curator of shit" and "anti-hygiene artist," Brisley sculpts and paints using his own excrement. "By hiding our waste, we are hiding who we really are." There is something unnatural, Brisley says, in our disgust of smells, bodily fluids, etc. When sexually aroused we are able to suspend the disgust normally associated with the fluids and functions of the human body; we are able to suspend disgust — to the point of orgasm, at least. We are also able to continue to remain romantically attached to close partners through ageing, even when the same bodily sights, sounds and smells from a stranger would disgust us. Brisley's rhetoric, like Diogenes' and Bataille's, focuses on the denial by human beings of what is natural to their species: a preference for an elevated ideal, that in its artificiality can only lead to dysfunction and disillusionment. However, in the same way that those like Diogenes, Bataille, or Brisley accuse the mass of humankind of an unhealthy obsession in the metaphysical and the supernatural, so cynics whose rhetoric is symbolized by feces run the risk of being dismissed as scatologists.

In another abject performance, Brisley lay for two weeks in a bath filled with black liquid and floating debris in a darkened gallery.[70] Yet it is not the magnitude of the filth that distinguishes Brisley from Diogenes. Regardless of the underlying cynical message, Goldberg claims that many of these performances were humorless and earnest in their serious statements concerning the ills of society. It would be unfair, though, to lay all the blame for this development on the artist. Audiences who frequent art centers and galleries must themselves take some responsibility for the art they consume. If the sometimes tongue-in-cheek work of the artist falls victim to the un-cynical, earnest reception of luvie-spectators, the artist may well simply decide to meet that expectation. Such a development denotes a return to the kind of artistic posturing that the Futurists and Dadaists set out to annihilate; the overtly serious— up its own arse — nature of much performance art during the 1960s and '70s undermining any truly cynical style. We continue to see this self-importance today in the work of Tracy Emin. Melvin Bragg even put it to her in a recent interview that her work was an irony-free zone.[71] Emin's reaction when two Japanese visitors jumped up and down on the installation of her squalid, unmade bed in a gallery space was to be outraged, rearrange the bed back into its (dis)organized state, and ask the gallery owners to sue the transgressors for damaging her art work! Emin is a prime candidate for Diogenes' truth test: exposing her work to ridicule to observe just how much joking around it can take.

The first sign of a re-emergence of Cynicism in art during the second half of the twentieth century was the role of punk in subverting its own youth culture as well as sticking its fingers up to society at large. This was an escape from the high art shown in galleries and a return to popular artistic forms of expression. Music and performance started to blend into a modern version of the anti-art entertainment introduced by the Futurists and Dadaists 50 years earlier: "The mood of many of these [punk art] works was disruptive and cynical. In many ways it came closest to some Futurist performances, in that it rejected establishment values and ideas, claiming art of the future as something completely integrated into life."[72]

The intention to shock, without the overt politics, and with the implicit intention of having a laugh at the expense of its victims, is what gave punk its Diogenean authenticity. However, even punk was to succumb to the now predictable fate of all late twentieth century avant-garde movements— to be subverted by the fashion and music industries, which quickly succeeded in taming it by imitation and mass marketing. Like punk fashion and punk rock, punk art eventually also took itself seriously, and like its early twentieth century predecessors gave in to large-scale performances.

The final revenge on art as a language of protest was ensured by gallery and artist entrepreneurs of the 1980s and '90s, aided and abetted by graphic and media artists who were also finding their feet. A new phenomenon, the "artist celebrity" was born, and, according to Goldberg, a "return to the bourgeois fold."[73] This phenomenon can best be illustrated by comparing our current fetishism with the signifier (brands such as the Nike "swoosh") with the similar branding now attached to art. The consumption of art is matched by artists' need to market their work in new ways. From Wharhol to Hockney to Damien Hirst, the art object, now produced in an art factory, bears no more than the artist's name and concept. It is becoming increasingly difficult to distinguish commercial, appropriated art (e.g., Benneton), from exploitation of the commercial by the real thing. How long before artists' names are listed on the stock exchange as their name value rises and falls? We have yet to witness if today's art schools, so saturated in the ethos of business and the commercial possibilities for art, produce a new generation of cynics. One can only await with interest what form they might take. Oddly, it is television rather than fine artists who are currently spawning cynics. Cartoon shows like the *Simpsons* and *South Park* took us somewhat by surprise, not because we weren't looking in the direction of our TV sets for cynicism — and certainly not at cartoon shows— but because our kids claimed them before we discovered the cynical sub-text that was aimed at us.

6

Contemporary Faces of Cynicism: Action, Laughter and Silence

> Cognitive kynicism is a form of dealing with knowledge, a form of relativization, ironic treatment, application and sublation. It is the answer of the will to live to that which has suffered at the hands of theories and ideologies—partly a spiritual art of survival, partly intellectual resistance, partly satire, partly "critique."— *Peter Sloterdijk*[1]

The formal systems and truth statements one normally encounters in a doctrine were absent in the philosophy of Diogenes; nevertheless, one was able to detect a consistent (largely non-verbal) discourse underscored by the way the Cynic conducted every aspect of his or her life. In contemporary presentations of cynicism there exists no such consistent style of discourse. As we understand it today, cynicism is expressed through many different media and in an infinite variety of styles. And like most other aspects of life today, cynicism has also given itself over to specialisms.

Today we encounter our philosophy within other camps, wearing different faces, and split along different fault lines. The hippie or new age traveler, though adopting the ascetic lifestyle we associate with the Cynics, may also be intensely political or mystical, which the Cynics definitely were not; behind Ivan Illich's biting polemic against the health care industry, is a deeply ideological thinker; and the witty and outrageous social commentary provided by writers such as the creators of *South Park* and *Team America* or Britain's *Ali G*, is subverted and undermined by the media machine that promoted it in the first place. In fact, nothing threatens cynicism more today than success and media over-exposure as evidenced by Cartman key rings and air freshener. In marked contrast to their

Cynic predecessors, contemporary cynics have a short shelf life, as they sell out; get bought out; become hackneyed, clichéd or worn out; or are simply upstaged by newer and more outrageous successors.

Consider for a moment what might occur if we could bring Diogenes back today: we encounter him masturbating and shouting abuse at passersby in one of our city center parks. Leaving aside that Western society is considerably less tolerant today than it was in ancient Athens, and that in all likelihood our hero would be whisked away by the forces of law and order for an urgent psychiatric assessment, how would Diogenes have dealt with being hounded by media attention instead of sticks and insults? Would his cynicism be destroyed by the entertainment value of the spectacle he offered? Could he resist the celebrity status that I and other writers impose on him in the pages of our books? The reader is left here to contemplate the spectacle of Diogenes being interviewed on late-night TV to move on and consider just how today's cynics operate in the media and mercantile driven world we now inhabit.

According to Peter Sloterdijk, "… kynical anti-philosophy possesses three essential media by which intelligence can free itself from 'theory' and discourse: action, laughter, and silence.[2] These three media will form the structure for this chapter, in which some, but by no means all, contemporary cynical modes of discourse will be introduced and discussed. What these cynical devices share in common, be they loud noises or loud silences, is first, that they touch the reader's emotions and imagination in some way to produce a *reaction* (anger, surprise, laughter, outrage, etc.), and second, as a consequence of this reaction, produce some critical thinking. It is also important here to distinguish the cynic from other rebels, those who may employ similar means in order to meet different ends: entertainment, alienation, promotion of a particular sub-culture, or to exhibit an air of cool.

Examining the distinctive styles employed in contemporary expressions of cynicism, it becomes clear that in spite of the obvious differences, there are also many continuities between ancient and contemporary cynics, both in their philosophical standpoint and their overall intention. The links between each of these contemporary modes and ancient Cynicism are discussed here, and some of the current targets of the cynic's scorn are also critiqued. The styles discussed vary from the heavy, serious polemic to the cartoon strip. And although the writers and commentators discussed in the following pages would not necessarily describe *themselves* as cynics, what will be shown here is the way that a particular style, in itself, can amplify and reinforce the cynical message just as much as can the personality invoking it.

As the expectations of a society change, so do its archetypal character heroes, some of the more enduring of whom, such as the doctor, the scientist, the politician, and the priest, have all suffered bad press in recent years, literally as well as metaphorically. In the same way that we create these heroic representatives of society, so too do we create anti-heroic characters. Of these, certain cynical types may well be put forward as candidates: The Dadaists, discussed previously, or their more recent punk cousins come to mind. Yet one person's icon of virtue is another person's villain, and there are certain professions which manage to meet the requirements of both. Of these, the journalist provides a good example, particularly because he or she also contributes to the changing public attitudes of many other characters in public life. Having already dealt to some extent with philosophers, priests, scientists, and artists elsewhere in the book, this chapter shifts its attention to doctors, managers, academics, and journalists. The cynical modes under which these characters of our age will be discussed include the polemic, journalism, parody, satire, and the scholarly critique.

ACTION

> Enlightenment possesses at its core a polemical realism that declares war on appearances.... Truth is not discovered innocently without a struggle, but rather is won in toilsome victory.... The world bursts at the seams with problems, dangers, deceptions, and abysses as soon as the gaze of mistrusting investigation penetrates it.— *Peter Sloterdijk*[3]

In the antics of the Dadaists we witnessed a return of head-on Cynical assault at its vicious best. Not only through the deployment of militant irony did the Dadaists wage their war on banality, but also through the use of unambiguous insults and even physical assaults. There are today other forms of in-your-face cynical combat more commonly deployed than performance art, although not, perhaps, so obviously associated with cynical discourse. Of these, the polemic, the newspaper column, and the film documentary have been singled out, since in each case we find examples of cynicism used in both the negative and positive application of the term. This is problematic when discussing characters like the journalist in particular, to whom the label of *cynicism* (the antipathy of Diogenes' philosophy) is commonly applied. The action in all three cases relies more on hard-hitting words and images than it does on a direct physical engagement with its audience, yet, as with the ancient Cynics and their Dadaist legatees, all rely on promoting controversy and outrage for their main effect.

The Polemicist

As with its Cynic antecedent the diatribe, the dictionary definition of polemic includes "verbal attack." From its root meaning war (*polemus*), the polemic is a sometimes savage, no-holds-barred attack, in which the author attempts to systematically demolish perceived fallacious or exaggerated claims around a particular issue, often a strongly held doctrinal belief. If the polemic is controversial, it is because it sets out to be so. According to Sloterdijk, cynical thinking can arise only when two views of things have become possible: an official, or *veiled* view, and an unofficial, or *naked* view. "In a culture in which one is regularly told lies, one wants to know not merely the truth but the *naked* truth."[4] For Sloterdijk, the polemic always revolves around this conception of the truth as naked truth. But the legitimacy of the polemicist's target is not one of universal, absolute truths. It is to be located in the all-too-human emotions of the author.

It is not my intention here to discuss the polemic in its popularized political context; any political points which arise here should be regarded as secondary to the main discussion. However, a politically sensitive subject does serve well to illustrate the polemical style. Modern health care makes an ideal target for the cynic precisely because society (at least until recent negative publicity such as the murder of his patients by the British doctor, Harold Shipman) still considers health care workers, if not gods or angels, certainly deserving of public admiration. Sloterdijk's "war on appearances" can, therefore, be tested to the full by examining the cynic's case against medicine, an eloquent example of which is provided in the following extract from Ian Kennedy's polemical work, *The Unmasking of Medicine*:

> The nature of modern medicine makes it positively deleterious to the health and well-being of the population. We have been willing participants in allowing the creation of a myth, because it seems to serve our interests to believe that health can be achieved, illness can be vanquished and death postponed until further notice.... Science has destroyed our faith in religion. Reason has challenged our trust in magic. What more appropriate result could there be than the appearance of new magicians and priests wrapped in the cloak of science and reason?[5]

As will be explored further in the final chapter, the new magicians are no longer even doctors. The doctor's role has now been combined with that of the priest and the scientist to create a new hybrid: the therapist — offering God, science and healing all in one package. As with Kennedy's work, Ivan Illich's attack on the medical establishment in *Limits to Medicine: Medical Nemesis, the Expropriation of Health*, is typical of the polemical style and raises issues far beyond the central theme of his book. Perhaps the biggest complement paid to Illich's work is that it so outraged the medical establishment it spawned a counter attack (David F. Horrobin's *Medical Hubris: A Reply to Ivan Illich*) that challenged Illich's original critique point-by-point. As if to underline that polemical truths only represent the truths as seen by the author, here we have two polemics colliding head-on. In order to decipher which polemic is un-cynical, one may apply Diogenes' truth criteria: that which is the most vulnerable to ridicule. It is also the one which supports received wisdom and claims universal, moral authority. Ultimately, of course, any truth, even the cynic's truth, is fair game for cynical treatment.

There is no room in the polemic for reasoned and balanced argument. The assumption is that the subject against which the polemic is aimed amounts to a lie of such proportions, a lie which popular culture has sanctified beyond normal criticism, so that in order to dent its fortified status there is only room to put the opposing case in equal and opposite measure. It is for this reason that the written polemic, like the scholarly critique, may employ some very un-cynical methods to attack its target. In Illich's polemic, he draws heavily on research data to counter other research used to underpin the myth of modern health care. The central theme of Illich's book is *iatrogenesis*, harm caused *by* medical intervention. Illich claims that after more than a century in pursuit of medical utopia, and contrary to current conventional wisdom, it is improved social conditions such as housing and improved nutrition, not medical services, that have been important in producing better health. With *cultural* iatrogenesis we are informed that "the ultimate backlash of hygienic progress ... consists in the paralysis of the healthy responses to suffering, impairment, and death."[6] Cultural iatrogenesis occurs when people accept health management designed on the engineering model and collude with the medics in an attempt to produce something called "better health." *Social* iatrogenesis is obtained when medical bureaucracy creates ill-health by increasing stress and creating dependence. New painful needs are generated by lowering levels of tolerance to discomfort or pain at the same time as the right to self-care is abolished. Third, Illich describes *industrial* iatrogenesis in which the goal of the industrialization of desire and the engineering of corresponding ritual responses has been created:

> Industrial hubris has destroyed the mythical framework of limits to irrational fantasies, has made technical answers to mad dreams seem rational, and has turned the pursuit of destructive values into a conspiracy between purveyor and client.... If the species is to survive the

loss of its traditional myths, it must learn to cope rationally and politically with its envious, greedy, and lazy dreams.[7]

Kennedy concurs with Illich's analysis, warning us not to relinquish responsibility over our own lives to doctors simply because we become ill. Illness he says, wrongly implies a deviation from a normal state, like a machine which malfunctions when it does not perform according to the design.[8] Although biological metaphors are often used in management and industry as though they somehow have a high moral as well as scientific value, it is the reverse metaphor: developing medicine on an industrial, mechanistic model that illuminates most graphically the flaws of medical science. Scientific exactitude and objectivity of the term illness are called into question in the opening paragraph of Kennedy's book when he informs us that in 1974 the American Psychiatric Association decided by a vote that homosexuality was not an illness.[9] Scientific fact, it seems, can be altered not only by further scientific discovery but by changing social views and values. However, one condemns icons of virtue such as doctors or charity workers at one's peril. The polemic attacks not only issues but peoples' underlying values—what they stand for. Polemical attacks can be seen as personally offensive to the sensibility of right-minded people. An extreme example of naked polemical discourse, one that is guaranteed to send a shudder of horror and outrage through those who conscientiously send their donations to good causes, is given in the following example of high cynicism from Jean Baudrillard:

> We have long denounced the capitalistic, economic exploitation of the poverty of the "other half of the world." We must today denounce the moral and sentimental exploitation of that poverty—charity cannibalism being worse than oppressive violence.... Their destitution and our bad conscience are, in effect, all part of the waste-products of history—the main thing is to recycle them to produce a new energy source ... material exploitation is only there to extract that spiritual raw material that is the misery of peoples, which serves as psychological nourishment for the rich countries and media nourishment for our daily lives. Other people's destitution becomes our adventure playground ... we are the consumers of the ever delightful spectacle of poverty and catastrophe, and of the moving spectacle of our own efforts to alleviate it ... when we run out of disasters from elsewhere or when they can no longer be traded like coffee or other commodities, the West will be forced to produce its own catastrophe for itself.... When we have finished sucking out the destiny of others, we shall have to invent one for ourselves.[10]

Yet it would be a mistake to reject or ignore such discourse simply because one finds it uncomfortable. For those who never bother to look behind the veneer, who never question the wisdom of experts, who are seduced by "overwhelming evidence," or who are caught up in feelings of sentimentality, it might take the shock[ing] attack of a polemical discourse to jolt one back to a more enlightened and informed position. However, one has to calculate the risk with gloves-off cynicism that it may reinforce the converted but frighten off or antagonize those yet to be convinced.

As with the scholarly critique, the polemic relies on serious argument rather than ironic ridicule for its cynical attack, and although a certain irony may be detected (as with Baudrillard's example above), it is not used in a way that introduces humor into the text. The polemic, like its distant cousin the diatribe, has a specific target that it seeks to demolish. Furthermore, there is often an emotionally-charged sense of injustice (if sometimes based purely on ideological opposition) at the outrageous stance of its target's position; emotion which may be exposed to the reader, or disguised. Take Norman Finklestein's polemic against the appropriation of a certain period of Jewish history for political and financial profit.[11] One of the criticisms leveled against *The Holocaust Industry* was that it was a rant, lacking in scholarly rigor. But unleashed cynicism *is* a rant: that's what gives the polemic its bite. So if the data contained in the pages of Finkelstein's book felt more like a blast of buckshot than scientific argumentation, then he succeeded as a master of the polemic. That he does not identify himself as a cynic (indeed, he accuses Jewish organizations of a *cynical* manipulation of the Holocaust memory) emphasizes the difficulty today of promoting the term cynic in its positive context.

The main distinction, then, between the scholarly critique (discussed later in this chapter) and the polemic is that the former relies on reasoned argument and academic thoroughness to persuade the reader as to the validity of its thesis, and in the polemic the reader is treated to an all-out frontal attack, demanding that the target be fractured by the sheer force of its assault. Another feature of the polemic is that the anger or outrage felt by the author toward the quarry can be reproduced in the reader. Equally, however, such emotions can backfire on the author as Finklestein's mailbox testifies. The polemicist will have calculated this, inviting controversy: a negative reaction to the skirmish in an ironic attempt to turn up the volume of the debate. In this respect, the polemicist employs strategies also used by the journalist.

The Columnist

> DID THE PRESS OVERKILL DIANA? Were newspapers guilty of hounding the Diana story to death in order to make money for themselves? — *Private Eye*[12]

The Diana as perceived by the public at large, was, with her own connivance, one of the media's most celebrated creations. They gave birth to the myth of the fairy-tale princess, or when it suited them, sad victim of the Windsors or blatant opportunist, whatever suited the moment. But when, just at the point that Diana threatened to undermine the various media images by changing her persona yet again, the icon was salvaged and immortalized in the most spectacular way. Regardless of the finger that pointed at the driver following the inquest report into the fatal crash, no one doubted that the press had played a role in Diana's (the woman's not the icon's) final demise. *Private Eye's* cynical satire had a dual target. One, the gross displays of sentimentality associated with the final tragedy, the other, the negative label of *cynicism* associated with a certain element of the journalistic profession. The term *cynicism*, frequently applied to those hacks who hound celebrities in the hope of snatching a picture of exposed flesh or a story of impropriety, serves to highlight the more common usage of the term today. There are also journalists who display cynicism of another kind: our positive, modern cynics, those who seek to expose the public lies—rather than the private lives—of the rich and powerful. As *cynical* journalists intrude into the lives of the famous simply to titillate a voyeuristic public, so their cynical cousin seeks to expose the great lies with which powerful individuals and organizations hide dirty deals behind a smoke-screen of honest respectability. That is not to say, however, that in the final analysis one type of journalist has a moral lead on the other; both types clearly seek a sensational story. That is the business of journalism.

It was Prince Charles himself, speaking to an audience of newspaper editors in March, 2001, who unwittingly provided us with a potent definition that covers both these types of cynicism. For while Charles clearly intended his comments on cynicism in a disparaging way, his definition could equally be claimed by advocates of positive cynicism: "Cynicism is so often the agent of destruction—the corrosive acid that eats away unseen—and we need to be aware that, like a drug, it is a dangerous substance." Charles was castigating his journalistic audience for the worrying trend in journalism to "blame others when things go wrong." Instead of a culture of complaining, he said, journalists had a responsibility to "celebrate the profound values of our nation."[13] What Prince Charles has clearly failed to grasp is that cynicism (as opposed to *cynicism*) is not a by-product of the whining and disaffected, but a positive and deliberate strategy to eat away and destroy (preferably *seen*) the very celebration of superficial values which Charles believes makes his nation great.

The Monica Lewinski scandal that rocked President Clinton's presidency also involved both journalistic types: the kind of journalism with which we associate royal watchers, as well as the serious investigative journalism of the Watergate type (which placed those journalists at some personal risk). However, the distinction between *cynical* and cynical journalism is becoming increasingly hard to distinguish, particularly those aspects of the profession typified by the foreign or the war correspondent. As Baudrillard put it, our own insatiable appetite for sucking out the destiny of others, our need to exploit the misery of other people in order to provide media nourishment for our daily lives, is proving a serious challenge for the objectivity and integrity of journalists of all persuasions.

The premature death at age 61 of newspaper columnist Auberon Waugh (son of the British writer Evelyn Waugh) in January, 2001, surfaced among many journalists in a feast of columns, reviews and letters either hailing him as a hero or castigating him as a villain. He had made many friends as well as enemies during his controversial career, which included working on such diverse publications as *The Spectator, Private Eye,* the *New Statesman,* the *Sunday* and *Daily Telegraph,* the *Daily Mirror,* and the *Literary Review,* of which he was the editor. Often characterized as right-wing, Waugh was in fact allied to no political interest group, but was fiercely independent and chose his friends from across the political divide. It was a tribute to Waugh's contribution to journalism that his death triggered the bloody battle of words it did between journalists themselves: the Waughite tendency supporting the right to say it how it is, no matter how offensive, and the politically correct, idealist tendency of those who still believe that politicians are fundamentally trying to make the world a better place for us to live in, and how cheap it is of hacks like Waugh to prop up the bar at El Vino's and pour scorn on their efforts.

Waugh's trademark was to say it like it was. Waugh, for example, according to Charles Moore, editor of the *Daily Telegraph,* was the only person outside of the IRA to publicly voice the opinion that he wished Margaret Thatcher had died in the Brighton bombing.[14] This was hardly the sentiment of a right-wing bigot, unless the remark was read as misogynistic, a trait of which Waugh was also accused. The simple formula that made Waugh's journalism so uniquely authentic was that he had the guts and integrity to publish just the kind of heart-felt rant that we shoot off to our pals every night in the pub, uncensored. The following comments (from editors and journalistic colleagues) characterize Waugh as a figure in the mold of American columnist H.L. Mencken: someone who always spoke his own mind and was political hostage to no one:

He greatly disliked morality wherever it came from.— *Charles Moore*[15]

A writer with a talent for vituperation and a taste for vendettas ...
In his idiosyncratic way, he was part of an authentic mood of revulsion
against the bossy authoritarianism from both left and right.— *Geoffrey
Wheatcroft*[16]

The irony is that he was more liberal in his attitudes than many self-
proclaimed liberals. He simply couldn't stand the bossiness of modern
society — one group of self-appointed nannies deciding what the rest
of us can and can't do.— *Henry Porter*[17]

One of the reasons I think he was so good was that he never fell into
the error of thinking that he was influential. In common with all the
best journalists, he knew that what he wrote was here today and gone
tomorrow and that its impact was minimal.— *Richard Ingrams*[18]

By contrast, in Polly Toynbee's obituary to Waugh published in the
Guardian newspaper on January 19, 2001, under the heading "Ghastly
Man," we encounter the kind of scorn that Waugh produced in yet other
journalists. Toynbee's characterization of Waugh, once again, opens up the
debate about who and what is a cynic. Toynbee cast Waugh as a *cynic* in
the negative use of the term:

> The world of Auberon Waugh is a coterie of reactionary fogies ...
> Effete, drunken, snobbish, sneering, racist and sexist, they spit poison
> at anyone vulgar enough to want to improve anything at all. Liberal-
> ism is the archenemy.... While do-nothing conservatism is their mode,
> they enjoy extremism of any complexion and excoriate the dreary toil
> of incremental improvement.... "Political correctness" is the tired, lazy
> little label attached to all change for the better.... Knee-jerk abuse of
> any politician was Waugh's stock in trade when he was a political com-
> mentator. It was not, as he pretended, a badge of some kind of honesty
> but quite the contrary, an idle unwillingness to engage with any politi-
> cian's attempt to make life better for anyone else.[19]

That Waugh was a cynic there can be no doubt. However, when one
contrasts Toynbee's posthumous attack on Waugh with the responses her
own commentary invited, it becomes clear that the *kind* of cynic he was
depends as much on the character of the witness as it does on the character of the accused. You either embrace cynicism or are repelled by it
depending on your appetite for derision. Examine the case for the defense:

> He stood for all the things that attracted me to journalism in the first
> place, all the things Polly Toynbee most disapproves of — long
> lunches and gossip and laughter and a mischievous (yes!), and above
> all irreverent (oh please!) response to pomposity and received opin-
> ion.— *Lynn Barber*[20]

The writer's sense of the absurd would have been equally tickled by
Polly Toynbee's reaction to his demise, last week. Writing in just the

kind of "no laughs please, we're left-wing" manner he despised, Toynbee bludgeoned the dead man from her high horse for — sin of all
sins—poking fun at the ways of the world.... He thrashed bores and
left them lying comatosed in a pool of ridicule.— *Cristina Odone*[21]

There are many left wing people who take things at face value and
many liberals who congratulate themselves on their moral superiority
when all they are doing is restating the bleeding obvious. The earnest-
ness of each of these groups is a signal that they don't really grasp
what's going on. People who live on this level and never travel anywhere else are unlikely to make jokes about plane crashes.... Their
humourlessness is a symptom of their lack of judgment.... "They"—
the enemy—are people whose souls are cold and whose bullet-point
priorities close the window on imagination and genuine freedom of
thought while increasing their own claims to ethical superiority.
— *Charlotte Raven*[22]

Auberon Waugh (despite a certain hedonistic streak) was a journalist of the Diogenes school: fearless, abusive, and witty. Moreover, the
brouhaha following Waugh's death provides a unique opportunity to study
a modern cynic of the Diogenes mold. Not a cynic of Diogenes' stature
perhaps, maybe in the vast scheme of things a fairly jaded cynic. But a
closer examination of Waugh's public performance underscores, once
again, many of the classical features that punctuate our philosophy. Take
the easy labeling of Waugh as a right-wing bigot. Such a response to
Waugh's cynicism exposes its own form of bigotry, a bigotry symbolic of
the kind of superficial objections used against better-known cynics such
as Diogenes, Nietzsche or Mencken. Such flippant characterization is frequently to be encountered among those made uncomfortable or even fearful of the cynic's ridicule. In fact, like his cynic ancestors, Waugh's politics
— if he had any — did not shake out along narrow party lines, being entirely
unpredictable. True cynics find their meaning outside of the narrow preoccupations of partisan politicking. If they stand for anything at all it is
the right to say whatever they want, in whatever way they want, and to
hell with people's sensibilities. In terms of cynical irony, Waugh's disin-
hibited remarks are just the kind of strategy used by the Dadaist, Richard
Huelsenbeck, when he announced that he was in favor of war because
"things have to collide." This is certainly how Charles Moore sees Waugh
when he comments that "as always with him it was done in a comical way
but it was something nobody else would have dared say."[23]

In terms of the discussion here, whether Waugh was a good bloke or
a sneering snob is entirely irrelevant. It is simply a matter of taste and personal opinion best left to those who knew the man well. Toynbee may be
correct that Waugh's humor was probably pub humor, but that does not

diminish its credibility and authority: if anything, it enhances it. Toynbee in her denunciation of Waugh and defense of liberalism attaches herself to the Icarian pose of sincere politics that cynics cannot resist but cast down. Whatever one may feel personally for a cynic, and Waugh may well have presented to some as obnoxious, cannot, and does not, deny the essential role of those who disturb the propaganda of political ideologues from both the left and the right. In fact, among the comments discussing Waugh's personal attributes we are provided with a clue concerning what appears to be a common trait among certain cynics:

> I often wondered about this part of Bron's character. It seemed so odd that a man who hated bullies and vindictiveness was capable of being both. Perhaps it was because he had so little self-pity and assumed that people were as robust as he was…. But surprisingly these [his obvious failings] did not actually include snobbery, racism and sexism. — *Henry Porter*[24]

There is certainly a robustness among cynics, a disregard for the way others perceive them, which makes them appear brutal and uncaring even when the opposite is actually the case. The mistake that most critics of cynicism make is to focus on what the cynic *says* rather than what they *show* when they say it. An easy target for Toynbee was a line from the diary that Waugh wrote in *Private Eye* for 16 years. In a spoof wine column Waugh compared one wine to "a bunch of dead chrysanthemums on the grave of a still-born West Indian baby." Down to the use of the colonial term West Indian — essential to the powerful image evoked by this line — to accuse Waugh of being a racist for conjuring up such an image completely misses its ironic distortion. Of course it's distasteful; that was the whole point!

Focusing on the person rather than on the performance is not the only trap that critics of cynicism fall into. By thinking purely in terms of the politics of left and right, commentators like Toynbee show a complete misunderstanding of what drives their cynical cousins: a basic distrust of *all* politicians. Whatever else Waugh may have been, he was a relentless cynical thorn in the side of liberal timidity and authoritarian morality. As such, he also bore one of the primary hallmarks of the ancient Cynics. What made his journalistic endeavors particularly unusual in today's age of media control was that he was his own person, and spoke on behalf of no one but himself. Contrary, then, to Toynbee's assessment, the *cynicism*, as opposed to cynicism, of journalism today does not emanate from dissidents like Waugh, but rather from those who serve powerful interests, not least their alignment to political interests. It is the Toynbees of this world, not the Waughs, who are the journalists most likely to have a corrupting influence on public opinion. They achieve this by reinforcing the rhetoric: the illusions, oversimplifications and empty slogans of whichever political party currently claims their editorial bias.

The Documentary Film Maker

> Money is abstraction in action. To hell with value, business is business ... wherever private wealth emerges, there is always someone around who assures us he has 'earned' it in the most moral way, by "his own sweat." Only out of resentment could anyone want to find fault with good businessmen.... The cynical function of money reveals itself in its power to entangle higher values in dirty deals.— *Peter Sloterdijk*[25]

In his role as creator and host of BBC's *TV Nation*, Michael Moore is another cynical journalist in the Diogenes mode: larger than life, in your face, breaking convention, and attacking from the outside. He is appropriately characterized on the cover of his second book, *Stupid White Men*, as a blue denim (proletariat uniform) wearing colossus, wielding the sword of truth over a board room table of grey-suited, middle-aged, corporate crooks. Moore's brand of cynicism favors direct action over subtle irony. Political undertones aside, there can be no doubt that Moore is an exemplary practitioner of the parrhesiast's art. Unfortunately, the success of Moore's satirical style of journalism resulted in the TV show's producers packaging Moore's formula in a way that made it a cliché of the original show, devoid of its freshness and cutting edge. The original format was replaced with recognizable and predictable stunts that were now played mainly for laughs. The media has an uncanny talent for spotting original cynics and then creating parodies of their satirical genius. Natural cynics such as Britain's Alexi Sayle and Sacha Baron Cohen (*Ali G*) have seen their fresh originality and annihilating wit undermined with predictable character turns that are played to death, or worse, accompanied by obligatory songs and dancing girls. This scary ability to replace genuine cynicism with bland variety is a theme that will be returned to. Modern cynics, it seems, are less inclined to adopt the ascetic lifestyle of their ancient cousin; finding it hard to resist the rewards that society is prepared to bestow on those who have a marketable talent. Does this make the modern cynic any less cynical? To the extent one is prepared to sell one's cynicism for fame and fortune, probably yes; but then how many of us would turn down a major TV contract for artistic purity? For now, let us return to the unleashed Michael Moore at his cynical best.

Moore started out as a local newspaper reporter in Flint, Michigan, home of General Motors. His 1989 film documentary, *Roger & Me*, set out a distinctive style of journalism that he was to return to and surpass in his 2002 film, *Bowling for Columbine*. The entertainment value of *Roger & Me* came from the spectacle of Moore and his colleagues embarrassing and humiliating some of our top business moguls. Yet underlying the entertainment are some of the most fundamental and important social and ethical issues facing the world of corporate management today. In *Roger & Me*, Moore filmed his search for General Motors chairman Roger Smith. The aim of the film is to invite Smith back to Flint to witness the aftermath — the death of a community —caused by the closure of General Motors plants. Moore, not surprisingly, fails in his mission, although he does get a brief and reluctant word with GM's chairman at the end of the two-hour film. Throughout the rest of the documentary, the audience witnesses the unfolding human tragedy through the individual lives of its participants. There are also some amusing spectacles of embarrassed corporate publicity agents squirming under Moore's relentless, polite and witty interrogation.

The story of Flint was continued in the opening page of Moore's first book, *Downsize This: Random Threats from an Unarmed American*, when he juxtaposed two apparently identical photographic images. One, the aftermath of the 1995 Oklahoma federal building bombing, the other, a demolished General Motors car factory in Flint in 1996. The two images are supported by the caption "What is Terrorism?" The message is clear: is the deliberate massacre of people in the Oklahoma bombing any more terroristic than the human tragedy of broken marriages, suicides, drug and alcohol addiction, poverty, domestic violence, and all of the other human and social disasters that followed in the wake of destroying the local economy of a whole community? For Moore, the human and financial cost of the latter amounts to a pernicious form corporate terrorism that is being repeated all over the world. Moore's charge of corporate terrorism is reinforced in that General Motors' decision to close some Michigan plants did not happen at a time when the company was in difficulties, but at a time when it was making record profits. One might have assumed that its workers would have shared in this success, but 240,000 of them were put out of work in order that GM could relocate to Latin America, where wages were a fraction of those the company paid its Flint workers, and its profits even bigger.[25] There are two observations worth noting here. First, Moore's project was well underway before the mass demonstrations against global capitalism witnessed by many Western capitals at the turn of the millennium. Second, in the wake of the destruction of the World Trade Center and subsequent events of the Iraqi war, Moore's Oklahoma/ Flint analogy had been eclipsed, something Moore would later address in his 2004 movie, *Fahrenheit 9/11*.

But cynicism is at its best when addressing the small story, and in a chapter of *Downsize This*, titled "Why Doesn't GM Sell Crack?" Moore relates a conversation he had with the owner of an American company during a plane trip. Posing the question of how much profit is enough, Moore uses the example that GM's profits the previous year of $7 billion, could be boosted to $7.1 billion by closing another plant in a U.S. town and relocating to Mexico, albeit at the expense of the community. The response he gets is that it is GM's duty to make the extra $0.1 billion. Moore persists, "Why ruin thousands of families for the sake of $0.1 billion? Do you think its *moral*?" The answer: Its not an issue of morality; profit is supreme. "So why doesn't GM sell crack?," Moore responds, to which the baffled executive replies, "Because it's illegal!"

The suggestion that legality be the sole criterion for business ethics invites further analysis. Much has been written on the relationship between ethics and the law, and after the heady days of 1960s' and '70s' liberalism, there is increasing evidence that politicians are attempting once more to legislate for individuals' moral behavior. Cynic thinking on the law has a long history. Diogenes and Crates both questioned the validity of man-made laws, claiming that moral behavior could not be prescribed on the basis of its legality, and in any case, laws varied from one country to another. Moore's example of illegal drugs is a good case in point. In many Islamic states the sale or even consumption of alcohol is punishable by the severest penalties. Yet in many Western countries, where the damage caused to the health of populations by alcohol or tobacco far exceeds that caused by other drugs, their use is not only legitimized but celebrated. It is the hypocrisy of criminalizing one activity while providing respectability to another that produces cynical contempt: the whiskey soaked judge passing moral judgment on the heroine addict.

Moore asks us to remember the American Dream. "If you work hard, and your company prospers, you too shall prosper." It is the lie (and death) of the American Dream which is the serious point exposed by Moore's cynicism. It raises the question of how much longer governments should tolerate (and Moore is not backward in telling us why he thinks they do) clearing up the human and economic waste left behind by large private corporations in their frenzied rush to create more and more personal wealth and power.[27] But as is typical of other cynics, Moore is not proposing any grand solution or Marxist-style revolution. It is the hypocrisy on all sides of the social and political spectrum that he exposes, as evidenced in his chapter titled *Why are Union Leaders so F#!@ing Stupid?* Those who witnessed Moore campaigning for the Democrats in the presidential election of 2004 may be excused for thinking that he had undergone a political conversion. The truth is far more likely that Moore had spotted the ideal platform from which to exploit his ongoing polemic against George W. Bush.

The cynical journalist then, like other cynics, is an apolitical animal; however, he or she is also operating in an arena of high political drama, one in which the political and business stakes are high. In such an arena, as evidenced by Auberon Waugh's obituaries, the cynic's legacy can often survive the cynic. Maybe not as long as Diogenes' legacy has prevailed, but long enough to lay down some lasting images, including the visual images of news footage and photography. The actual image is then added to by the cynic in a way that produces the second, cynical image. The reader is left at this point with the images created by the aftermath of two bombings: Waugh's image of the Brighton bombing and Moore's image of the Oklahoma bombing. Tasteless or inspired depending on one's ability to transcend taboos relating to murder, they demand, and get, a response.

LAUGHTER AND RIDICULE

"He's not the Messiah ... he's a very naughty boy," says Brian's mother, addressing the assembled multitude in Monty Python's spoof film, *The Life of Brian*. Outrage and indignation followed the release of the film in 1979, yet claims that it was a tasteless and offensive attack on Christianity — and Christ in particular — somewhat miss the point of the film. The fact that a hapless bystander (Christ only has a brief passing role in the film) could be mistaken for the Messiah reveals the sheer stupidity of those who unquestioningly accept the words and actions of others as a blueprint by which to order their own lives. However, although the message is clearly cynical, what makes this particular dialogue interesting is the form in which the cynicism is presented. Critique by ridicule is a tradition that can be traced back directly to the Cynics and beyond into carnavalized folklore. The Cynic Menippus of Gadara, through imitations of his work by better known writers such as Lucian, Seneca and William Blake, had a major influence on European satirical literature and other art forms.

Parody and other forms of ridicule

> The most recent, infamous handbook by this Aristotle, *Rhetoric*, is nothing less than a catechism of marketing, a motivational enquiry into what appeals and what doesn't, what's believed and what's rejected. Now you know the irrational stimuli that govern the actions of your fellows, he says, and therefore your fellows are at your mercy. Push their buttons: they are yours.— *Umberto Eco*[28]

Lucian's description of Menippus as "the secret dog who bites as he laughs" captures the essence of Sloterdijk's second essential cynical medium. The point of cynical humor not being laughter for laughter's sake, but, as with other modes of cynicism, a device to lay its target open to unmerciful critical exposure. In order to undermine the academic arrogance and pseudo-intellectual fraud of his own time, the satire of Menippus involved the simple formula of taking the words and philosophic genres of learned sages, and inserting into them incongruous verses, songs and curses to emphasize their absurdity. In Lucian's satire *Dialogues of the Dead*,[29] philosophers and ancient mythical heroes, in spite of their different chronological places in history, meet in Hades to ridicule each other. William Blake turned upside down the moral positions occupied by good and evil, heaven and hell, God and the Devil, to subvert the received notions that attached to these concepts.

In the above 1993 passage from Umberto Eco, we are provided with a modern example of the parodic mixing of historical genres with contemporary concerns. Set in Classical Greece in the style of a Cynic diatribe, Eco's parody simultaneously ridicules Aristotle and modern management psychology. Eco's satirical dig at the genre, the philosopher, and the topic under discussion, provides ample evidence of the multi-layered potential of parody as a conduit for cynical discourse. It is an interesting coincidence that the earliest written mention of the noun *parodia* has been found in Aristotle's *Poetics*.[30] The modern dictionary definition of parody as: "A humorous exaggerated imitation of an author, literary work, style, etc." is considerably expanded in Margaret Rose's text on the subject *Parody: Ancient, Modern, and Postmodern*. Evidence shows that from the earliest times there were two main usages of the form: the purely comical and the critical-ridiculing, although then as now, the humor and the ridicule are often intertwined. Sloterdijk provides a practical example of these dual benefits when he describes Diogenes' truth test: exposing the claims of the serious sciences to ridicule and observing how much joking around they can take. Truth, says Sloterdijk, not only can stand mockery, but is "freshened by any ironic gesture directed at it." Conversely, whatever cannot stand satire is false.[31] Christopher Stone reinforces this strategy when he writes that "... ridicule is society's most effective means of curing inelasticity. It explodes the pompous, corrects the well-meaning eccentric, cools the fanatical, and prevents the incompetent from achieving success. Truth will prevail over it, falsehood will cower under it.[32]

In Eco's parody concerning Aristotle's *Rhetoric* from his book *Misreadings*, he placed modern ideas in an historical setting and genre. In his parody of the Columbus landing from the same book,[33] the event is historical but the medium postmodern, that is to say, postmodern in the context of Baudrillard's thesis of hyper-reality. We are presented with an account of the Columbus landing via the medium of modern TV news reporting. At least two targets are exploited here: the fragility of historical truths and the banality of television newscasting; in particular, the way in which the primary concern of the newscasters is not the momentous event which is taking place but the trivial concerns of themselves and of each other. The vagaries and obsessions of reporters and guest experts often color and alter the facts which we the viewers receive of actual events. Watching the news coverage of the 2003 Iraq War, for example, an alien visitor may well have concluded that the whole event was staged for the benefit of those who were reporting the events. If one needs to increase one's cynicism of news reporting any further, the next time a news item of a war or earthquake disaster is televised, try placing the whole event in the context of an Eco spoof or a Monty Python sketch; not to ridicule the victims of the event, but to highlight the *cynicism* (in its negative context) of those whose business is reporting on other peoples' lives.

"In fourteen hundred and ninety-two Columbus sailed the ocean blue ... and then what?"[34] Like Eco, Julian Barnes pours cynicism on the validity and significance of historical truths in his book *A History of the World in Ten and a Half Chapters*. He draws attention to the historical facts and figures that have been drummed into generations of receptive minds, and stuck there, without anyone knowing what use to make of them in the future:

> And then what? Everyone became wiser? ... Stopped making the old mistakes, or new mistakes, or new versions of old mistakes? (And does history repeat itself, the first time as tragedy, the second time as farce? No, that's too grand, too considered a process. History just burps, and we taste again that raw-onion sandwich it swallowed centuries ago.)
> Dates don't tell the truth. They bawl at us—left, right, left, right, pick 'em up there you miserable shower. They want to make us think we're always progressing, always going forward. But what happened after 1492?[35]

The truth concerning Columbus' voyage is even stranger than Barnes' or Eco's fiction. Five hundred years after Columbus supposedly discovered the New World, a Russian toxicologist accidentally found significant traces of cocaine and nicotine in the tissues of Egyptian mummies.[36] Outraged historians and scientists who had staked their reputations on the irrefutable evidence that Columbus discovered the Americas attempted to discredit the validity of Svetla Balabanova's findings. However, one by one, through repeat studies of their own, most have acknowledged that the only explanation for these findings is that the ancient Egyptians, or others trading with them, were making transoceanic crossings to the Americas thousands of years before Columbus. The purpose of discussing Eco's and

Barnes' work, however, is not to highlight the exploits of the Spanish mariner and explorer, fascinating as they may be. Both writers engage in cynical and iconoclastic treatment of their quarry, and if one analyzes the genres employed, it is noticeable that Eco relies more on parody, whereas Barnes tends more toward satire. Both also apply a liberal dose of irony. To summarize the difference: irony may be said to work with one code concealing two messages; satire, as sending one largely unambiguous message to the reader through a single code; and parody contains at least two codes which are potentially both ironic and satiric. The cynic, of course, has no need of analyzing these terms in a reductionist way; it is enough to get the joke.

Cartoon and Comedy

The *Dilbert* books by Scott Adams have been among management's best selling texts. They are clearly cynical, but being presented as humor, using cartoon characters, this somehow made the cynicism acceptable to a mass audience. As with satire, of which it may be a form, the cartoon is often removed from serious dialogue, which also makes it less threatening to its target. Of course, everyone is able to identify with the seriousness of the underlying message, which is what makes the cartoon humorous: all of life's stereotypes are instantly recognizable. Only context separates comedy from tragedy. Adams opens *The Dilbert Principle* with a self-deprecating dig at management writers themselves: "These days it seems like any idiot with a laptop computer can churn out a business book and make a few bucks. That's certainly what I'm hoping."[37]

Although the presentation is different, like Michael Moore, Adams uses countless real-life examples from people who have written to, or e-mailed him, as the subjects of his work. All of management's dogma and idiosyncrasies are laid bare and exposed to ridicule. Picking up Michael Moore's theme, the first of Adams' *Great Lies of Management* is that "Employees are our most valuable asset!" Further examples of Adams' brand of ridicule are provided below:

> Change is caused by consultants. Then you need consultants to tell you how to handle change. When you're done changing you need consultants to tell you that the environment has changed and you'd better change again.[38]

> Everybody knows that business plans are created after decisions have been made by the executives of your company. Therefore, nobody believes your assumptions anyway. So you're not being unethical when you use ludicrous assumptions, you're just lying to keep your job.[39]

But as Adams points out, no matter how bizarre he makes his jokes, people come back at him with even more bizarre real-life examples. People buy Adams' books and share his humor precisely because they identify with what he is saying. It can come as a relief that someone is making mirth out of a situation that nearly caused you to quit your job. For having experienced so many lies, so much wasted energy, human tragedy, and downright hypocrisy in our workplaces, many of us simply laugh at it, shrug it off, and put up a comic strip on our office wall because, as the dust jacket on Adams' book tells us, "murdering the boss is not an acceptable option."

That is not to say that cartoons always represent harmless fun. Cartoon parodies of sentimental family entertainment figures such as Mickey Mouse, Snow White and Rupert the Bear landed the editors of the satirical magazine *OZ* in court on obscenity charges: "the cartoons of Robert Crumb and S. Clay Wilson [were] designed to shock the bourgeoisie as they had not been shocked since Dada.'[40] The cartoon on which the trial focused from the 1970s' "School Kids" issue of *OZ* was a montage by a 15-year-old schoolboy who had simply super-imposed Rupert's head on a character sporting an erect penis in six frames of a Crumb cartoon, completing the parody with Rupert's famous rhyming couplets. The absurdity of the central charge that the publication was an "obscene article intended to arouse lustful and perverted desires in the minds of young people"[41] lay in the fact that the issue was created by school kids and giggled over by adults. The cartoon as a genre has, in fact, always had a serious adult following, even if, sinisterly of late, the satire and irony is often dropped and replaced by real pornography.

As regards the comic-absurd aspect of cartoon, there is a self-imposed irony in people laughing at a situation when it is externalized while feeling helpless to respond to (even being traumatized by) the same situation when it occurs on a personal level. Britain, in particular, has a reputation for outrageous satire and a willingness to send itself up. Satirical comedy such as *Monty Python* led to a long line of fringe performance that has become rapidly absorbed into mainstream British entertainment. Shocking to begin with (such as *Spitting Image's* latex caricatures of politicians and members of the Royal Family cavorting around, vomiting, fornicating, and hurling abuse at each other), such words and images soon become clichéd and old hat as the shock threshold increases or changes. The human emotions we engage with when enjoying the spectacle of TV satire such as *Spitting Image* have a parallel in the traditional experience of carnival. Both provide merriment by breaking taboos and ridiculing powerful members of society. A major difference is that TV has turned us into passive, armchair heretics, a long way off from the sensuous revelry of carnival. We have become as lazy about the energy we expend on subverting the society in which we live as we have in most other aspects of our lives.

In stark contrast to some American stand-up comics of the late 1950s and early '60s such as Lenny Bruce, Mort Sahl and Dick Gregory — those who were prepared to face not only the censorship of being labeled un-American but even jail for the right to express their cynical views — by the 1990s the pervasive weapon of political correctness had begun to place certain satirical targets off-limits, providing a safe haven for politicians as well as the minority groups whose protection they so patronizingly claimed to represent. Yet their phony discourse has exposed many of today's politicians to an even greater wave of ridicule than their reactionary, brash predecessors. Thankfully there are signs that many younger satirists are not prepared to play by the same rules as their politically motivated older colleagues. Theirs is not an ideological war but a return to good old-fashioned anti-ideology.

The young Jewish actor who played *Ali G* successfully trampled over political correctness by parodying a streetwise black kid in order to escape the conventions of those who are supposed to know better. One is confounded by the reactions of his guests to his ironically naive questions. For although fully aware that he is an actor, and that *they* are being ridiculed, they nevertheless respond to him as though *he* were the fool; even slipping into pidgin English to reinforce their point just in case he really is the buffoon he plays. The surprise is, that for a nation that normally has no problem laughing at itself, the swing of the pendulum toward dour self-consciousness is taking a worryingly long time to make its return journey. And, as though to further frustrate a return to unbridled sarcasm, hard-hitting satire these days is either confined to the fringe, or like *Ali G*, rewarded with the kind of TV show and box office movie success that strips it of its cynical integrity. In any event, British humor has always had a strange relationship with the day-to-day life of the average Brit. The necessary alter-ego which helps to maintain the individual's sanity is being severely tested by the current fashion for taking things seriously.

So how does one reconcile these two sides of the British character and temperament? Is there something about the British psyche that requires a split personality to function: grey-suited businessman by day, football hooligan at the weekend? Are unbridled public displays of mirth or violent behavior a safety valve for a fundamentally repressed private inner character — one who will split their sides laughing at the waiter Manuel being berated by the owner of *Fawlty Towers*, but would rather die than offer a complaint if faced personally with bad hotel service?

Unlike their American cousin (for whom complaining has become a national institution), when it comes down to individual responses, the British penchant for politeness makes a stand against even a gross affront often go unchallenged. On being served in a restaurant with a meal which one would not give to a dog, the average British customer on being asked the (usually rhetorical) question, "Is everything satisfactory, sir?" (they always ask the man), will give the customary reply, "Oh, yes, excellent, thank you," and leave a generous tip into the bargain. Cynicism in Britain is synonymous with being a bit deranged. If you *do* complain about a meal or other service, a look of shocked surprise appears on the face of the waiter or shop assistant, who does not really want to know what you think anyway: "But you're the first person who's ever complained!"; which of course invalidates your complaint, your sanity, and your desirability as a customer all in one go.

It is not out of flippancy that this section concludes with the seemingly trivial example of exposing the fraud of a restaurant meal. If cynicism is to work as a positive strategy, one has to start practicing in small ways, and making a stand against being taken for a sucker, especially when one should be the one calling the shots—paying for a service—would be a relatively safe place to start.

SILENCE: A PLEA FOR
INTELLECTUAL QUIET

> Total Quality Management, Business Process Re-engineering and the rhetoric of "Empowerment" feed the ever-growing need for symbolic novelty within the managerialist scheme of things.... Without penetrating the veneer of managerial concepts, categories and ideologies, management education as a potentially constructive activity will remain impotent as an educational process; unable to liberate thought, extend vision and legitimate novel expressions of the human imagination.— *Robert Chia & Stuart Morgan*[40]

> The hubris of management is to pretend that Fortuna does not exist or that she may be permanently coaxed or placated into servility. Disregarding the chaotic qualities of life or seeking to control them, tame them or "disqualify" them through forecasting, planning and other lawlike techniques amounts to a set of wish-fulfilling illusions, which may in the short run relieve feelings of anxiety and powerlessness, but, if anything, accentuates our long-run vulnerability to it.— *Yiannis Gabriel*[41]

Chapter 1 discussed the way in which Cynicism may unwittingly have helped to pave the way for Christianity through its purging effects on existing faiths and beliefs. This section will look at how cynicism (acknowledging that it refuses to offer alternative doctrines itself) can open up a spiritual void from which new ideas often emerge. The silence that concerns us here is not the type of silence one witnesses in cynical posturing such as that demonstrated by Diogenes and his lamp. This type of silence is cynical *action*. It has the same effect as the noise of a diatribe or a polemical attack: to shock or to create discomfort, forcing the observer from a position of passive indifference to have a view — any view. The silence discussed here, though an effect of cynicism, is not itself inherently cynical. Yet when combined with cynical action or laughter this contemplative silence does form an essential and deliberate part of the cynics' strategy. It forces the audience to provide its own answers, even rephrase its questions — do some critical thinking. It is in this part of the cynical process that an altered perception of the cynics' target becomes possible: a cynical enlightenment. Silence in this context is the antithesis of the meaningless, obfuscating overuse of language as represented by modern day academic discourse with its soothing explanations and answers about the world. The new quasi-scientific discipline of "management," currently one of the most popular areas of study in universities across the world, serves here as an ideal target for the cynic.

The authors of the two passages quoted above are not intentionally operating from the standpoint of the cynic. Even so, their critique, exposing as it does the illusory truths emanating from within their own field of study, does take a cynical stab at academia from within its own domain. Yet what these and other similar critiques are calling for, in spite of the noise they themselves generate, is silence: the need to create a contemplative void inside the deafening roar of answers and explanations about the world. This is the role for which the cynic is ideally suited. Before going on to consider cynical silence, it is first necessary to briefly discuss the way in which the scholarly critique itself may be used as a vehicle for cynicism.

It has been acknowledged that Diogenes despised academics. And, as has also been noted, Nietzsche, Foucault, Baudrillard, and Lyotard all produced treatises denouncing knowledge institutions, even though they delivered their discourse from within those very same institutions. This is not, however, an unreasonable approach, since contemporary cynics no longer need to function, as did their Cynic ancestors, from the outside. Neither do they need to exile themselves to Sloterdijk's lone and lofty perch of world-hating introspection. Today's cynic can work as effectively, if not more effectively, from within the representative structures they seek to criticize as they can from the outside shouting in. The ability to be heard is fundamental for the cynic seeking to effect change from within, and, as most scholars tend to refer to other scholarly texts, cynical scholars will naturally seek to exploit this medium to communicate their message. The downside of much scholarly discourse is that for the most part the readership is confined to other academics, those who share the heavily-coded language and stylistic nuances that exclude others from an understanding of the text. That is not to say that even if most of us *could* de-code scholarly discourse it would all necessarily make sense anyway. My conjecture is that although any critical, thinking person can expose the verbosity or arrogance of academia in a general sense, only the cynical scholar can truly lift the lid on false argument emanating from within academia itself.

And yet there are some clear risks for the scholarly cynic who adopts a cynical stance. Not the charge of treachery that insider cynics may be branded by those within their own profession, for they will have calculated this risk. In playing by the rules of academia, in observing all of those theoretical embellishments, it can sometimes appear that writers are condoning and colluding with the very thing they seek to criticize. Nevertheless, there is a direct motivational link between the original critique of Diogenes and that of the modern scholarly critique. For unlike the use of critique as employed by Kant and Marx (the submission of buried assumptions to public examination), we are provided by Foucault with a concept of critique that represents an attitude or virtue much closer to that of the Cynics: "I would say that critique is the movement by which the subject is given the right to discover the truth [by exercising] an art of voluntary insubordination of thoughtful disobedience."[44]

This meaning of critique is reinforced in Bewes' and Sloterdijk's combined definition of Cynicism as "a strategic mode of thinking, the universally widespread way in which enlightened people see to it that they are not taken for suckers."[45] For Foucault, in order to find truth:

> one had to be ready to *convert* one's self and one's whole way of seeing the world ... rupture with oneself and one's past ... jettison false opinions, evil masters, and old habits. And this entailed not only a kind of ongoing "critique," ... but also an ongoing combat and struggle in which the outcome was ambiguous, reversible, and always uncertain.[46]

The link between the critique of Diogenes and the modern cynical critique can be focused on Sloterdijk's claim that Diogenes' main theoretical achievement consisted in defending reality against the theorists' delusion that they have conceptualized it. What the cynical scholar attempts to do is to challenge theories to be more realistic. And if the cynicism of the scholarly critique is to be found in the sub-text of serious academic argumentation, it is no less cynical for that. The two critiques quoted at the beginning of this section and further discussed below provide not only useful evidence of modern scholarly cynicism but add to the more general debate about cynicism itself. The target of the first of these critiques is the popularizing of critical theory abstracted from its concrete foundations and presented as dogma. In their essay "Educating the Philosopher-Manager," Chia and Morgan call for a shift in management education priorities toward cultivating what they describe as a "negative capability." This concept (in the jargon of academia) involves cultivating a refusal to be seduced by contemporary modes of thought which are a feature of the dominant signifying systems. These grand narrative statements, deceive and disorient our senses, disable critical thought and restrict our vision.[47] Although the style is different — diametrically different from the minimalism of Diogenes— there are direct parallels here between the authors' concept of negative capability, and many of the features of cynicism discussed elsewhere in this book.

The cannibalization of philosophical thought over time has made it impossible to identify the knowledge base on which many contemporary theories are founded, assuming that they have a legitimate knowledge base at all. Chia and Morgan are fully aware of the futility of such a search. They are not proposing here that even if we could discover the philosophical provenance of some of the sillier management theories, that this would necessarily throw any further light on their utility. On the contrary, in order for the philosopher-manager to open up a new vision in the arena of managerial practices, they suggest that we stop systematically sifting through the ossified layers of assumptions, entrenched dogmas, ideologies and traditions which have served to imprison and impoverish thought. Managers must suspend their "haste in wanting to know," and mediate on sensual experiences which would otherwise be lost without trace. We are urged in this critique to engage in some intellectual quietness.

The authors refer to Susan Sontag's claim that in our need to intellectualize and interpret everything around us we have lost the ability to feel. Sontag describes the classical dilemma of our culture: "the hypertrophy of the intellect at the expense of energy and sensual capability, interpretation is the revenge of the intellect upon art ... to interpret is to impoverish, to deplete the world — in order to set up a shadow of meanings."[48] Cynicism is, of course, itself an interpretive process. All of that prodding and poking around, even the ridiculing, is carried out by the cynic with the express purpose of drawing attention to what he or she feels is the lie behind the mask of truth: the cynic's version of the truth, obscured by the deceptive truth of false representation. Interpretation works in (at least) two directions. One involves building up layer upon layer of new interpretation and explanation to stretch a concept so that it fits new audiences or new generations of audiences. The other, cynical form of interpretation, involves exposing the raw motivation that gave birth to a concept or idea in the first place, removing the first type of interpretive layering to reinterpret meaning. Not (meaning) in the uplifting, spiritual sense of finding God, nor in the sense of providing universal laws, but meaning in terms of the underlying reason for any espoused position or stance; even if that includes an ideological belief or simple truth claim. Does green packaging on the supermarket shelf symbolize genuine concern for the environment or the company's desire to increase its market share of the product? It is not the cynic's concern that the outcome may be both. It is the incongruity between the prevailing message and the underlying intent that sparks the cynic's scorn.

Neither is the call for some intellectual quietness itself an anti-interpretive stance. It is one that recognizes the value of engaging with ideas on an emotional rather than an intellectual level. A parallel is the way one seeks to understand music through the sensual effect of its rhythms and tones as opposed to focusing on an analysis of the musical score. Another example can be found in the way many people attempt to record the essential experience of a foreign trip on film; for in the act of filming or photographing, a barrier is created between the individual and the experience they are trying to capture. Such gut feelings have been dismissed in the prevailing fashion for scientific proof and objectivity, the limitations of which we are only just beginning to acknowledge.

One explanation for our need to consume novel management concepts and ideologies is that in times of uncertainty and stress, some of us need to reach for the reassuring comfort of the rituals that management models provide. By engaging in this ritualistic behavior, tinkering around with the superficial aspects of our working environment, the illusion can be created that one is the author of more fundamental change, an illusion that also helps to avoid facing the more complex, difficult or creative decisions that the capricious and chaotic reality of our working life demands. The role of Machiavelli's Fortuna in our working and domestic lives is the theme of Yiannis Gabriel's critique, "The Hubris of Management." Gabriel challenges the presumption among many management scholars and practitioners, "that everything *is, can be* and *must be* predicated, planned for and controlled through the use of scientific knowledge." As well as serving a political and cultural function, in which the power and privilege of managers is legitimized, Gabriel maintains that this myth of control also serves as a "defence against anxiety," a "wish-fulfilling fantasy" for those who prefer self-delusion to dealing with the chaotic reality that most organizations represent.[49]

In the same way that theoretical models are consumed in order to give some false meaning to working lives that are unpredictable and often devoid of (non-financial) rewards, so in a more general sense, our appetite for new goods and services fills the aching void created by the spiritual desolation of modern life.[50] We work, to earn, to consume — to what? Many of us, or at least those of us in a position to choose, could benefit from a cynical re-evaluation of the way we contribute, not only to our workplace environment, but to our own welfare, replacing consumption for consumption's sake with a more satisfying diet aimed at filling that spiritual void. And, for those of us whose spiritual needs cannot be quenched by religion — who regard God as simply another chaos-controlling illusion to make sense of a confusing world — we might turn to our cynicism for spiritual comfort: the comfort of knowing that since the world is chaotic anyway, one might as well make the best of it.

It is necessary at this point to explore further the relationship between the interpretive, noisy role of the cynic, and the anti-interpretive silent role of Chia's and Morgan's philosopher manager. In particular, how the cynic may contribute to creating an environment where silent reflection can take place. The effects of silence on discourse are described in the following passage by Sontag:

> Everyone has experienced how, when punctuated by long silences, words weigh more; they become almost palpable. Or how, when one talks less, one begins feeling more fully one's physical presence in a given space. Silence undermines "bad speech," by which I mean dissociated speech — speech dissociated from the body (and, therefore from feeling), ... Unmoored from the body, speech deteriorates. It becomes false, inane, ignoble, weightless. Silence can inhibit or counteract this tendency, providing a kind of ballast, monitoring and even correcting language when it becomes unauthentic.[51]

The thesis proposed by Chia and Morgan suggests that in order to reflect on what we are being presented, to separate the message from the noise, we need to create more silence in our working environments. Lyotard concurs with this need for silence, advising us to value the intensity of experience and suggesting that, if we are always theorizing about things we cannot enjoy them for their own sake.[52] In Lyotard's view there should be a shift from the dominance of dry, abstract thinking to a greater appreciation of the emotional; that we should move from criticism to hedonistic affirmation.

However, before intellectual quietness can be achieved, some conceptual ground-clearing needs to be undertaken in order to create the right conditions for productive listening to take place.[53] Paradoxically, sometimes the only way to undertake this ground-clearing is by first raising a commotion, the kind of commotion raised by Diogenes which (allegedly) allowed Christianity to flourish, or that raised by Nietzsche, trampling over Christianity, truth, history and science, and helping to set the scene for postmodernism: the kind of noise and tension which makes some silent reflection imperative. This is an ideal role for the cynic. The snag is, that having created some space in which to think, there are always those who cannot bear the silence — silence which can often be felt as tension — and who on viewing the blank canvas of ideas have the irresistible urge to fill it in. This is Gabriel's insecure manager, who without plans and interpretive devices feels nervous and out of control. Any attempt by the cynic to break with the representative structures of the past will increase feelings of insecurity in those tethered to the received wisdom that such structures provide. The perception that the progress of the past has faltered opens up an uncomfortable void. And into the void, restoring order to a world that was once explained by scientific certitude, creeps a new realism represented by a montage of half-baked concepts and ideologies, purloined from any cultural or historical setting and oblivious of their original significance.

For some, this pastiche of knowledge itself provides a welcome blank canvas in the history of ideas; for others, it represents a free-floating grand narrative from which new ideas can be molded. The postmodern world is one in which the signifier has taken over from the signified, in which the gloss on top dominates. The news item, the packaging, the political soundbite, the company mission statement, and the promotional video, now *represent* the product rather than simply *presenting* it. An even more worrying aspect of this postmodern phenomenon is that regardless of consumers' knowledge that the content will not match the promise of the packaging, they consume it anyway. It is a game in which all have become willing participants. Many management models and theories (not to mention new-age therapies which will be explored in the following chapter) are no different in this respect. The fact that they promise everything and deliver little does not dampen the appetite of those whose comfort they seek.

In another paper, "On Paragrammatic Uses of Organizational Theory,"[54] Gabriel develops the proposal that even these nonsensical theories can be made good use of in the right hands. He uses the analogy of the bricolage cook who browses recipe books, not to study their formulaic wisdom but to subvert, abuse, reject, modify, and generally appropriate any ideas that he or she can fashion for his or her own uses. For Gabriel, this opportunistic plundering of ideas is the way that intelligent people relate theory to practice, and practice to theory. They invent "paragrammes" to create real solutions for real problems, rather than turning to those formulaic prescriptions whose promises will always fall short of the task in hand.

That much of today's knowledge is not rooted in critique and debate is a product of a certain acquiescence to, or disengagement from, the constant spin and dogma that daily assault and insult our senses. Furthermore, theories, models, and the whole paraphernalia of the knowledge industry help to create an illusion of order and provide a smokescreen behind which those who cannot cope with chaos and conflict can hide. Modern politics provides us with a good example of this new grand narrative: banality posing as critical dialogue. Like many managers in large organizations, politicians are under increasing pressure to follow a corporate line. Gone seem to be the days when it was accepted, even encouraged, to openly disagree with or have a heated debate with your boss or colleague. Such actions are now regarded as a heretical act of disloyalty. It is a facet of modern political discourse that passion and commitment no longer have a place, precisely because you can disagree with a passionately-held belief. Due to the lack of any real conflict in the public sphere today, modern democracies are hardly democratic at all. Liberal theory has promoted a conception of politics that seeks to eradicate the contest and debate that is the life blood of robust democratic politics.[55] In its place has been substituted a legal and administrative edifice, producing sets of procedures and institutions designed to preserve peace, promote fairness, and achieve consensus. The American presidential election result of 2000 demonstrated that ultimately the preservation of these administrative institutions was more important than trying to figure out the will of the electorate.

The new language of tyranny that so effectively smothers passion and dissent in politics has filtered through to every aspect of our lives. Lyotard emphasizes the constraints that organizations put on conversation.[56] The first way they do this is by interrupting discursive potentials in the communication networks so that there are things that should not be said. The second way is by privileging certain classes of statements, so that there are things which should be said, and ways of saying them. Bureaucratization is the outer limit of this tendency. It is acknowledged by at least one management theorist[57] that "lying through our teeth" has become a widely-encouraged practice in organizations that do not really want to hear the truth anymore. In spite of all the rhetoric about honesty, acknowledging failure has become a dangerous occupation in most organizations. In this context we would do well to remain aware that competence is never an established fact but rather depends on whether or not the statement proposed is considered by one's peers to be of any worth. Things are judged good because they conform to the criteria accepted in one's social circle, and culture is the consensus that makes it possible to distinguish "one who knows" from "one who doesn't."[58] But not everyone can tolerate the stress of functioning in the daily workplace while being expected to use insincere soundbite statements and having to suppress strong emotions. Sooner or later there is likely to be a reaction to the continual emphasis on political correctness or the swearing of allegiance to a company's mission statement that even the company director thinks is bunkum. And, despite all that sloganizing about equal opportunities, everyone knows why the other guy got the job, so next time try a different approach.

Intellectual quietness, as well as Machiavellian *virtu*, is what politics and contemporary management lack: filtering out the noise of all that frantic cerebral activity in order to be able to feel what is going on under our noses. The role of the cynic, whether in the workplace or within our institutions of learning, is to create some space for a re-evaluation of the status quo by casting serious doubt on its validity. As Gabriel reminds us, "Viewing management as a scientific discipline capable of taming the forces of unpredictability and disorder represents one of the chief illusions of the 20th century — an illusion that has sought to supplant the moral discourse of values with a supposedly technical discourse of means.[59]

In response to Gabriel's thesis on the commercial opportunities for the critique, and hence the probable devaluation of critique as critique, the modern cynic is faced with something of a dilemma. How does the cynic avoid his or her own critique from being appropriated to achieve the very goal the cynic was attempting to subvert in the first place? Might we even witness a meltdown of cynicism as its target learns to feed on its criticism for its own aggrandizement?

There is, of course, a greater threat to cynicism than the appropriation of the critique. This is the black hole in the history of ideas discussed earlier. The void of temporary silences created by the much heralded, but difficult to locate, end of modernism, is being filled once more by the inward rush of new ideologies anxious to inherit the ruffled mantel of God, science and philosophy. No matter how important cynical silences may be in the war against dogma, they can never provide but a temporary respite from relentless ideological crusades; of which none are harder to extinguish than those fuelled by that most noxious emotion of all: *sentimentality*. The following chapter discusses the challenge to cynicism represented by victimhood and the therapy culture, a contemporary mode of thinking and acting that exemplifies the very antithesis of cynical reason.

7

Cynical Responses to the 21st Century

> Religious man was born to be saved; psychological man was born to be pleased. The difference was established long ago, when "I believe," the cry of the ascetic, lost precedence to "one feels," the caveat of the therapeutic. And if the therapeutic is to win out, then surely the psychotherapist will be his secular spiritual guide.— *Philip Rieff*[1]

> heightened emotionalism for which there is as yet no adequate name ... is described by phrases such as "confessional culture," "'therapy culture," or more derogatorily as "psychobabble" or the "touchy feely" tendency ... the single most important characteristic of this phenomenon is its belief that the free expression of emotions is essential to mental health ... another characteristic is frequently the conviction that one's self-hood has been damaged by past emotional traumas and repression, and a consequent desire to confess or reveal such events, which has lead to an alternative description as the "victim culture."— *Dick Pountain & David Robins*[2]

Twentieth-century man and woman may have become more cynical about the expectation that medical science will vanquish illness and postpone death. Ian Kennedy's 20-year-old warnings in *The Unmasking of Medicine*, along with similar critiques of the health care industry, may well have contributed to this loss of faith. However, our range of expectations about what can and should be cured has grown, not diminished, over time. We have become more dependent than ever on the power of the healer that medicine helped to promote. Every aspect of our lives, from minor health problems to the direction our bed faces, to the color of our drapes, is now the subject of expert advice and intervention. We have simply transferred our hopes and dreams of deliverance from suffering in a new direction. As with priests and doctors, there is something inherent in the formal ther-

176

apeutic relationship that elevates therapists relative to the persons they designate as the clients. There are only two possibilities: to be the savior or the one in need of being saved; to be one who has seen the light or one still in the dark. Promises of "empowerment" have a seductive appeal, even when it must be obvious that with the ability to bestow power also comes the ability to take power away.

So who is the therapist? Although the therapist has been described as a representative character of our age,[3] it is difficult to come up with a universal definition for this species. The skills and experience necessary to practice in this role can require from seven years' or more formal training as a psychiatrist, psychologist or psychotherapist, to a half-day workshop in neuro-linguistic programming or laughter therapy, or indeed, no training at all. There is no correlation between the length of training and the benefits received. Nothing annoys a psychiatrist more than the patient who, after countless futile therapy sessions, discloses the secrets of his inner self to a visiting student because the one is capable of showing empathy and the other, in spite of training, is a cold fish. Having emphasized the unequal relationship between one who claims the power to heal and one who presents oneself as in need of healing, the counseling profession seems to attract more than its share of dysfunctional characters who often spend as much time *in* therapy as they do delivering it. Being in therapy oneself is compulsory in most psychotherapy schools, thereby ensuring an endless supply of therapy fodder and reinforcing the indispensable role of the therapist. Long-since discredited in the mental health services, the practice of putting peer pressure on people to make fools of themselves or disclose intimate details of their personal lives in front of perfect strangers is now commonly practiced by management trainers and others in the odd belief that it fosters trust, teamwork, or some other equally abstract goal. So what does our willingness to subject ourselves to such treatment tell us about modern man and woman?

If we are looking for a mood in today's world that represents the antithesis of cynicism, it can be found among the increasing numbers of people prepared to identify themselves as victims, not to mention those who are ever eager to exploit victimhood. If cynicism is a strategy for liberating oneself from a hostile world by claiming personal responsibility for one's emotional wellbeing, then victimhood is an attitude to life that involves handing over that responsibility to someone else; it can also be a strategy for blaming others for a lack in some aspect of one's life. No one would deny that there *are* victims: of a disabling disease or accident, of starvation, of an abusive partner or exploitative relationship, of crime, or of an oppressive regime. The main target of cynicism here is not those people for whom dependency on others is an absolute necessity, but the increasing numbers of people who seem to identify with victimhood as a deliberate choice of lifestyle.

GOD IS NOT DEAD

Why does victimhood and therapy culture present a challenge for twenty-first century cynics? Because these new faiths have supplanted the somewhat tarnished canons formally presented by religion and science. The postmodern doctrine expressed by therapy culture is a rag-bag of new values, created from the appropriated fragments of many existing religions, cultural beliefs, and quasi-philosophical and scientific theories. As in Christianity, there is also something fundamentally evangelical at its core. In 1966, in his book *The Power of the Therapeutic*, Philip Rieff was already warning that religiously-inclined therapists were engaged in the absurd task of trying to teach contented people just how discontented they really were.[4] Rieff also pre-announced MacIntyre's description of the therapist as a representative character of our age: "As cultures change, so do the modal types of personality that are their bearers. The kind of man I see emerging, as our culture fades into the next, resembles the kind once called 'spiritual'—because such a man desires to preserve the inherited morality freed from its hard external crust of institutionalized discipline."[5]

We could conclude from this analysis that therapy culture represents a continuation of the Christian tradition, stripped of the features that make that tradition less acceptable in the modern world. This jettisoning of the past may (in some cases) include a belief in the supernatural, but there is little evidence of any willingness to free morality from the new institutionalized laws of which therapists, as the new spiritual leaders, are the enforcers. For example, the abandonment of one's dysfunctional behavior (as defined by the therapist) for more acceptable forms of behavior may determine whether one is allowed to continue with the therapeutic program. Alcoholics Anonymous, one of the longer-established helping organizations, begins its 12-step program with the following acknowledgement: "We admitted we were *powerless* over alcohol — that our lives had become *unmanageable* [my italics]."[6] The two words "powerless" and "unmanageable" already confer a state of dependency, not so much on alcohol as on the agent who *does* have the power to manage the individual's life. Spiritual faith in the program or the healer, a handing over of oneself to a higher power, is often the price expected for a cure. The huge popularity and proliferation of nonsensical new-age therapies testifies to the immense spiritual void that clearly exists in postmodern man and woman.

Although both the priest and the therapist rely on the fear of moral sickness to swell the ranks of their followers, the therapist ensures the added success of his or her church by applying the principles of that other new religion: consumerism. The therapist is very adept at creating the illusion that the client is calling all the shots. This is the force of the market in action, implying that the therapist is simply meeting the needs of a customer. As Gerard Egan observes in *The Skilled Helper*, "The goals of helping must be based on the needs of the clients."[7] *Needs*, of course, are not the things that most people necessarily *want*; they are the things that the therapist determines to be healthy outcomes for the client. The following observation by Rieff highlights this aspect of therapy and at the same time reinforces the claim that therapy culture represents the very antipathy of cynicism: "I doubt that Western men can be persuaded again to the Greek opinion that the secret of happiness is to have as few needs as possible."[8]

CHRISTIANS, JEWS, ARABS AND WOMEN: THE ABUSED AND THE ABUSER

Norman Finkelstein's polemic, *The Holocaust Industry*, forces Jews to reconsider their own position on this issue. Witness the phenomenon recently gaining popularity in Europe and in the United States, "Second Generation Holocaust Survivors." To put it bluntly (and Finkelstein does), as the generation of living survivors of the actual Nazi holocaust[9] is decreasing, their children and grandchildren are eager to inherit the emotional and political capital that has been attached to that event. Those who perished in the Holocaust clearly *were* victims; they were murdered by the Nazis. Those who escaped were also victims;[10] they lost their families, their homes, and were forced to flee their homelands as refugees. That a third generation should choose to cast itself as victims of the Nazi holocaust, particularly those brought up in the safety and security of a comfortable home in the West, is absurd when compared to those who are still suffering real horrors around the world today. Finkelstein's analysis of the Nazi holocaust also highlights how a whole nation or a people can identify with victimhood in a way that insulates them from the normal condemnation meted out by other civilized people when they (the self-proclaimed victims) engage in atrocities against others:

The Holocaust has proven to be an indispensable ideological weapon. Through its deployment, one of the world's most formidable military powers, with a horrendous human rights record, has cast itself as a "victim" state, and the most successful ethnic group in the United States has likewise acquired victim status. Considerable dividends accrue from this specious victimhood — in particular, immunity to criticism, however justified.[11]

That Finkelstein has been branded by some a self-hating Jew is ample testimony to the fact that he has now joined the ranks of other, more famous, cynics such as Diogenes the self-hating Greek, or Nietzsche the self-hating German: those people who bear no allegiance to anything as arbitrary as a country and for whom their race or their nationality is simply a chance event. But before one can be self-hating, one must first be able to identify (positively or negatively) with the object of that hate, and though cynics might not deny their birth heritage they would not affirm their existence by anything as limiting. It is a badge of the cynics that they throw off blind allegiance to any narrowly-defined group, choosing instead to classify themselves in an altogether more epic and humane way, as citizens of the cosmos: cosmopolitans. Again, one has to pose the question: "Just how more civilized has the world become over the last two millennia?" The cynic's home can be anywhere the cynic feels some natural affinity, from the World Wide Web to the global homogeneity of a university campus; wherever he or she feels comfortable in cosmopolitan surroundings. Nostalgia (from *nostos*: a return home) is not so much for a place one has left but an imaginary home one has yet to find; in this context nostalgia and utopia can have the same meaning. For the majority of people, however, it would seem that a physical rather than virtual homeland remains a singularly powerful need. In *Scapegoat: The Jews, Israel, and Women's Liberation*, Andrea Dworkin describes the near sexual desire experienced by some Palestinians to feel the soil of their own land on their bare feet.[12] Cynicism directed at this desire for a physical homeland should always be qualified by an acknowledgement of the unique psychology that is experienced by those who are dispossessed, and that only they can be feel.

The fiercely political, revolutionary, and dogmatic stance taken by Dworkin on behalf of womanhood rules her out as a cynic, yet in other respects Dworkin employs the kind of in-your-face polemical strategy that many cynics can only envy. She is also an accomplished exponent of the diatribe, inviting confrontation as a strategy to hijack her critics. More importantly, for the purposes of the discussion here, she is a victim who rejects victimhood. It is perhaps less important to pigeonhole one-off characters like Dworkin into a genre, than simply acknowledge their contribution to a particular debate. Like her or loathe her, she is hard to ignore, having more in common with Diogenes than many of the contemporary cynics previously referred to. True cynics do not subscribe to any grand narrative, preferring to challenge received wisdom and truth claims. Dworkin, on the other hand, is the author of grand narrative; she exchanges one dogma for another. And although Dworkin's and Finkelstein's assessment of the Holocaust may be markedly different, what both these writers have in common is a powerful and controversial point of view; and a polemical style that ensures their views are not ignored.

Dworkin draws parallels among the fates of Jews, Palestinians, and women, in presenting her own critique on victimhood. She also offers some fairly radical strategies for women to escape the centuries of oppressive treatment that they have endured. Unlike Cixous and those feminists who acknowledge men's femininity, who see the liberation of women in society through a feminization of society as a whole (a loosening of the patriarchal ties that have dominated Western society since the time of Homer), Dworkin seems to advocate not only the masculinization of women but some good old-fashioned revolution into the bargain. She sends out the call to womanhood to see to it that:

> she does not starve or surgically remodel herself; instead she becomes strong and literate in self-defense, aggressive in taking up space and demanding respect. She makes assault against her very expensive through both civil action and the skilled use of violence. She stops being a weak Jew.... She has a right to execute any man who batters, rapes, or prostitutes her or uses her in prostitution. She has the right to organize retaliation ... she has an obligation to defend herself from intrusion, attack, or invasion; she will fight back and she can be counted on to win, whether from strength or from intelligence. She begins to value life by valuing her own.
> Put concretely, women need land and guns or other armament or defense; or women need to organize nonviolently in great masses that grow out of small demonstrations using civil disobedience.... Remember that men are biologically vulnerable: they wear their genitals on the outside of their bodies; it is easier for women to hurt men than men to get inside women — except that women don't want to hurt men and men do want to get inside of women. One must turn this around: men must be more aware of their fragility and vulnerability.[13]

Whether one agrees with Dworkin's politics or not, she makes an important contribution to the study of victimhood. Rather than dismiss her work out of hand because one cannot reconcile oneself with her thesis, it is worth exploring in some detail how Dworkin arrives at the scary (not only for men) conclusion quoted above. One should also be aware that Dworkin herself has repeatedly been the victim of male violence. A major part of Dworkin's text involves page upon page of very graphic — paradoxically almost pornographic — descriptions of the unimaginable, unspeakable, and unthinkable things that men have done to women (and to a lesser extent in the case of the Nazi Holocaust, that men and women have done to men): women having babies ripped out of their bellies or their genitals cut out, gang rapes, beatings and murders, not to mention long-standing practices in certain cultures such as foot binding and female circumcision. Even though an awareness of this human desecration clearly forms an essential basis for Dworkin's arguments, one wonders if it is necessary to devote literally hundreds of pages to such descriptions, many of which are repeated in different chapters of her book. A risk of presenting this endless catalogue of horrors — to distil and concentrate graphic descriptions of the whole of man's inhumanity to women in one sitting — -must be to desensitize or anaesthetize the reader to such images. The predictable clichés one has come to expect from radical feminism are further reinforced by the emotional rhetoric that Dworkin attaches to these events:

> The female fear of men has its roots in men's physical contempt for women, expressed in kidnapping, killing, forced marriage, rape, prostitution, genital mutilation, battery, and imposed separation or segregation. The male fear of women may come from the birth trauma, fear of castration, infantile dependence or the tooth fairy; but it is a fear that is old and big.[14]

Any criticism of Dworkin aside, what she says about the Holocaust poses some fundamental questions concerning victimhood. According to Dworkin, following the Holocaust the stereotypical Jewish man was seen as weak, passive and pacifist: metaphorically and literally castrated.[15] A consequence of this portrait of the effeminate Jewish male, which both fed into the Holocaust and resulted from it, has been to achieve in one generation a complete make-over of the Israeli Jew as the antithesis of his stereotype Yiddish cousin. Following the Holocaust, says Dworkin, Jewish pacifism was dead, "killed by the Nazis along with the six million. There would be no more feminized, gentle Jewish male, no more 'Yid'."[16] Hatred was a necessary ingredient to fuel this process of masculinization, which even though it underpins her own strategy for women's liberation, Dworkin, nevertheless (and in agreement with Finkelstein), criticizes in its effects on Palestinian Arabs:

> The masculinity of Israeli soldiers frankly goes off the charts: normalizing Jewishness has meant normalizing violence — ordered and disciplined ... Israeli virility has changed the meaning of being a Jew so profoundly that the enemies of Israel do it honor.... Israeli men are

admired for being hard, cold, cruel; the stigmatized smartness of the Jewish scholar has been transferred into strategic skill and an unnerving capacity to use force, including torture and assassination, against a perceived enemy.[17]

Israel, according to Dworkin, is nearly an apartheid state, in which the emasculation of Arabs is a necessary price to pay for Jewish men's own castration by the Nazis. And, as though to reinforce the now commonly accepted maxim about victims of abuse becoming the abusers, it is not only the Arabs who are having to pay the price for Jewish men's newfound masculinity: "Wife beating in Israel is ubiquitous ... aggravated by religious law, which makes the husband the sole dispenser of divorce and turns women who leave husbands without divorce into refugees."[18] Dworkin cites an Israeli newspaper report in which 112 women were reported killed by their husbands during one eight-month period in 1998. On her substantive theme of scapegoating, Dworkin draws a parallel between prostitutes and Palestinian Arabs, both of whom provide scapegoats: prostitutes for women and Palestinians for Jews. It is by casting the other in this role, she says, that the one group elevates its own self-worth in comparison to the other. The 'inferior and abject' represented by prostitutes or Palestinians "defines a material bottom beneath which one cannot sink."[19] Without the Palestinians, the Sephardic Jews would be at the bottom of the hierarchical pecking order in Israel; "dominance requires contempt for an inferior."[20]

Dworkin presents a cyclical logic, a resolution to which seems utterly elusive: "Any group or person treated like a woman, feminized, also lacks meaningful sovereignty and is also seen as morally bankrupt."[21] It is surprising then, that although in her conclusion Dworkin advocates the masculinization of women, a rising up of womankind and violent insurrection against their male tormentors, she also acknowledges the cycle of violence that such a strategy inevitably brings. As the Israelis seek revenge for the Holocaust, she tells us, so will the Arabs seek revenge for *their* holocaust. "The claim for moral equivalency is terrifying and wrong; but it is a scream intent to get a hearing ... to reach the consciences of the indifferent."[22] Dworkin was not to know that within a year of publishing her book in 2000, the revenge of Islam would have been exercised in the most spectacular form, and within the very heart of America.

THE ELIMINATION OF SUFFERING

Among the indifferent to the concept of victimhood, and consequently the need for victim retribution, is the cynic notion of cosmopolitanism.

Apart from attempting to stand outside of national, ethnic and religious demarcations, cynicism is neither particularly feminine nor masculine in orientation. The cynic's utopia, if it existed at all, would reject countries, borders, ethnic and religious difference, in favor of a shifting cosmopolitan world where, if cultures and sub-cultures existed at all, they would be based on individual preference and choice. To be fair to Dworkin, reconciling the aspirational differences of men and women is an altogether more elusive goal. Nevertheless, there are those feminists, referred to earlier, who unlike Dworkin, seeking as she does the liberation of women through their masculinization, rather seek to promote the feminine side of humans which has hitherto been suppressed. Corresponding with the more aggressive side of human nature that Dworkin describes, Hélène Cixous acknowledges that humans do seem to gain satisfaction from destructive and auto-destructive behavior. In choosing life, their own survival, people alternatively choose to either kill or to save others. The sad reality is that more often they choose to kill the other.[23] Cixous proposes that the exchange between suffering and joy is not only indispensable but essential to life. One cannot know joy without suffering. This is not the suffering of the victim. The victim's suffering is an abstract suffering: the *claim* to have suffered hurt or injustice which can then be traded as a commodity to buy, among other things, pity, prestige, and compensation. The victim's claim to have suffered is traded for a perpetual state of beatitude, the supreme and blessed preserve of the self-righteous, those who will never know true happiness. "Happiness ... arises out of chance, hazard, accident, events, fortune, the fortuitous. Beatitude is not the height of, but the opposite of this free and gratuitous happiness."[24] This Nietzschean conception of happiness, described here by Henri Birault, and corresponding to Cixous's proposition, has shades of Epicureanism: the crust of bread and a drink of water which provide greater pleasure to one willing to experience the pain of thirst or hunger than does a lavish banquet.[25] The prevailing belief today could not be more different: happiness is to be attained through sound planning, a strong moral code of conduct, and fixed guarantees about the future, whether investment in a pension plan or a deity. Real happiness is always deferred in our preoccupation with managing and predicting our own destiny. Cixous points out that in this way we deprive ourselves of the real secrets of the universe because we no longer know how to let ourselves feel, or even allow ourselves to feel what we feel. "We receive what happens to us with 'received feelings' " and do not profit from it in any way:

> We do not know how to suffer, this perhaps is the worst. It is our
> greatest loss. And we do not know how to enjoy. Suffering and joy
> have the same root. Knowing how to suffer is knowing how to have joy

in suffering. Knowing how to enjoy is knowing how to have such intense joy that it almost becomes suffering. Good suffering.[26]

As Gabriel said, life is capricious; it cannot be planned and controlled. And it is through unexpected and often painful unknown events throwing us off our comfortable and planned course that one rediscovers what one never had: "a strange profit." Such experiences Cixous describes as *entredeux*, those moments when we are not entirely living and not entirely dead, when we are not ourselves, when we witness our otherness. Such moments can be brought about, for instance, by the violent loss of someone who is a part of us, one's house burning down, a grave illness, even the option (if not the right) one has to take one's own life: "everything that makes the course of life interrupted." Sometimes we are the authors of *entredeux*, sometimes not. "We respond straight ahead and think sideways ... we 'take decisions': in a stroke, we come down on one side — we cut out a part of ourself."[27] In suffering, Cixous tells us, "there is a whole maneuver of the unconscious, of the soul, of the body, that makes us come to bear the unbearable." But this maneuver does not lead us to being expropriated; "to not being the victim but rather the subject of the suffering."[28] A new sensation of being is produced by such events. In being ripped from the familiar and the predictable, one is forced to reappraise who and what one is. Freud recognized this profit when he described the secondary function that accompanies illness.[29]

Yet today, the therapist, the counselor, the healer, seek to rob us of the profit we might gain from our own suffering. In their endeavors to understand, explain, predict, manage, rationalize, and expel our suffering, the therapist turns victimhood rather than suffering into a virtue. In ancient Greece the Cynics adopted the deliberate strategy of exposing themselves to pain and hardship all the better to get closer to that joy which Cixous tells us can only be found in equal measure to suffering. The Cynics *trained* to endure suffering, acknowledging the way the world is, and not the way we would like it to be. For the Cynic it was natural and healthy to suffer, to be disillusioned, to question without receiving answers. It was through suffering that the Cynics found the strength to endure life. Not passively as victims, but by owning and employing their suffering in a way that also produced moments of joy. Extreme as the Cynics' strategy might seem, it does serve to highlight the unhelpfulness of presenting suffering (particularly expressions of mental suffering) as something to be avoided, hidden away, cured. Therapy for the mind, whether chemical or psychological, has come to represent that unhappiness is an unacceptable condition, something to be cured. Perhaps there is just too much pressure on modern man and woman to be happy.

To add to Dworkin's catalogue of men's crimes against women, it should be acknowledged that having messed with their minds (as well as their bodies) in the first place, women have suffered the additional indignity of being the main targets and casualties of the therapy industry; and are today also its main proponents:

> So they [men] made death out of us. They invented marriage coun-
> selors. Sex clinics. Sex educators. Psychoanalysts. Psychotherapists.
> Priests in ready-to-wear and haute couture. Leaders in group dynam-
> ics. Inseminators of creativity. Initiators of free expression.... All
> these charlatans of our shared misery. These predators of our
> confinement. These fungi of our despair. And those women. Instead of
> screaming "liars." They screamed "thank you." Instead of screaming
> "enough." They screamed "I'm cured." Those men turned us into dead
> women.— Jeanne Hyvrard[30]

Below, crime writer James Ellroy gives an autobiographical account of his personal investigation into his mother's 38-year-old murder. Here he explores the types of women who responded to his requests for information:

> They were middle aged and in therapy. They defined themselves in
> therapeutic terms. They lived therapy and talked therapy and used
> therapeutic jargon to express their sincere beliefs that their fathers
> really could have killed my mother.... They were victims. They saw
> the world in victim predator terms. They saw me as a victim. They
> wanted to create victim predator families. They wanted to claim me as
> a brother and anoint my mother and their fathers as dysfunctional
> parents.... They were evangelical recruiters. They moved me and
> scared me. I replayed the tapes and nailed the source of my fear. The
> women sounded smug. They were entrenched and content in their vic-
> timhood.[31]

In this work, Ellroy also responds to the therapeutic myth of closure in his own uniquely cynical style: "I wanted to find the fool who invented closure and shove a big closure plaque up his ass."[32] Closure, of course, involves the psycho-therapeutic goal that one can, and should, shut the book on even the most violent traumas in one's life, and move forward, now equipped with a better understanding of oneself as a result: the personalization of the illusory march of progress. The concept of closure reinforces the pseudoscientific myth that in today's enlightened times, it is unnecessary to accept anything as uncivilized as psychological pain; that after a decent period of time we should be ready to delete any disturbing memories, thereby authenticating the efficacy and critical role of the therapist. It is not surprising in the face of all this frenetic activity to put our lives to rights, that among those who fall into the victim role are people in relative positions of power whom one would not normally associate as victims. But then again, we have already discussed ways in which power can be sought by identifying oneself as a victim. In the following critique on victimhood (one that reflects many of Jean-François Lyotard's observations about power in the educational system), Rebecca Stringer claims just that, when she turns her attack on the academic feminist:

> Victim feminism has been breeding in the academy since the late 1970s, ... it reaches the status of an intellectual infection of women's studies departments and is expressed most potently in academic feminist writings on pornography, sex, and rape. A particular victim feminist "type" emerges from their writings. It is the figure of the feminist / intellectual / philosopher / academic who promulgates victim feminism and alone benefits from it.[33]

In the same way that the language of political correctness has seeped into our unconscious, so students of our universities, both male and female, have uncritically absorbed ideas such as victim feminism. Stringer and others are now ready to point to the pay-off of identifying with this on-campus culture: the paradoxical twist that those who associate themselves with powerlessness and oppression are rewarded with power and status within the university.

THE PROFIT AND THE
LANGUAGE OF SUFFERING

A crass feature of victim culture is to be found in current attitudes to charity, which, as Baudrillard suggests, can be used as a means by which those who are better off assuage their guilt and justify the maintenance of their relatively privileged lives by making some token recognition to those who really are victims, at the same time gaining entertainment value from the spectacle.[34] Typical of this unsophisticated behavior is the arrogant oblivion that sending a juggling troupe to Kosovo might seriously irritate brutalized refugees rather than provide them any degree of comfort. Some people seem to have an overwhelming need to appropriate the lives of others as though to compensate for some lack in their own lives; who, unlike the cynic, are uncomfortable with their own solitude. Cixous refers to appropriation as the use and abuse of owning: "even when it seems most innocent it is still totally destructive. Pity is destructive; badly thought out love is destructive; ill-measured understanding is annihilating."[35]

The annual media circus that is Red Nose Day in Britain, whereby the whole country indulges in an orgy of fund raising (stopping traffic and dominating TV) provides a graphic illustration of charity gone mad. As well as providing masses of free publicity for media hungry show business celebrities, Red Nose Day provides an excuse for the sentimental British public to make fools of themselves as only they know how: that strange desire the British have to cross-dress in public, for adults to dress as children or wheel each other around in perambulators, to cover themselves with custard or slime. Only devotees of the *Benny Hill Show* or *Carry On* films, with their delight in the smutty innuendo and pantomime humor, could possibly understand the underlying drive for this strange behavior. This is not carnival but an act of pure infantile regression at the expense of those who are supposedly the beneficiaries of this embarrassing spectacle. The following extract from a satirical performance by Lesley Gannon sums up the arrogance and ill-measured understanding described by Cixous of the Western do-gooder personality:

> NAR[RATOR]: Lydia Allheart was one of the students following the college's Community Theatre modules and has succeeded in carving out a career in this area. We spoke to her in her London offices.
> INT[ERVIEWER]: So, what have you been doing since you were in the show?
> LYD[IA]: Well, I've been terrifically lucky really. I've got to work with some really fantastic people in the community and basically through my work really made a difference to those communities. I always believed that theatre was a very powerful tool, if used correctly and so I started going into communities, identifying problems within them, and used theatre to solve those problems.
> INT: And what sort of problems have you solved
> LYD: Erm, unemployment, drug addiction, homelessness...
> INT: When you say you solved those problems...
> LYD: It's just fantastic to see how grateful the people are. Often they're quite ... common really and they don't properly understand about the arts ...
> INT: And what did you get from this kind of work?
> LYD: Lottery money ... And a real sense of achievement.
> INT: There have been a few problems though I understand ...
> LYD: Oh God, you're going to talk about that thing aren't you.... It was all a terrible mix-up really, I blame the translators myself, you know their English isn't brilliant ... we had arranged, or thought we had arranged to take out a piece of theatre to help the people of this particular village cope with what had been happening to them.... Well when we got there, Christ, I mean we're talking about a war zone remember, they thought we were bringing medical supplies or something and weren't terribly pleased to see us— we put on the play anyway — which was really amazing, performing right there in the thick of

it — tremendous atmosphere, I mean the people loved it, of course they didn't understand a lot of it, but they gave us a tremendous response afterwards. Sadly, because of the mix-up no one seemed to know who was paying us and so regrettably we've had to put it in the hands of our lawyers.[36]

Just in case we should feel deprived between live coverage of actual wars, a BBC radio series in Britain, *From Our Own Correspondent*, features off-duty war correspondents interviewing each other on their courageous exploits. Presented like a parody of a natural history documentary, hushed and earnest voices from the war zone describe the latest scene of carnage, making it clear to the listener that the reporter is doing all he possibly can not to contaminate the battle or disturb the huddled group of crying refugees as he goes about his journalistic business. Just as with the natural history drama, one can only speculate how much of the sound effects (gasps of surprise, excitement and mock dismay) are manufactured in the studio.

The more one studies the phenomena of victim, charity and therapy culture, the more one cannot escape the moral, emotional, and financial profits that attach to them. In *Cool Rules*, Pountain and Robins offer their own explanation concerning the pay-off for victimhood, and although claiming that Cool (like cynicism) represents the antithesis of therapy culture, the authors also point to an interesting link between the two:

> To discover that one is a victim is to make oneself special, to remove oneself from the ranks of the ordinary.... Demanding an equal share of the historical pain of the Holocaust and other great historical tragedies ... pursuit of psychic integrity through suffering ... the great historical injustices of our own childhood mistreatment, becomes elevated to the question of questionable testimony.[37]

The fact that one should feel the need to claim the pain of one's ancestors to make one feel special; feel jealous of the events that gave them fame, underscores the suffocating predictability today of many people's middle class, safe but boring lives. Do we really, as Dadaist Richard Heulsenbeck's ironic pronouncement suggests, *need* wars to make things collide? In considering the kind of general victim mentality that is creeping into the Western psyche and which threatens to disable large numbers of these otherwise intelligent, middle class people, it is helpful to consider the phenomenon of relative deprivation. "We are faced every day" Pountain and Robins tell us, "with images of the richest, most beautiful and most fulfilled people on the planet and compared to them, everyone feels like a loser."[38] What Pountain and Robins fail to emphasize is that most of these images are in any case mythological: the airbrushed lie of the media machine's ever-inventive pallet. And since most of these beautiful fakes spend more time on the therapist's couch than the rest of us, or are frantically trying to buy immortality with plastic surgery and other beautifying treatments, it is also very unlikely that they are truly fulfilled. Relative deprivation is a means by which comparatively affluent people can identify directly with victim culture. Celebrities and those too privileged to claim that they are victims themselves may achieve this state of virtuousness by associating themselves with "good causes."

If one is looking for an external feature of this new culture, then the anxiety produced by today's self-conscious attitude to language provides a useful indicator. This is the way that caring people show that they care and demonstrate their membership in the enlightened species. Such people are so hypersensitive to victim culture, so terrified of victimizing others by a careless slip of the tongue, that speech is often accompanied by an embarrassing display of affirmative signals: inappropriate sugary tones; pregnant pauses; rapid nodding to affirm that one is listening; a shiftiness around the eyes; and fingered "scare" quotes to underscore that a word may have more than one meaning. Those who strain to speak in the voice of victims or survivors also reflect the growing moral elevation and superiority of the victim in society, an inflation of political rhetoric in which it becomes fashionable to identify with, or represent, the underdog.[39]

The new discourse of survivalism is the antipathy of cynical rebellion in one important respect: the deepest injury inflicted by victimization is that it can destroy any sense of personal responsibility, and hence capacity for resistance. It also represents a worrying shift from the way the noncynic has traditionally addressed grievances: the moral agent becomes the passive victim; the political protest the whine of self-pity.[40] And in contrast to the cynic's liberating garb of self-mockery, those who wear the mantle of self-pity are under compulsion to take themselves very seriously. This external humorlessness (not to be confused with the distress of those who *have* suffered) goes with the sinister territory that victimhood engenders.

Morag Shiach in "Millennial Fears" claims that the cultural moment of our millennium is marked by an intensification of fear and circulation of anxieties as it relates to the language our time: "to inhabit a linguistic system is to live in a state of fear."[41] This fear, Shiach says, is further characterized by hazards that are becoming increasingly imperceptible to the victims. And here, it is unnecessary to rehearse for the reader the repertoire of linguistic and non-linguistic devices employed by cynics to ensure that *they* do not become victims of language. Diogenes must have sensed the pathological path that humankind was treading, the dangers of the gap that was stretching open between people's idealistic expectations and their baser human instincts. Over the past two thousand years, in spite of the best efforts of priests, scientists, lawmakers, and now armies of consultants, therapists and counselors, the *physical* appearance of the world may certainly have changed, but all have failed to deliver on human health and happiness. This provides for modern-day cynics a much richer source of data to portray human being's catastrophic record than Diogenes had available. What is more surprising, perhaps, considering the repeated evidence of people's failure to achieve paradise on earth, is that so much effort continues to be invested in false ideologies and beliefs, shunning any cynical revolt. Like Diogenes' own critics, today's purveyors of truth and beauty continue to marginalize modern cynics like Nietzsche and Bataille as curiosities or raving madmen for daring to puncture their empty dreams. And because we are simply unable to carry forward the wisdom some acquire in old age, regardless of our technological advancements, we do not progress as a species emotionally or intellectually. We repeat the same follies as each generation continues to look to the grand narratives of science, religion, politics and philosophy to provide our lives with meaning.

Perhaps the Cynics' revolt against the world parallels, in one respect, the child's eventual revolt from its parents and from the world its parents represent: an acknowledgement that life is cyclical and must be renewed and refreshed if it is to remain vital and human. In this respect, we are *not* our history. On the contrary, our history gives to us the possibility of starting anew, to continually re-invent ourselves. As with Bataille's allegory of the fall of value systems, it is not a stabilizing process in which one system is elevated to replace that which has been cast down. It is rather a continuous process of repetition.[42] Such a vital, cynical force may explain the subtitle in Navia's book, *Antisthenes of Athens: Setting the World Aright,* although whether this was a deliberate mission in a revolutionary sense, or an instinctual reaction against the perceived flaws of mainstream society, remains open to interpretation. Nietzsche understood this irresistible urge; so did the Dadaists, and so do many postmodernist philosophers; except that the latter, in their arrogance, believed they were the first to discover the disintegration of history (perfectly understood by all cynics from Diogenes onward). As Navia writes, "the structure of Cynicism is the obliteration of the structure of the world, on the assumption that ... 'everything that is deserves to perish'."[43] Or, to put it another way, Slavoj Zizek's morbid reality that "every birth marks the beginning of decomposition."[44]

Afterword

Tribute to a Formidable Cynic of Our Age

"True cynics are often the kindest people, for they see the hollowness of life, and from the realization of that hollowness is generated a kind of cosmic pity."
Raymond Federman, The Twofold Vibration

There can be no conclusion to this book. Conclusion, that is, in the sense of a summary thesis on cynicism. Neither do I present the reader with a neat climactic ending or lessons for the future. The use of such devices would be to betray everything that cynicism stands for. What has been written on these pages amounts to no more than one introduction to a little-known philosophy, prompted by the imaginings of one life out of millions of others. As Nietzsche put it, "It is only *my* truth." The real conclusion of this book will never be known except in the exchange between the words on these pages and the thoughts of the individual reader. The most important part of this book for me was the process of writing it and digesting the thoughts of others who had written before me. My greatest wish is that someone else will pick up the torch of cynicism that I have tried to re-kindle and write another book, inspired in part by the pages contained here.

That at least was my intention. Then, just as I was completing the final chapter of this book, I made a remarkable discovery — I stumbled across a real cynic. I had been searching for a living cynic, a real Diogenean cynic, ever since I had started writing the book. But either they were too political or they did not laugh or they were too scholarly or like me they could only *tell* the reader about cynicism. What I was searching for was someone like Diogenes, one of those rare beings who lives his philosophy, someone who could show us what cynicism is rather than simply describe it. I am grateful to Raymond Federman for doing just that.

If Diogenes had sought out his tub as a symbolic gesture for his cynicism, Raymond Federman's cynicism was born from a tub. Or to be more precise, the small upstairs closet in a Paris apartment into which he had been hastily thrust by his mother just before she, his father and his two sisters were rounded up in the *Rafle du Vel d'Hiv'* and taken to Auschwitz to be killed. The 14-year-old boy who hid in the closet started his new life with no more than a small package of his own warm feces wrapped in newspaper (*The Voice in the Closet*). Federman describes being "born voiceless at a hole's edge" on 16th July 1942. But he did not remain voiceless. In his 40-year career as a writer he has never stopped talking.

Sidelined by the literary establishment for daring to revive (in both content and form) the chaos and orgy of Dionysus that once made writing explode the senses, Federman has never attained the celebrity status of other contemporary French philosophers. This is not because he avoids accolades but because he has a stubborn commitment to his art. In *Take It Or Leave It*, the longest cynical rant in history, he refused to allow the publisher to include any page numbers. No single writer of our age has captured the true spirit of Diogenes more than Raymond Federman. No, not even his old friend Samuel Beckett whom he idolizes and quotes at every opportunity. But then Federman was the very first Beckettian. When his Ph.D. board challenged Federman that Beckett was a charlatan, he retorted angrily, "You'll see, Beckett will win the Nobel prize for literature in ten years time"—he predicted the exact year! Federman integrates all of the essential modes of cynical discourse — action, laughter and silence — into his prolific writing. The victim who refuses to see himself as a victim was given in that small closet not only the gift of life, but the gift to make others laugh—laugh at a world that he knows to be truly absurd, laugh at himself, laugh at *The Laugh That Laughs at the Laugh*.

And yet, typical of all great cynics, Federman is before his time. He may not reach the legendary status he deserves until after, as he puts it, he has changed tense. Published in 20 languages, he remains unknown in Britain and sadly overlooked in his host country. But here is a living example of Burkhardt's all-sided-man. Emerging from Federman's fiction are some remarkable facts and near misses, including his exploits as a down-and-out in New York City (and several other cities); as a gambler; as a paratrooper in the 82nd Airborne Division; failing to qualify for the 1948 Olympic swimming team by a tenth of a second; and blowing saxophone with Charlie Parker.

With Federman now living in the sun on his emeritus distinguished professor's pension and promoting wider recognition of his works in numerous new and revised publications, one might question his credentials as a cynic. And yet, with the following line from *To Whom It May Concern*, Federman anticipates the question. "I am caught," he says, "between the desire for fame and the need for oblivion." And herein lies the cynical paradox. If Diogenes had not become a celebrity, surely Alexander would have had no reason to cast him in his shadow; an act which produced the response that assured Diogenes his celebrity status for all time. To give a voice to cynicism we must have some celebrated exponents of the art. Public cynics, like avant-garde artists, cannot avoid the respectability conferred on them with the passing of time. In the very act of achieving recognition, cynics are pulled down from their lofty perch. Federman anticipated this possibility also when as an unpublished writer he wrote to a friend, "I want to shock the bourgeois (before I become one myself) a little."

And so, the reader who has made it to the final pages of this book will after all be subjected to a climactic conclusion. For in Federman's writing can be found first hand (as opposed to my own second-hand accounts) a parallel reference to every theme that I have discussed in the preceding pages. Regrettably only fragments of Federman's diatribes can be reproduced here. His aphorisms speak for themselves, but to fully appreciate the rage and humor of his diatribes, and his absolute *commitment* against the object of his anger and obsession, total immersion is recommended.

CLASSICAL CYNICISM

> he thinks this is the defining act
> the actualization of a central image
> that of a man standing
> on the edge of an abyss
> pissing into a hard wind
> not a mistake not an idle gesture
> but the assertion of presence
> > *Here & Elsewhere*
> > (Macon, GA: Six Gallery Press, 2003)

> I disturb people, I make them uncomfortable, and that is my purpose, and I shall exploit this, to push down their throats what I have to tell them
> > *The Laugh That Laughs at the Laugh*
> > (Edited by Eckhard Gerdes. San Jose,
> > CA: Writers Club, 2002)

RENAISSANCE CYNICISM

in Politics TRUE POLITICS there is no room for sentimentality ... it's all played beyond good and evil and if you are one of
the losers then Bang! it's you who takes it on the head but if
you're on the side of the guys who are winning then it's you who
gives it to the other guy it's just a matter of being on the right
side at the right time and then you're one of those who those
who those who those who those who those who fuck the rest
of humanity who beat the shits out of the other guy with con-
tusive clubs with hammers and nails and electric shocks and
fingers in the ass and needles in the arm and kicks in the belly
and cigarette burns while

> *the rest of humanity continues to vomit its*
> *guts while shouting stupid slogans!*

Therefore you don't think I'm going to take you seriously
because of a little question like that? Politics my friend (yes you
with the mustache) you can shove it up your ass in little cap-
sules (Psitt!) in square round or oval pills (Psitt!) it's delicious
for constipation believe me!

> *Take It or Leave It*
> (Normal, IL: Fiction Collective Two, 1997)

NIETZSCHE

in the dark I sneaked out
of the window and climbed
behind a cloud to look for god
but all I found were my own footprints
Here & Elsewhere

Fuck MODESTY! Scorn and contempt and hatred that's what
one learns from ZSCH damn right scorn and not modesty or
humility or resignation or submission or fear! One must shit
and piss on all human weakness well, gentlemen, I assure you
he shitted and pissed all over it, and this is why he could call
himself without any modesty the FIRST if not the ONLY ONE
to have totally squarely integrally radically and definitely shoved
aside religion morality responsibility and of course the LITTLE
JESUS and his OLD MAN heaven and hell and all the rest

> *Take It or Leave It*

THE POSTMODERN CYNIC

when we fall into the great void
we recede backwards
at the speed of light
towards our origin
so that we can
be launched
again
into the spiral
of our unfinished destiny
Here & Elsewhere

I was sad to see postmodernism disappear before we could
explain it, I kind of liked postmodernism, I was happy in the
postmodern condition, as happy if not happier than the previous condition. I don't remember what that was called but I was
glad to get out of it
Aunt Rachel's Fur
(Tallahassee, FL: Fiction Collective Two, 2001)

THE CYNICAL ARTIST

What determines the degree of completion of a work is not all
the exigencies of art or of truth, it is fatigue, and, even more
so, disgust.... There is no true art without a strong dosage of
banality. The one who uses the unusual in a consistent manner
quickly bores his audience, for nothing is more unbearable than
the uniformity of the exceptional.
Take It or Leave It

ACTION

gentlemen between you and I and without blushing America is
hard to take to swallow hard to conquer because do I dare suggest it America it's a big fat broad that one must seize with one's
arms squeeze passionately a big sexy bitch with enormous teats
a splendid ass and a lovely furry cunt and if you want to possess to explore to search that magnificent bit of geography you
have to go a long way and have the desire and the courage not
only to speak about it but do something about it and the problem with most Americans is that they don't have the guts nor
the initiative to fuck the hell out of their mother land and so
instead of really trying to shove their dicks into it they justify
their cowardice by simply dropping their pants in front of it

and jerk off like a bunch of kids where in fact me gentlemen I
wanted to penetrate that mother land yes I wanted to explode
to burst inside her ass and inside her cunt I wanted my sperm
to flow between her gorgeous cheeks one good time and that's
why I decided to love it to love it without shame
Take It or Leave It

LAUGHTER

Seriousness is a quality for those who have no other qualities.
Smiles on Washington Square
(Los Angeles: Sun and Moon, 1985)

Ah the laughing act: doesn't work for you guys because you
guys laugh Japanese style delicately with your hands in front of
your mouth as if you were coughing! What the hell you guys
think that laughter is some kind of sickness?
Take It or Leave It

SILENCE

It was not going very well already in the kingdom of literature
since le nouveau roman that great triumph of sing-my-ass we
were going quite copiously robbe-grilladized semiotized in full
from salsify to chinese lanterns but now we are truly moving
tumbling into shit here we are fallen crestfallen to the under-
level of undersollersism into the invertebrate desensibilized by
barthist analism zerofied offhandedly materialized getting closer
to objects and facts than causes emasculated scientifically by
shameless daily gossiping superjerking scenarios moving now
towards the immense the endless organic debacle towards the
great deluge of low-down tricks the crashup of confusionism
masturbatory telquelism drifting on the lacanian raft derrid-
ian barge shipwrecked in other words on the sea of fucked up
literature where civilization can be measured assessed rather by
the distance man places between himself and his excrement
Take It or Leave It

That's the problem with talking too much. Eventually you reveal
yourself. But when you don't talk you become a suspiciously
suspicious character.
Double or Nothing
(Normal, IL: Fiction Collective Two, 1998)

Therapy Culture

This fucking world is saturated with false hopes ... we are
drowning in a cesspool of theosophical emanations, cosmic
influences, occult powers, spiritual visitations, stellar vibrations
and divine farts, and yes yes it's all shit, de la merde molle et
fumante, do you hear me, de la saloperie, de la crasse
> *The Twofold Vibration*
> (Los Angeles: Green Integer, 2000)

AND FINALLY

We all live like cockroaches in the crevices of our twisted imagination
> *Smiles on Washington Square*

One suffers and one suffers from not suffering enough
> *The Twofold Vibration*

having oscillated all my life
between the torments
of superficial idleness
and the horror
of disinterested action
I find myself at last
in a situation
where to do nothing
exclusively
becomes an act of
the highest value
> *Here & Elsewhere*

Notes

Chapter 1

1. Luis E. Navia, *Classical Cynicism: A Critical Study* (Westport, CT: Greenwood Press, 1996), 29.

2. A. J. Malherbe, *The Cynic Epistles* (Atlanta: Scholars Press), 1977.

3. Navia, *Classical Cynicism,* 21.

4. Eduard Zeller, *Outlines of the History of Greek Philosophy* (New York: Dover Publications, 1980), 75–78.

5. Navia, *Classical Cynicism,* 51–52.

6. Ibid., 15–16.

7. Ibid., 16.

8. Ibid.

9. Ibid., 19.

10. Luis E. Navia, *Antisthenes of Athens: Setting the World Aright* (Westport, CT: Greenwood Press, 2001), 91.

11. Navia, *Classical Cynicism,* 8.

12. R. Bracht Branham, Introduction to R. Bracht Branham & Marie-Odile Goulet Caze (eds.), *The Cynics: The Cynic Movement in Antiquity and Its Legacy* (Berkeley: University of California Press, 1996), 8–10.

13. Martha C. Nussbaum, *The Therapy of Desire* (Princeton, NJ: Princeton University Press, 1994), 8.

14. R.W. Sharples, *Stoics, Epicureans and Sceptics* (London: Routledge, 1996).

15. Navia, *Classical Cynicism.*

16. Luis E. Navia, *Diogenes of Sinope: The Man in the Tub* (Westport, CT: Greenwood Press, 1998), 47.

17. See: D. R. Dudley, *A History of Cynicism: From Diogenes to the 6th Century AD* (London: Methuen & Co. Ltd., 1937) 146; Marcel Schwob, *King in the Golden Mask and Other Stories* (Manchester: Carcanet New Press, 1982), 129; Navia, *Classical Cynicism,* 14.

18. Dudley, 15.

19. Navia, *Diogenes,* 89.

20. Navia, *Classical Cynicism,* 10.

21. Simon Blackburn, *Oxford Dictionary of Philosophy* (Oxford: Oxford University Press, 1996), 410. The dates attributed to Diogenes in the table are from sources other than Blackburn. There is no absolute agreement on Diogenes' date of birth, but more agreement as to the date of his death: the same year (some accounts say the same day) as Alexander, 323 B.C. Given the various accounts of Diogenes living to 80 or 90 years of age, together with firm evidence that he was involved in a currency scandal in Sinope in the year 396, make even the birth date of 404 B.C. seem too late (Blackburn gives c. 400–325). Navia suggests in *Classical Cynicism* that in order for Diogenes to have met Antisthenes, and to have been old enough to have been involved in the currency scandal of 396, we should push the date of his birth back to at least 413.

22. Dudley, 95.

23. Ibid., 143.

24. Ibid., 124.

25. Ibid.

26. Sharples, 11.

27. Navia, *Classical Cynicism,* 58–59.

28. Dudley, 103.

29. Navia, *Classical Cynicism,* 70.

30. Dudley, 104.

31. Zeller, 112–115.

32. R. J. Hankinson, *The Sceptics* (London: Routledge, 1995), 4.

33. Sharples, 9.

34. Dudley, 118.

35. Sharples, 30–31.

36. Ibid., 113.

37. Ibid., 56.

38. Ibid., 85.

39. Ibid., 127.

40. Zeller, 210–212.

41. Nussbaum, 316.

42. Ibid., 319.

43. Sharples, 126.

44. Farrand Sayre, *Diogenes of Synope: A Study of Greek Cynicism* (Baltimore: J.H.Furst, 1938), 27.

45. Ibid., 24.

46. Diogenes Laertius, *Lives of Eminent Philosophers,* vol. 2 (Cambridge, MA: Harvard University Press, 1995), 25.

47. Dudley, 66.

48. Gerald F. Downing, *Cynics and Christian Origins* (Edinburgh: T&T Clark, 1992), 30.

49. Diogenes Laertius, cit. Dudley, 30.

50. R. Bracht Branham, "Defacing the Currency: Diogenes' Rhetoric and the Invention of Cynicism," in R. Bracht Branham and Marie-Odile Goulet-Caze (eds.), *The Cynic Movement in Antiquity and Its Legacy* (Berkeley: University of California Press, 1996), 98–99.

51. Derek Krueger, "The Bawdy and Society," in R. Bracht Branham and Marie-Odile Goulet-Caze (eds.), 234.

52. Dudley, 180. Also note that the precise means of Diogenes' own death is left to symbolic fiction, the one consistent "fact" seeming to be that he was on his way to the Olympic games when his death occurred. Some stories have it, that in imitating animals to the end, he ate raw squid or octopus. Another version has him bitten by a dog while fighting with it over the octopus. There are other even more fanciful stories, but all of these simply add the Cynic's reputation as an absurd figure, and detract from his serious contribution to the philosophy of life.

53. Krueger, 236.

54. Julia Kristeva, *Powers of Horror: An Essay on Abjection* (New York: Columbia University Press, 1982), 2–3.

55. Samuel Beckett, *The Expelled and Other Novellas* (London: Penguin, 1973), 79–91.

56. Peter Sloterdijk, *Critique of Cynical Reason* (London: Verso, 1988), 151.

57. Kristeva, 4, makes a further distinction: between amorality, which flaunts man-made laws for a "higher" purpose, and immorality, which fragments the borders between humanity and inhumanity. However, having made this distinction, Kristeva fails to discuss the subjectivity that inevitably exists between these two positions. The view, for example, that one person's freedom fighter can be another person's terrorist; the distinction between a just war in which society confers honors for the taking of human life in the pursuit of a higher ideal, and those who have indulged in barbarity and murder. The Cynics, who rejected man-made laws and prevailing moral codes, would for the most part have stood outside of moral categories such as good/evil, pure/impure, sacred/profane, religious/pagan — those things which produce in most of us the potential for guilt and sin.

58. Kristeva, 56.

59. Dudley, 22.

60. Navia, *Antisthenes,* 92.

61. Dudley, 36.

62. Plato, *The Republic* (Harmondsworth: Penguin, 1955), 209.

63. Aristotle, *Politics, Books I & II* (Oxford: Clarendon Press, 1999), 134.

64. Dudley, 36–37.

65. Navia, *Diogenes,* 27.

66. Marcel Schwob, *The King in the Golden Mask and Other Stories* (Manchester: Carcanet New Press, 1982), 128–130.

67. Dudley, 174.

68. Malherbe, 213.

69. Downing, 302.

70. Sayre, 24.

71. Navia, *Classical Cynicism,* 85.

72. Ibid., 96.

73. Navia, *Diogenes,* 109.

74. Navia, *Diogenes,* 109.

75. Dudley, 28.

76. Sayre, 17.

77. Ibid., 13.

78. Laertius, *Lives,* vol. 2, 41.

79. Dio Chrysostom, *Discourses 1–11,* Loeb Classical Library (Cambridge MA: Harvard University Press, 1961), 177.

80. Ibid., 169–233. Dio Chrysostom (c. A.D. 40–120) was a Roman intellectual of Greek descent, Stoic, and sometime Cynic. His version of the Diogenes/ Alexander story is given in his *The Fourth Discourse on Kingship.*

81. Michel Foucault , *Fearless Speech* (Los Angeles: Semiotext(e), 2001), 12.

82. Ibid., 18–19.

83. Ibid., 110–111.

84. Sayre, 77.

85. Downing, 47.

86. Dudley, 39.

87. Downing, 36.

87. Laertius, Vol 2, 51.

89. Downing, 37.

90. Navia, *Diogenes,* 29.

91. Malherbe, 57.

92. Downing, 117–118.

93. Navia, *Diogenes,* 56.

94. Dudley, 35.

95. Navia, *Classical Cynicism,* 101.

96. Ibid., 137.

97. Sayre, 5.

98. Dudley, 105.

99. Sayre, 13.

100. Navia, *Diogenes,* 113–128.

101. Ibid., 74.

102. A.A. Long, "The Socratic Tradition: Diogenes, Crates, and Hellenistic Ethics," in R. Bracht Branham and Marie-Odile Goulet-Caze (eds.), *The Cynics: The Cynic Movement in Antiquity and Its Legacy* (Berkeley: University of California Press), 1996, 30.

103. Dudley, 118.

104. Navia, *Classical Cynicism,* 96, 104.

105. Navia, *Diogenes,* 75.

106. Dudley, 118.

107. Downing, 49.

108. Such criticism includes that of the modern publishers of Laertius' text.

109. Branham, "Defacing the Currency," 89.

110. Ibid., 82–83.

111. Ibid., 93.

112. Krueger, 236.

113. Dudley, 111.

114. Bion was also the first author to have employed the menippea in his writings.

115. Mikhail Bakhtin, *Problems of Dostoevesky's Poetics* (Minneapolis: University of Minnesota Press, 1999), 12.

116. *Concise English Dictionary of Current English* (Oxford: Oxford University Press, 1995).

117. Sayre, 103.

118. Laertius, Vol. 2, 45.

119. Ibid., 59.

120. Sayre, 103.

121. Plato (from *Phaedrus*), cit. Navia, *Diogenes,* 55.

122. Laertius, Vol. 2, 5.

123. Long, 33.

124. Laertius, Vol. 1, 109.

125. Branham, Introduction, 10–11.

126. Bakhtin, 120.

127. Ibid., 113.

128. Navia, *Classical Cynicism,* 156; Downing, 182.

129. Branham, Introduction, 11.

130. Navia, *Classical Cynicism,* 158.

131. Margaret A. Rose, *Parody: Ancient, Modern, & Postmodern* (Cambridge: Cambridge University Press, 1993), 85–86.

132. Bakhtin, 113.

133. Ibid., 81.

134. Clearly those aspects of carnival which provide an excuse for overindulgence in eating, drinking, and fornicating, would not have appealed to Cynic asceticism.

135. Jacques Lacan, cit. Fred Botting and Scott Wilson, *Bataille* (Basingstoke: Palgrave, 2001), 189.

136. Nietzsche from *Genealogy of Morals,* cit. James Miller, *The Passion of Michel Foucault* (Cambridge, Mass: Harvard University Press, 2000), 223.

137. Navia, *Antisthenes*, 100.

138. Navia, 102.

139. Kristeva, 126.

140. Ibid., 4.

141. Navia, *Antisthenes*, 102.

142. Navia, *Diogenes*, 121–122. Aristotle, cit. Navia, etc.

143. Michel Serres, *Detachment* (Athens: Ohio University Press, 1990), 93.

144. Navia, *Classical Cynicism*, 67.

Chapter 2

1. Jacob Burckhardt, *The Civilization of the Renaissance in Italy* (London: Penguin Books, 1990), 98.

2. Ibid., 4.

3. Peter Burke, introduction to Burckhardt, 4–5.

4. James Hankins, "Humanism and the Origins of Modern Political Thought," in Jill Kraye (ed.), *The Cambridge Companion to Renaissance Humanism* (Cambridge: Cambridge University Press, 1998), 123.

5. Burckhardt, 98.

6. Ibid., 99.

7. Ibid., 99.

8. Ibid., 100–101.

9. Ibid., 106.

10. Ibid., 290–291.

11. Ibid., 314.

12. Nicholas Mann, "The Origins of Humanism" in Jill Kraye (ed.), *The Cambridge Companion to Renaissance Humanism*, Cambridge: Cambridge University Press, 1998, 1–2.

13. Hankins, 125.

14. Burckhardt, 317.

15. Ibid., 164–165.

16. Burckhardt, 313.

17. Ibid., 274.

18. Ibid., 272.

19. Ibid., 120.

20. Ibid., 288.

21. Peter Burke, introduction to Burckhardt, 24.

22. Burckhardt, 34–35.

23. Ibid., 45.

24. Ibid., 48.

25. Ibid., 41.

26. Michel Foucault, cit. Paul Rabinow, *The Foucault Reader* (London: Penguin Books, 1984) 370.

27. Burckhardt, 103.

28. Ibid., 182.

29. Ibid., 289.

30. Ibid., 30, 50.

31. DeFranco Sacchetti cit. Burckhardt, 233.

32. Ibid., 234.

33. Ibid., 251.

34. Ibid., 280.

35. Matteo Bandello, cit. Burckhardt, 281.

36. Burckhardt, 251.

37. Ibid., 112–113.

38. Ibid., 273.

39. Ibid., 256.

40. Ibid., 257.

41. Ibid., 263.

42. Ibid., 263–264.

43. Ibid., 268.

44. Hankins, 135.

45. Georges Bataille, *The Accursed Share*, vols. 1,2 (New York: Zone Books, 1993), 380.

46. Bernard Crick, introduction to Niccolò Machiavelli, *The Discourses* (London: Penguin Books, 1998), 16.

47. Niccolò Machiavelli, *The Discourses* (London: Penguin Books, 1998), 268.

48. Ibid., 21.

49. Ibid., 16.

50. Hankins, 120–121.

51. Machiavelli, *The Discourses*, 18.

52. Niccolò Machiavelli, *The Prince* (Indianapolis: Hacket Publishing Company, 1995), 9–10.

53. Ibid., 71.

54. Ibid., 30–31.

55. Ibid., 51–52.

56. Machiavelli, *The Discourses*, 37.

57. Machiavelli, *The Prince*, 52.

58. Machiavelli, *The Discourses*, 17.

59. Ibid., 176–177.

60. Ibid., 290.

61. Richard Huelsenbeck cit. Sloterdjik, 392.

62. Machiavelli, *The Discourses*, 144–145.

63. Hankins, 134.

64. Machiavelli, *The Discourses*, 386.

65. Ibid., 98.

66. Ibid., 265.

67. Ibid., 252.

68. Machiavelli, *The Prince*, 18.

69. Ibid., 75–76.

70. Hankins, 136.

71. Ibid., 137.

72. Machiavelli, *The Discourses*, 200.

73. Ibid., 268.

74. Machiavelli cit. Burckhardt, 272.

75. Burckhardt, 272.

76. Although the genocidal acts that took place during the Renaissance have many parallels with the horrors of the Reformation, it is important to also distinguish the different driving forces behind these two barbaric periods of history. While binary opposites may be inadequate to capture the real essence of either they do help to underline the clash of cultures. The campaigns of Luther and Calvin, in contrast to those of the Renaissance despot, have more in common with those of Hitler: the revenge of the philistine over the intellectual, the suppression of literary and artistic freedom over its censorship, conformity over the individual, order over chaos, xenophobia over cosmopolitanism, etc.

Chapter 3

1. Walter Kaufmann, *Nietzsche: Philosopher, Psychologist, Antichrist* (Princeton NJ: Princeton University Press, 1999), 366.

2. H. L. Mencken, introduction to Friedrich Nietzsche, *The Antichrist* (Tucson: See Sharp Press, 1999), 6.

3. Friedrich Nietzsche, *Thoughts Out of Season*, Part II, *Complete Works* (London: George Allen & Unwin, 1909), 33.

4. Madan Sarup, *An Introductory Guide to Post-Structuralism and Postmodernism* (London: Harvester Wheatsheaf, 1993), 5.

5. Georges Bataille, *The Accursed Share*, vols. 1,2 (New York: Zone Books, 1993), 380.

6. Luis Navia, *Classical Cynicism: A critical study* (Westport, CT: Greenwood Press, 1996), 82.

7. Anthony A. Long, "The Socratic Tradition: Diogenes, Crates, and Hellenistic Ethics," in R. Bracht Branham and Marie-Odile Goulet-Caze (eds.), *The Cynics: The Cynic Movement in Antiquity and Its Legacy* (Berkeley: University of California Press, 1996), 29.

8. Heinrich Niehues-Probsting, "The Modern Reception of Cynicism: Diogenes in the Enlightenment," in R. Bracht Branham and Marie-Odile Goulet-Caze (eds.), *The Cynics: The Cynic Movement in Antiquity and Its Legacy* (Berkeley: University of California Press, 1996), 353–354.

9. Friedrich Nietzsche, *Twilight of the Idols: or, How to Philosophize with the Hammer* (Indianapolis: Hackett Publishing Co. Inc., 1997), 11.

10. Sarup, 105–106.

11. Friedrich Nietzsche, *Ecce Homo: How One Becomes What One Is* (London: Penguin Books, 1992), 43.

12. Kaufmann, 409.

13. Friedrich Nietzsche, *Beyond Good and Evil: Prelude to a Philosophy of the Future*, in *Complete Works* (Edinburgh: T.N. Foulis, 1909), 39.

14. Niehues-Probsting, 354.

15. Kaufmann, 365.

16. Ibid., 71.

17. Niehues-Probsting, 359. Elizabeth Forster-Nietzsche in np. cit. Nietzsche.

18. Alain de Botton, *The Consolations of Philosophy* (London: Hamish Hamilton, 2000), 219.

19. Niehues-Probsting, 357.

20. Kaufmann, 32.

21. Ibid., 69.

22. Kaufmann, 89: "The use of the word 'existential' is not meant to fix Nietzsche's position in the history of ideas, to regulate him to any school, or to imply anything more than we are about to develop explicitly."

23. de Botton, 205.

24. Kathleen J. Wininger, "Nietzsche's Women & Women on Nietzsche," in Kelly Oliver and Marilyn Pearsall (eds.),

Feminist Interpretations of Friedrich Niet-zsche (University Park, PA: Pennsylvania State University Press, 1998), 244.

25. Dave Robinson, *Nietzsche and Postmodernism* (Cambridge: Icon Books, 1999), 27.

26. Ibid., 66.

27. Kaufmann, 204.

28. Robinson, 15, 77.

29. Alan D. Schrift, "Nietzsche's Contest: Nietzsche and the Culture Wars," in Alan D. Schrift (ed.), *Why Nietzsche Still: Reflections on Drama, Culture, and Politics* (Berkeley: University of California Press, 2000), 198. Nietzsche likened Homeric competitions to Dionysian festivals: "the highest site on which dramas of culture should be fought."

30. Nietzsche, *Twilight of the Idols,* 89–90.

31. Robinson, 66.

32. Leonard Shlain, *The Alphabet Versus the Goddess: Male Words Female Images* (London: Alan Lane, Penguin Press, 1998), 138.

33. Ibid., 141.

34. Friedrich Nietzsche, *Philosophy in the Tragic Age of the Greeks* (Washington, DC: Regnery, 1962), 34.

35. Nietzsche, *Twilight of the Idols,* 57–58.

36. David B. Allison, "Musical Psychodramatics: ecstasis in Nietzsche," in Alan D. Schrift (ed.), *Why Nietzsche Still: Reflections on Drama, Culture, and Politics* (Berkeley: University of California Press, 2000), 77n.

37. E. M. Cioran, *Tears and Saints* (Chicago: University of Chicago Press, 1995), 8.

38. Nietzsche, in Niehues-Probsting, 354.

39. Georges Bataille, 1993, Vol. III, 401.

40. Niehues-Probsting, 355.

41. Kaufmann, 413.

42. Kaufmann, 66–67.

43. Kelly Oliver and Marilyn Pearsall, "Introduction: Why Feminists Read Nietzsche," in *Feminist Interpretations of Friedrich Nietzsche* (University Park, PA: Pennsylvania State University Press, 1998), 8.

44. Jacques Derrida, "The Question of Style," in Kelly Oliver and Marilyn Pearsall (eds.), *Feminist Interpretations of Friedrich Nietzsche* (University Park, PA: Pennsylvania State University Press, 1998), 57.

45. Kelly Oliver, "Woman as Truth in Nietzsche's Writing," in Kelly Oliver and Marilyn Pearsall (eds.), *Feminist Interpretations of Friedrich Nietzsche* (University Park, PA: Pennsylvania State University Press, 1998), 68.

46. Morag Shiach, *Helene Cixous: A Politics of Writing* (London: Routledge, 1991), 27. Shiach also notes: "Cixous alludes to Nietzsche's remark that 'I fear we are not getting rid of God because we still believe in grammar' and goes on to suggest that such belief, and such fear, must be challenged by a writing that will undermine the apparent relations between grammatical structure and the real world" (79). Also note: Susan Sellers (ed.), *The Helene Cixous Reader* (London: Routledge, 1994), xxix.

47. Shiach, 67.

48. Tracy Strong, Introduction to Nietzsche, *Twilight of the Idols,* xvii.

49. Nietzsche, *Twilight of the Idols,* 6.

50. Nietzsche, *Beyond Good & Evil,* 87.

51. Ibid., 97.

52. Ibid., 101.

53. Martin Stoddard (ed.), *Sayings of F. Nietzsche* (London: Gerald Duckworth and Co., 1993), 35.

54. Ibid., 21.

55. Kaufmann, 72.

56. Nietzsche, in Kaufmann, 81.

57. Sarup, 91.

58. H.L. Mencken, Introduction to Nietzsche, *The Antichrist,* 16.

59. Sean Burke, *The Death and Return of the Author: Criticism and Subjectivity in Barthes, Foucault, and Derrida* (Edinburgh: Edinburgh University Press, 1998) 111.

60. Kaufmann, 84.

61. Ibid., 17.

62. Ibid., 285.

63. Nietzsche, *Philosophy in the Tragic Age of the Greeks,* 30.

64. Kaufmann, 288–289.

65. Ibid., 45.

66. Nietzsche, *Ecce Homo,* 96.

67. Maudemarie Clark, "Nietzsche's Misogyny," in Kelly Oliver and Marilyn Pearsall (eds.), *Feminist Interpretations of Friedrich Nietzsche* (University Park, PA: Pennsylvania State University Press, 1998), 189.

68. Nietzsche, *Ecce Homo,* 17.

69. Nietzsche, *Twilight of the Idols,* 44.

70. Robinson, 54–55.

71. Nietzsche, *Thoughts Out of Season,* 52.

72. Ibid., 20–21.

73. Robinson, 47.

74. Ibid., 4.

75. Kaufmann, 94.

76. Alasdair MacIntyre, *After Virtue* (Gerald Duckworth & Co., 1999), 258.

77. Nietzsche, *Thoughts Out of Season,* 173–174.

78. Ibid., 190.

79. Ibid., 32.

80. Ibid., 60–61.

81. Nietzsche, *The Antichrist,* 23.

82. Nietzsche, *Thoughts Out of Season,* 52.

83. Ibid., 63–64.

84. Nietzsche, *Twilight of the Idols,* 18–19.

85. Nietzsche, *Ecce Homo,* 21.

86. Ibid., 98.

87. Nietzsche, *Thoughts Out of Season,* 96–97.

88. Sarup, 91.

89. Friedrich Nietzsche, *Philosophy and Truth* (Atlantic Highlands, NJ: Humanities Press, 1979), 84.

90. Mencken, introduction to Nietzsche, 10–11.

91. Nietzsche, *Twilight of the Idols,* 33.

92. Nietzsche, *Ecce Homo,* 96.

93. Samuel Beckett, *Trilogy: Malloy, Malone Dies, the Unnamable* (London: Calder Publications, 1994), 193.

94. Mencken, introduction to Nietzsche, *The Antichrist,* 10–11.

95. Nietzsche, *Twilight of the Idols,* 38.

96. Nietzsche, *Philosophy and Truth,* 79.

97. Dana R. Villa, "Democratizing the Agon," in Alan D. Schrift (ed.), *Why Neitzsche Still: Reflections on Drama, Culture, and Politics* (Berkeley: University of California Press, 2000), 229.

98. Alphonso Lingis, "Satyrs and Centaurs: Miscegenation and the Master Race," in Alan D. Schrift (ed.), *Why Neitzsche Still: Reflections on Drama, Culture, and Politics* (Berkeley: University of California Press, 2000), 159.

99. Robinson, 26–27.

100. Nietzsche, *Thoughts Out of Season,* 25.

101. Ibid., 25–26.

102. Bataille, 1993, Vol. II, 163.

103. Timothy Bewes, *Cynicism and Postmodernity* (London: Verso, 1997), 171.

104. Peter Sloterdijk, *Critique of Cynical Reason* (London: Verso, 1988), 119.

105. Nietzsche, *Thoughts Out of Season,* 40.

106. Branham and Goulet-Caze, 362–363.

Chapter 4

1. Timothy Bewes, *Cynicism and Postmodernity* (London: Verso, 1997), 2.

2. In spite of his postmodernist credentials Lacan, like Freud, attempts to capture human behavior within a totalizing, scientific system complete with identifiable "stages" and ordered categories. Feeling and emotion give way to intellectual theories which are not even supported by the clinical case histories offered by Freud. And when Sokal and Bricmont criticize postmodern authors such as Julia Kristeva for setting out to produce theories to support poetic language and other literary genres, they are right when they point out that since "their style is usually heavy and pompous, so it is highly unlikely that their goal is principally literary or poetic." Many other so-called postmodern texts, notably those of Roland Barthes, Baudrillard and Nietzsche himself, *are* highly poetic, even if they do not set out to be so.

3. Jürgen Habermas, cit. Fredric Jameson, "Postmodernism and Consumer Society," in Hal Foster (ed.), *Postmodern Culture* (London: Pluto Press, 1985), 112.

4. Madan Sarup, *An Introductory Guide to Post-Structuralism and Postmodernism* (London: Harvester Wheatsheaf, 1993), 168.

5. Jürgen Habermas, "Modernity — An Incomplete Project," in Hal Foster (ed.), *Postmodern Culture* (London: Pluto Press, 1985), 4.

6. Peter Sloterdijk, *Critique of Cynical Reason* (London: Verso, 1988), 119.

7. Luis Navia, *Diogenes of Sinope: The Man in the Tub* (Westport, CT: Greenwood Press, 1998), 73.

8. Bewes, 171.

9. Navia, *Diogenes*, 76.

10. Hal Foster, *The Return of the Real* (Cambridge, MA: MIT Press, 1996), 207.

11. Sarup, 69.

12. Alan Sokal and Jean Bricmont, *Intellectual Impostures: Postmodern Philosophers' Abuse of Science* (London: Profile Books, 1999), 192.

13. Alan Sokal, "Transgressing the Boundaries: Toward a transformative hermeneutics of quantum gravity," *Social Text* 46/47 (Spring/Summer 1996): 17–252.

14. Sokal and Bricmont, 13.

15. Ibid., 21.

16. Ibid., 5.

17. Ibid., 6.

18. Jean-François Lyotard, *The Postmodern Condition: A Report on Knowledge* (Atlantic Highlands, NJ: Humanities Press, 1993), 7–8.

19. James Miller, *The Passion of Michel Foucault* (Cambridge, MA: Harvard University Press, 2000), 151–152.

20. Sarup, 72.

21. Jean Baudrillard, *Impossible Exchange* (London: Verso, 2001), 4.

22. Ibid., 5.

23. Lyotard, 29.

24. Ibid., 26.

25. Sokal and Bricmont, 184.

26. Ibid., 80.

27. Sokal and Bricmont, 78.

28. Ibid., 50.

29. Dio Chrysostom, *Discourses 1–11*, Loeb Classical Library (Cambridge MA: Harvard University Press, 1961), 411–415.

30. Sokal and Bricmont, 138.

31. Ibid., 143.

32. Ibid., 140–141.

33. Miller, 152.

34. Baudrillard, *Impossible Exchange*, 23.

35. Sokal and Bricmont, 61.

36. Richard Coker, BBC Two, *Horizon*, January 2000.

37. Lauree Garrett, BBC Two, *Horizon*, January 2000.

38. Dilly Barlow (Narrator), BBC Two, *Horizon*, January 2000.

39. Robert Daum, University of Chicago, BBC Two, *Horizon*, January 2000.

40. Dilly Barlow (Narrator), BBC Two, *Horizon*, January 2000.

41. Sokal and Bricmont, 130.

42. Sokal and Bricmont, 87.

43. Sarup, 153.

44. Ibid., 154.

45. Ibid., 154.

46. Ibid., 155.

47. Ibid., 183.

48. Ibid., 186.

49. Ibid., 180.

50. Sokal and Bricmont, 278.

51. Ibid., 55–56.

52. Sarup, 186.

53. Baudrillard, *Impossible Exchange*, 13.

54. Louise-Ferdinand Céline cit., Julia Kristeva, *Powers of Horror: An Essay on Abjection* (New York: Columbia University Press, 1982), 150.

55. Baudrillard, *Impossible Exchange*, 9.

56. Emile Cioran, cit. Baudrillard, Ibid., 128.

57. Jean Baudrillard, *The Spirit of Terrorism*; Slavoj Zizek, *Welcome to the Desert of the Real!*; Paul Virilio, *Ground Zero*; all published by London: Verso, 2002.

58. Baudrillard, *The Spirit of Terrorism* (London: Verso, 2002), 4.

59. Miller, 18.

60. Foucault's final lectures in his seminar on *parrhesia*, "Discourse and Truth," are published in English as: Michel Foucault, *Fearless Speech* (Los Angeles: Semiotext(e), 2001). Foucault's analysis of Dio Chrysostom's version of Diogenes' meeting with Alexander is discussed in Chapter 1 of this book.

61. Miller, 360.

62. Ibid., 66.

63. Ibid., 5.

64. Michel Foucault in Paul Rabinow (ed.), *The Foucault Reader* (London: Penguin, 1984), 374.

65. Miller, 163.

66. Ibid., 294.

67. Fredric Jameson, "Postmodernism and Consumer Society," in Hal Foster (ed.), *Postmodern Culture* (London: Pluto Press, 1985), 112.

68. Miller, 103.

69. Henri Gouhier, cit. Miller, 104.

70. Miller, 105.

71. Ibid., 218–219.

72. Ibid., 17.

73. Ibid., 48.

74. *Ibid.,* 152.

75. Foucault, cit. Miller, 152.

76. Sarup, 80.

77. Sarup, 81.

78. Sarup, 83.

79. Alan Sheridan, *Michel Foucault: The Will to Truth* (London: Routledge, 1980), 184.

80. Sarup, 84.

81. Foucault, cit. Miller, 20.

82. Foucault, cit. Miller, 55.

83. Ibid.

84. Thomas Flynn, "Foucault as Parrhesiast: His last course at the Collège de France (1984)," in James Bernauer and David Rasmussen (eds.), *The Final Foucault* (Cambridge, MA: MIT Press, 1994), 116.

85. Ibid., 102.

86. Ibid., 103.

87. Ibid., 115.

88. Ibid., 109–110.

89. Miller, 31.

90. Bewes, 28; Sloterdijk, 5.

Chapter 5

1. Luis Navia, *Antisthenes of Athens: Setting the World Aright* (Westport, CT: Greenwood Press, 2001), 95.

2. Peter Sloterdijk, *Critique of Cynical Reason* (London: Verso, 1988), 391.

3. Renata Salecl, *(Per)Versions of Love and Hate* (London: Verso, 1998), 104–109.

4. Jim McCarthy, *Political Theatre During the Spanish Civil War* (Cardiff: University of Wales Press, 1999), 2.

5. Luis E. Navia, *Diogenes of Sinope: The man in the tub* (Westport, CT: Greenwood Press, 1998), 61–62.

6. RoseLee Goldberg, *Performance Art: From Futurism to the Present* (London: Thames and Hudson, 1988), 7.

7. Ibid., 8–9.

8. Sloterdijk, 391–392.

9. BBC Radio 4, "In Our Time," 15 November 2001.

10. See Chapter 1.

11. Georges Bataille, *Visions of Excess: Selected Writings, 1927–1939* (Minneapolis: University of Minnesota Press, 1985), 40.

12. Goldberg, 11.

13. Ibid., 16.

14. Ibid.

15. See Chapter 1.

16. Goldberg, 17.

17. Ibid.

18. Ibid., 26.

19. Ibid., 38–39.

20. Ibid., 39.

21. Ibid., 50.

22. Hugo Ball, cit. Ibid., 52.

23. Goldberg, 52.

24. Ibid., 62.

25. Malcome Green (translation and introduction), *Blago Bung, Blago Bung, Bosso Fataka!— First Texts of German Dada by Hugo Ball, Richard Huelsenbeck Walter Sterner* (London: Atlas Press, 1995), 17, 19.

26. Ibid., 15.

27. Sloterdijk, 399.

28. Ibid., 239.

29. Richard Huelsenbeck, cit. Ibid., 392.

30. Sloterdijk, 392.
31. Green, 35–36.
32. Sloterdijk, 392.
33. Hans Richter, cit. Green, 33.
34. Sloterdijk, 397
35. Oskar Schlemmer, cit. Goldberg, 102.
36. Ibid., 103.
37. Goldberg, 75–76.
38. Raoul Hausmann, cit. Sloterdijk, 397.
39. Hal Foster, *The Return of the Real* (Cambridge, MA: MIT Press, 1996), 1.
40. Hugo Ball's diary 25 November 1915, cit. Green, 38.
41. Foster, 112.
42. Ibid., 21.
43. Bataille, 241.
44. Joseph Beuys, cit. Goldberg, 150.
45. Joseph Beuys (Exhibition) The Secret Block for a Secret Person in Ireland, Royal Academy of Arts, 22 July to 16 September 1999.
46. Donald Kuspit, "Joseph Beuys: Between Showman and Shaman," in David Thistlewood, *Joseph Beuys: Diverging Critiques* (Liverpool: Liverpool University Press, 1995), 30–31.
47. Andrea Duncan, "Rockets Must Rust: Beuys and the work of iron in nature," in David Thistlewood, *Joseph Beuys: Diverging Critiques* (Liverpool: Liverpool University Press, 1995), 85.
48. Robert Storr, cit. Donald Kuspit, "Joseph Beuys: the Body of the Artist," in David Thistlewood, *Joseph Beuys: Diverging Critiques* (Liverpool: Liverpool University Press, 1995), 32.
49. David Thistlewood, *Joseph Beuys: Diverging Critiques* (Liverpool: Liverpool University Press, 1995), 22.
50. Goldberg, 156.
51. Ibid., 159.
52. Ibid., 165.
53. Kathy O'Dell, *Contract with the Skin: Masochism Performance Art and the 1970s* (Minneapolis: University of Minnesota Press, 1998), (figures) 7–12.
54. Salecl, 161.
55. Goldberg, 165.
56. O'Dell argues that it is unhelpful in the context of this discussion to narrow one's definition of masochism to that given in psychiatry to describe a "clinical condition" in which must be included: "recurrent, intense sexually arousing fantasies, sexual urges, or behavior involving the act (real, not simulated) of being humiliated, beaten, bound or otherwise made to suffer" (*Diagnostic Statistical Manual of Mental Disorders*, cit. O'Dell, 3).
57. Salecl, 160.
58. Julia Kristeva, *Powers of Horror: An essay on abjection* (New York: Columbia University Press, 1982), 102.
59. James Miller, *The Passion of Michel Foucault* (Cambridge, MA: Harvard University Press, 2000), 272.
60. Michel Foucault, cit. Miller, 27.
61 André Stitt, cit. Simon Herbert, "Disparate Pockets," *Art & Design*, 5, no. 3/4 (1989): 78.
62. Herbert, 78.
63. O'Dell, 6.
64. Bataille, 57.
65. Channel 4 (UK), *Anatomy of Disgust*, 29 August 2000.
66. Channel 4 (UK), *The Anatomists*, 12 and 26 March 2002.
67. *The Observer*, "Body Worlds: Fascination beneath the surface," 20 May, 2001.
68. Channel 4 (UK), *The Anatomists*, 12 March 2002.
69. *The Observer*, "Body Worlds."
70. Goldberg, 165.
71. ITV (UK) *South Bank Show*, 19 August 2001.
72. Goldberg, 182.
73. Goldberg, 183.

Chapter 6

1. Peter Sloterdijk, *Critique of Cynical Reason* (London: Verso, 1988), 292.
2. Ibid., 290.
3. Ibid., 330.
4. Ibid., 218.
5. Ian Kennedy, *The Unmasking of Medicine* (London: Granada Publishing, 1983), 25.

6. Ivan Illich, *Limits to Medicine: Medical Nemesis— the Expropriation of Health* (London: Pelican Books, 1976, 42.

7. Ibid., 265.

8. Kennedy, 2–6.

9. Ibid., 1.

10. Jean Baudrillard, *The Illusion of the End* (Cambridge: Polity Press, 1994), 66–69.

11. Norman G. Finkelstein, *The Holocaust Industry: Reflections on the Exploitation of Jewish Suffering* (London: Verso, 2000).

12. Ian Hislop (ed.), *The Private Eye Annual 1998* (London: Pressdram Ltd., 1998).

13. *The Daily Telegraph*, "Time for the media to curb cynicism and celebrate what's good about our country." 12 March 2001. Charles' speech took place at a special service to mark the 300th anniversary of the publication of the first British daily newspaper.

14. Charles Moore, "Moore pays tribute to Waugh," *The Guardian*, 17 January 2001.

15. Ibid.

16. Geoffrey Wheatcroft, "Auberon Waugh," *The Guardian*, 18 January 2001.

17. Henry Porter, "Waugh at Peace," *The Guardian*, 18 January 2001.

18. Richard Ingrams, "Waugh Games" *The Observer*, 21 January 2001.

19. Polly Toynbee, "Ghastly Man," *The Guardian*, 19 January 2001.

20. Lynn Barber, "Waugh Stories," *The Observer*, 21 January 2001.

21. Cristina Odone, "A party that never laughs," *The Observer*, 21 January 2001.

22. Charlotte Raven, "Love across the divide," *The Guardian*, 23 January 2001.

23. Charles Moore, "Moore pays tribute to Waugh," *The Guardian*, 17 January 2001.

24. Henry Porter, "Waugh at Peace."

25. Sloterdijk, 315–316.

26. Michael Moore, *Downsize This: Random Threats from an Unarmed American* (London: Boxtree, 1997), 10.

27. Ibid., 11.

28. Umberto Eco, *Misreadings* (London: Picador, 1993), 111.

29. Lucian, "Dialogues of the Dead," *Lucian,* vol. 7, Loeb Classical Library (Cambridge, MA: Harvard University Press, 1928).

30. Margaret A. Rose, *Parody: Ancient, Modern, and Post-modern* (Cambridge and New York: Cambridge University Press, 1993), 7.

31. Sloterdijk, 288.

32. Christopher Stone, quoted in Rose, 26.

33. Eco, 135–137.

34. Julian Barnes, *A History of the World in Ten and a Half Chapters* (London: Picador, 1989), 83.

35. Ibid., 241.

36. Channel Four's *Equinox,* 8/9/96.

37. Adams, ix.

38. Scott Adams, *The Dilbert Principle* (London: Boxtree, 1996), 200.

39. Ibid.,165.

40. Dick Pountain and David Robins, *Cool Rules* (London: Reaktion Books, 2000), 78–79.

41. Francis Wheen, *The Sixties: A Fresh Look at the Decade of Change* (London: Century, 1982).

42. Robert Chia and Stuart Morgan, "Educating the Philosopher-Manager: Designing the times," *Management Learning,* 27, no. 1 (1996): 40.

43. Yiannis Gabriel, "The Hubris of Management," *Administrative Theory & Praxis,* 20, no. 3 (September 1998), 268.

44. Michel Foucault, cit. James Miller, *The Passion of Michel Foucault* (Cambridge, MA: Harvard University Press, 2000), 302.

45. Timothy Bewes, *Cynicism and Postmodernity* (London: Verso, 1997), 28.

46. Michel Foucault, cit. Miller, 325–326.

47. Chia and Morgan, 37.

48. Ibid., 51.

49. Gabriel, 257.

50. Christopher Lasch, *The Culture of Narcissism: American Life in an Age of Diminishing Expectations* (New York: W.W.Norton, 1979), 72–73.

51. Susan Sontag, *Styles of Radical Will* (London: Vintage, 1994), 20.

52. Madan Sarup, *An Introductory Guide to Post-Structuralism and Postmodernism* (London: Harvester Wheatsheaf, 1993), 100.

53. Chia and Morgan, 55.

54. Yiannis Gabriel, "On Paragrammatic Uses of Organizational Theory," *Organization Studies*, 23, no. 1 (2002): 133–151.

55. Dana R. Villa, "Democratizing the Agon," in Schrift (ed.), *Why Nietzsche Still: Reflections on Drama, Culture, and Politics* (Berkeley: University of California Press, 2000), 225.

56. Jean-François Lyotard, *The Postmodern Condition: A Report on Knowledge* (New Jersey: Humanities Press, 1993), 15.

57. Robert Fritz, *Corporate Tides* (Oxford: Butterworth-Heinemann, 1994), 18.

58. Lyotard, 17–24.

59. Yiannis Gabriel, "The Hubris of Management," 269.

Chapter 7

1. Philip Rieff, *The Triumph of the Therapeutic* (Harmondsworth: London, 1966), 22.

2. Pountain and Robins, *Cool Rules* (London: Reaktion Books, 2000), 156–157.

3. Alasdair MacIntyre, *After Virtue* (Gerald Duckworth & Co., 1999), 27–30.

4. Rieff, 207.

5. Ibid., 2.

6. Alcoholics Anonymous, http://www.aa.org/9 May 2001.

7. Gerard Egan, *The Skilled Helper: A Problem-Management Approach to Helping,* 5th edition (Pacific Grove: Brooks/Cole Publishing Company, 1994), 5.

8. Rieff, 15–16.

9. Norman Finkelstein distinguishes the Nazi holocaust from "The Holocaust" which he claims is the appropriated version, not to mention all the other less publicized holocausts.

10. Despite the victim status attached to those who clearly suffered at the hands of the Nazis, Finkelstein normalizes his

relationship to his mother by emphasizing that, "to me she is simply my Mum." Interview with Fergal Keane, *Taking a Stand*, BBC Radio 4, 30 January 2001.

11. Norman G. Finkelstein, *The Holocaust Industry: Reflections on the Exploitation of Jewish Suffering* (London: Verso, 2000), 3.

12. Andrea Dworkin, *Scapegoat: The Jews, Israel, and Women's Liberation* (New York: The Free Press, 2000).

13. Ibid., 336–337.

14. Ibid., 74.

15. Ibid., 207.

16. Ibid., 97.

17. Ibid., 99.

18. Ibid., 214.

19. Ibid., 275.

20. Ibid., 278.

21. Ibid., 335.

22. Ibid., 291.

23. Hélène Cixous and Mireille Calle-Gruber, *Helene Cixous Rootprints* (New York: Routledge, 1997, 30).

24. Henri Birault, cit. Lyn Hejinian, *The Language of Inquiry* (Berkeley: University of California Press, 2000), 377.

25. R.W. Sharples, *Stoics, Epicureans and Sceptics* (London: Routledge, 1996), 126.

26. Cixous and Calle-Gruber, 12.

27. Ibid., 9.

28. Ibid., 19.

29. Sigmund Freud, *Fragment of the analysis,* vol. 8 (London: Penguin, 1977), 76.

30. Jeanne Hyvrard, *Mother Death* (Lincoln: University of Nebraska Press, 1988), 99.

31. James Ellroy, *My Dark Places* (London: Arrow Books, 1997), 296–297.

32. Ibid., 322.

33. Rebecca Stringer, "A Nietzschean Breed," in Schrift, Alan D. (ed.), *Why Nietzsche Still: Reflections on Drama, Culture, and Politics* (Berkeley: University of California Press, 2000), 253.

34. Jean Baudrillard, 66–69.

35. Hélène Cixous, "Extreme Fidelity," in Susan Sellers (ed.), *Writing Differences: Readings from the Seminar of*

Hélène Cixous (New York: St Martin's Press, 1988), 18–19.

36. Leslie Gannon, "Docu Soap," performance at *Ellipsis*, Chapter Arts Centre, Cardiff, 15 December 2001.

37. Pountain and Robins, 159.

38. Ibid., 149–151.

39. Christopher Lasch, *The Culture of Narcissism: American Life in an Age of Diminishing Expectations* (New York: W.W. Norton & Co., 1979), 67.

40. Ibid., 77.

41. Morag Shiach, "Millennial Fears: Hope and transformation in contemporary feminist writing," *Paragraph: A Journal of Modern Critical Theory*, 23, no. 3 (November 2000), 324–326.

42. Allan Stoekl in Georges Bataille, *Visions of Excess: Selected Writings, 1927–1939* (Minneapolis: University of Minnesota Press, 1985), xiv.

43. Luis E. Navia, *Antisthenes of Athens: Setting the World Aright* (Westport, CT: Greenwood Press, 2001), 103.

44. Slavoj Zizek, *The Plague of Fantasies* (London: Verso, 1997), 65.

Bibliography

Adams, Scott. *The Dilbert Principle*. London: Boxtree, 1996.

Aristotle. *Politics Books I & II*. Oxford: Clarendon Press, 1999.

Baily, Joe. *Pessimism*. London: Routledge, 1988.

Bakhtin, Mikhail. *Problems of Dostoevesky's Poetics*. Minneapolis: University of Minnesota Press, 1999.

Barber, Lynn. "Waugh Stories" in *The Observer*, 21 January 2001.

Barlow, Dilly, narrator. *Horizon*. BBC Two (British TV). January 2000.

Barnes, Julian. *A History of the World in Ten and a Half Chapters*. London: Picador, 1989.

Bataille, Georges. *The Accursed Share*. Vols. I and II. New York: Zone Books, 1993.

_____. *Story of the Eye*. London: Penguin, 1982.

_____. *Visions of Excess: Selected Writings, 1927–1939*. Minneapolis: University of Minnesota Press, 1985.

Baudrillard, Jean. *The Illusion of the End*. Cambridge: Polity Press, 1994.

_____. *Impossible Exchange*. London: Verso, 2001.

_____. *Simulations*. New York: Semiotext(e), 1983.

_____. *The Spirit of Terrorism*. London: Verso, 2002.

BBC Radio 4. *In Our Time*. 15 November 2001.

Beckett, Samuel. *The Expelled and Other Novellas*. London: Penguin, 1973.

_____. *Trilogy: Malloy, Malone Dies, the Unnamable*. London: Calder Publications Limited, 1994.

Bernauer, James, and David Rasmussen, eds. *The Final Foucault*. Cambridge, Mass: The MIT Press, 1994.

Beuys, Joseph. *The Secret Block for a Secret Person in Ireland*. Exhibition at the Royal Academy of Arts, 22 July to 16 September 1999.

Bewes, Timothy. *Cynicism and Postmodernity*. London: Verso, 1997.

Blackburn, Simon. *Oxford Dictionary of Philosophy*. Oxford: Oxford University Press, 1996.

Blake, William. *The Marriage of Heaven and Hell*. New York: Dover Publications, 1994.

"Body Worlds: Fascination Beneath the Surface" in *The Observer*, Sunday, 20 May 2001.

Botting, Fred, and Scott Wilson. *Bataille*. Basingstoke: Palgrave, 2001.

Bracht Branham, R., and Marie-Odile Goulet Caze, eds. *The Cynics: The Cynic Movement in Antiquity and Its Legacy*. Berkeley: University of California Press, 1996.

Burke, Sean. *The Death and Return of the Author: Criticism and Subjectivity in Barthes, Foucault, and Derrida*. Edinburgh: Edinburgh University Press, 1998.

Burckhardt, Jacob. *The Civilization of Renaissance in Italy*. London: Penguin Books, 1990.

Channel 4 (British TV). *The Anatomists*. 12 and 26 March 2002.

_____. *Anatomy of Disgust*. 29 August 2000.

_____. *Equinox*. 8 September 1996.

Charles, Prince of Windsor. Quoted in "Time for the Media to Curb Cynicism and Celebrate What's Good About Our Country" in *The Daily Telegraph*, 12 March 2001.

Chia, Robert, and Stuart Morgan. "Educating the Philosopher-Manager: Designing the Times" in *Management Learning*, Vol. 27, no. 1, 1996.

Chrysostom, Dio. *Volume 1, Discourses I-XI*. Loeb Classical Library, Cambridge, Mass.: Harvard University Press, 1961.

Cioran, E. M. *Tears and Saints*. Chicago: University of Chicago Press, 1995.

Cixous, Hélène, and Mireille Calle-Gruber. *Helene Cixous Rootprints*. New York: Routledge, 1997.

Coker, Richard. *Horizon*. BBC Two (British TV), January 2000.

Concise English Dictionary of Current English. Oxford: Oxford University Press, 1995.

Daum, Robert. *Horizon*. BBC Two (British TV). January 2000.

de Botton, Alain. *The Consolations of Philosophy*. London: Hamish Hamilton, 2000.

Deluze, Gilles. *Nietzsche and Philosophy*. London: Continuum, 2002.

Downing, F. Gerald. *Cynics and Christian Origins*. Edinburgh: T&T Clark, 1992.

Dudley, D. R. *A History of Cynicism: From Diogenes to the 6th Century AD*. London: Methuen, 1937.

Dworkin, Andrea. *Scapegoat: The Jews, Israel, and Women's Liberation*. New York: The Free Press, 2000.

Eco, Umberto. *Misreadings*. London: Picador, 1993.

Egan, Gerard. *The Skilled Helper: A Problem-Management Approach to Helping*. Pacific Grove: Brooks/Cole, 1994.

Ellroy, James. *My Dark Places*. London: Arrow Books, 1997.

Federman, Raymond. *Aunt Rachel's Fur*. Tallahassee, Fla.: Fiction Collective Two, 2001.

_____. *Double or Nothing*. Normal, Ill.: Fiction Collective Two, 1998.

_____. *Here & Elsewhere*, Macon, Ga.: Six Gallery Press, 2003.

_____. *Smiles on Washington Square*. Los Angeles: Sun and Moon Press, 1985.

_____. *Take It or Leave It*. Normal, Ill.: Fiction Collective Two, 1997.

_____. *The Twofold Vibration*. Los Angeles: Green Integer, 2000.

_____. *The Voice in the Closet*. Buffalo: Starcherone Books, 2001.

Finkelstein, Norman G. *The Holocaust Industry: Reflections on the Exploitation of Jewish Suffering*. London: Verso, 2000.

Foster, Hal. *The Return of the Real*. Cambridge, Mass.: The MIT Press, 1996.

_____, ed. *Postmodern Culture*. London: Pluto Press, 1985.

Foucault, Michel. *Fearless Speech*. Los Angeles: Semiotext(e), 2001.

Freud, Sigmund. *Fragment of the Analysis*. Vol. 8. London: Penguin, 1977.

Fritz, Robert. *Corporate Tides*. Oxford: Butterworth-Heinemann Ltd., 1994.

Gabriel, Yiannis. "The Hubris of Management" in *Administrative Theory & Praxis*. Vol. 20, no. 3, September 1998.

_____. "On Paragrammatic Uses of Organizational Theory" in *Organization Studies*. Vol. 23, no. 1, 2002.

Gannon, Leslie. "Docu Soap." Performance at Ellipsis, Chapter Arts Centre, Cardiff, UK, 15 December 2001.

Garrett, Lauree. *Horizon*. BBC Two (British TV). January 2000.

Gerdes, Eckhard, ed. *The Laugh That Laughs at the Laugh: Writing from and About the Pen Man*. n.p.: Raymond Federman, Lincoln: Writers Club Press, 2002.

Goldberg, RoseLee. *Performance Art: From Futurism to the Present.* London: Thames & Hudson, 1988.

Green, Malcome, ed. *Blago Bung Blago Bung Bosso Fataka! First Texts of German Dada by Hugo Ball, Richard Huelsenbeck Walter Sterner.* London: Atlas Press, 1995.

Hankins, James. "Humanism and the Origins of Modern Political Thought" in Jill Kraye, ed., *The Cambridge Companion to Renaissance Humanism.* Cambridge: Cambridge University Press, 1998.

Hankinson, R. J. *The Sceptics.* London: Routledge, 1995.

Hejinian, Lyn. *The Language of Inquiry.* Berkeley: University of California Press, 2000.

Herbert, Simon. "Disparate Pockets" in *Art & Design,* Vol. 5, no. 3/4, 1989.

Hislop, Ian, ed. *The Private Eye Annual 1998.* London: Pressdram Ltd., 1998.

Hyvrard, Jeanne. *Mother Death.* Lincoln: University of Nebraska Press, 1988.

Illich, Ivan. *Limits to Medicine: Medical Nemisis — The Expropriation of Health.* London: Pelican Books Ltd., 1976.

Ingrams, Richard. "Waugh Games" in *The Observer,* 21 Jan 2001.

Kaufmann, Walter. *Nietzsche: Philosopher, Psychologist, Antichrist.* Princeton, N.J.: Princeton University Press, 1999.

Kennedy, Ian. *The Unmasking of Medicine.* London: Granada, 1983.

Kraye, Jill, ed. *The Cambridge Companion to Renaissance Humanism.* Cambridge: Cambridge University Press, 1998.

Kristeva, Julia. *Powers of Horror: An Essay on Abjection.* New York: Columbia University Press, 1982.

Laertius, Diogenes. *Lives of Eminent Philosophers, Vol. I.* Cambridge, Mass.: Harvard University Press, 1995.

_____. *Lives of Eminent Philosophers, Vol. II.* Cambridge, Mass.: Harvard University Press, 1995.

Lasch, Christopher. *The Culture of Narcissism: American Life in an Age of Diminishing Expectations.* New York: W.W. Norton, 1979.

Lucian. "Dialogues of the Dead" in *Lucian Volume VII.* Loeb Classical Library. Cambridge, Mass.: Harvard University Press, 1928.

Lyotard, Jean-François. *The Postmodern Condition: A Report on Knowledge.* New Jersey: Humanities Press, 1993.

Machiavelli, Niccolò. *The Discourses.* London: Penguin Books, 1998.

_____. *The Prince.* Indianapolis: Hacket, 1995.

MacIntyre, Alasdair. *After Virtue.* London: Gerald Duckworth, 1999.

Malherbe, A. J. *The Cynic Epistles.* Atlanta: Scholars Press, 1977.

McCaffery, Larry, et al., eds. *Federman: From A to X-X-X-X: A Recyclopedic Narrative.* San Diego: San Diego State University Press, 1998.

McCarthy, Jim. *Political Theatre During the Spanish Civil War.* Wales: University of Wales Press, 1999.

Mencken, H. L. *A Mencken Chrestomathy.* New York: Vintage Books, 1982.

Miller, James. *The Passion of Michel Foucault.* Cambridge, Mass: Harvard University Press, 2000.

Moore, Charles. "Moore Pays Tribute to Waugh" in *The Guardian,* 17 January 2001.

Moore, Michael. *Downsize This: Random Threats from an Unarmed American.* London: Boxtree, 1997.

_____. *Stupid White Men.* New York: Harper Collins, 2001.

Navia, Luis E. *Antisthenes of Athens: Setting the World Aright.* New York: Greenwood Press, 2001.

_____. *Classical Cynicism: A Critical Study.* Westport, Conn.: Greenwood Press, 1996.

_____. *Diogenes of Sinope: The Man in the Tub.* New York: Greenwood Press, 1998.

Nietzsche, Friedrich. *The Antichrist.* Tucson: See Sharp Press, 1999.

_____. "Beyond Good and Evil: Prelude to a Philosophy of the Future" in *Complete Works*, Volume Five. Edinburgh: T.N. Foulis, 1909.

_____. *Ecce Homo: How One Becomes What One Is.* London: Penguin Books, 1992.

_____. *Philosophy and Truth.* New Jersey: Humanities Press, 1979.

_____. *Philosophy in the Tragic Age of the Greeks.* Washington, D.C.: Regnery, 1962.

_____. "Thoughts Out of Season, Part II" in *Complete Works*. London: George Allen & Unwin, 1909.

_____. *Thus Spoke Zarathustra.* London: Penguin, 1969.

_____. *Twilight of the Idols: Or, How to Philosophize with the Hammer.* Indianapolis: Hackett, 1997.

Nussbaum, Martha C. *The Therapy of Desire.* Princeton, NJ: Princeton University Press, 1994.

O'Dell, Kathy. *Contract with the Skin: Masochism Performance Art and the 1970s.* Minneapolis: University of Minnesota Press, 1998.

Odone, Cristina. "A Party That Never Laughs" in *The Observer*, 21 January 2001.

Oliver, Kelly, and Marilyn Pearsall, eds. *Feminist Interpretations of Friedrich Nietzsche.* University Park: The Pennsylvania State University Press, 1998.

Plato. *The Republic.* Harmondsworth: Penguin, 1955.

Porter, Henry. "Waugh at Peace" in *The Guardian*, Thursday, 18 January 2001.

Pountain, Dick, and David Robins. *Cool Rules.* London: Reaktion Books, 2000.

Rabinow, Paul, ed. *The Foucault Reader.* London: Penguin Books, 1984.

Raven, Charlotte. "Love Across the Divide" in *The Guardian*, 23 January 2001.

Rieff, Philip. *The Triumph of the Therapeutic.* Harmondsworth: Penguin, 1966.

Robinson, Dave. *Nietzsche and Postmodernism.* Cambridge: Icon Books, 1999.

Rose, Margaret A. *Parody: Ancient, Modern and Postmodern.* Cambridge: Cambridge University Press, 1993.

Salecl, Renata. *(Per)Versions of Love and Hate.* London: Verso, 1998.

Sarup, Madan. *An Introductory Guide to Post-Structuralism and Postmodernism.* London: Harvester Wheatsheaf, 1993.

Sayre, Farrand. *Diogenes of Synope: A Study of Greek Cynicism.* Baltimore: J.H. Furst, 1938.

Schrift, Alan D., ed. *Why Nietzsche Still: Reflections on Drama, Culture, and Politics.* Berkeley: University of California Press, 2000.

Schwob, Marcel. *King in the Golden Mask and Other Stories.* Manchester: Carcanet New Press, 1982.

Sellers, Susan, ed. *Writing Differences: Readings from the Seminar of Hélène Cixous.* New York: St. Martin's Press, 1988.

Serres, Michel. *Detachment.* Athens: Ohio University Press, 1990.

Sharples, R.W. *Stoics, Epicureans and Sceptics.* London: Routledge, 1996.

Sheridan, Alan. *Michel Foucault: The Will to Truth.* London: Routledge, 1980.

Shiach, Morag. *Helene Cixous: A Politics of Writing.* London: Routledge, 1991.

_____. "Millennial Fears: Hope and Transformation in Contemporary Feminist Writing" in *Paragraph: A Journal of Modern Critical Theory*. Volume 23, Number 3, November 2000. Edinburgh University Press.

Shlain, Leonard. *The Alphabet Versus the Goddess: Male Words, Female Images.* London: Alan Lane, Penguin, 1998.

Sloterdijk, Peter. *Critique of Cynical Reason.* London: Verso, 1988.

Sokal, Alan. "Transgressing the Boundaries: Toward a Transformative Hermeneutics of Quantum Gravity" in *Social Text*. No. 46/47, Spring/Summer 1996.

_____, and Jean Bricmont. *Intellectual Impostures: Postmodern Philosophers' Abuse of Science.* London: Profile Books, 1999.

South Bank Show. ITV (British TV). 19 August 2001.

Stoddard, Martin, ed. *Sayings of F. Nietzsche.* London: Gerald Duckworth, 1993.

Thistlewood, David. *Joseph Beuys Diverging Critiques.* Liverpool: Liverpool University Press, 1995.

Toynbee, Polly. "Ghastly Man" in *The Guardian,* 19 January 2001.

Turner, Paul, ed. *Lucian: Satirical Sketches.* Harmondsworth: Penguin, 1961.

Virilio, Paul. *Ground Zero.* London: Verso, 2002.

Wheatcroft, Geoffrey. "Auberon Waugh" in *The Guardian,* 18 January 2001.

Wheen, Francis. *The Sixties: A Fresh Look at the Decade of Change.* London: Century, 1982.

Zeller, Eduard. *Outlines of the History of Greek Philosophy.* New York: Dover Publications, 1980.

Zizek, Slavoj. *The Plague of Fantasies.* London: Verso, 1997.

_____. *Welcome to the Desert of the Real.* London: Verso, 2002.

Index